Jack Nicholson

DATE DUE			

201-9500   PRINTED IN U.S.A.

Jack Nicholson

Don Shiach

B.T. Batsford, London

Printed in Great Britain
by WBC Book Manufacturers
Bridgend, Wales

For the publishers

BT Batsford Ltd
583 Fulham Road
London
SW6 5BY

ISBN 0 7134 8430

791.43
SHI
2/00

A catalogue record for this book is available from
the British Library.

CONTENTS

1

INTRODUCTION

INTRODUCTION

Jack Nicholson is a phenomenon. I use that word not in a tone of excessive hagiography, but as an objective assessment of his status within the film industry, in which actors who are elevated to something called stardom are judged, firstly, by their ability to draw the customers in and, secondly, by their innate talent. Nicholson's 'superstardom' spans four decades and shows no sign of ending. Perhaps a few major stars of Hollywood's golden era, like Clark Gable, James Stewart and John Wayne, could match Nicholson's longevity as a perennial favourite and marquee draw, but not even their most fervent fans would class them in the same league as Nicholson as a 'serious' actor.

So why has Jack Nicholson been so popular for such a long time? Comparing him with the three stars above, he is not perceived as a romantic man of action like Gable, as solid, sincere and downhome like Stewart, or as macho and heroic as Wayne, so why has been such a success? Indeed, if we try to compare him with golden era Hollywood stars, it only emphasizes his uniqueness. Comparisons have been made with Humphrey Bogart, especially when Nicholson played private eyes as in *Chinatown* and *The Two Jakes*, and he does have some of Bogart's characteristic cynical worldliness and battered integrity, but it is far from a total match. Sometimes Nicholson reminds me of John Garfield, and it was Garfield who played Frank Chambers in the 1946 version of *The Postman Always Rings Twice*, the role that Nicholson took on in the 1981 remake. Garfield often played intelligent rebels from the American working class and this is a feature of Nicholson's work as well. He also has something of Robert Mitchum about him: the lazy slow drawl, the innate insolence, the coiled aggression waiting to be unleashed. However, Nicholson is not 'another anybody' because his success as a movie actor is the result of his own style and talent, and, importantly, the product of New Hollywood's need for a star who could embody rebelliousness, counterculture values, contemporary male uncertainties, as well as a Hollywood version of 'badness'.

NICHOLSON MYTHOLOGY

Movie stars, when they become established, acquire a certain screen persona, which is usually, but not always, inextricably linked with their 'private', off-screen image. Very often these star 'images' are deliberately manufactured by the publicity machine of the film industry with the active co-operation of all the media that feed off the aura that has attached itself to Hollywood, and certainly with the collusion of the stars themselves. No major movie star was ever 'created' without the full-time involvement of the individual concerned. Stardom does not just happen, that is just a self-serving myth of the movie industry, the sort of 'lie' that has Lana Turner being accidentally 'discovered' sitting on a stool in Schwab's. Stardom has to be worked at, you have to be ferociously ambitious, you have to be totally single-minded, you have to have something the industry wants at a particular time and behind you, you must have influential people with a vested interest in turning you into a star.

Nicholson, by his own admission, was very hungry in his youth for fame and success. He went after it, and he was lucky enough to be able to supply something that Hollywood had a demand for in the late sixties and early seventies, and thereafter he has generally guided his career astutely so that his status in the industry has remained secure. A movie star is a commodity, something the hucksters can sell to the movie-going public, a name on the marquee that will draw the suckers in. Nicholson's 'unique selling point' is what guarantees his huge fees and substantial percentage of the grosses of the movies he appears in. Jack Nicholson is now a seriously rich man, having earned a conservative $60 million from *Batman* alone. Nicholson's 'persona', the intermingling of the screen and private image, has much to do with his powerful position in the movie marketplace.

'That old devil Jack'. 'Badass Nicholson'. 'Hollywood's oldest wild child'. 'The star with the shortest fuse in Tinseltown'. All these things have been said and written about Nicholson and there is a confusion as to whether it is Nicholson, the actor who plays roles like those in the movies, or the 'real' Jack Nicholson who is being described. Perhaps there is no longer a 'real' Jack Nicholson because he has been subsumed by the 'Jack Nicholson' the world knows and (mostly) admires. Perhaps Nicholson doesn't any longer know who the hell he is. Perhaps he never did know and that is why he became an actor in order to hide behind a multiplicity of fictional characterizations, into which he could inject aspects of himself. We all play roles in life, but movie stars are especially burdened with role-playing, even when they are not on screen. Being a major movie star in the crazy celebrity culture we live in means you're 'on call' most of the time. We think we know these people, but we don't; what we know is a shadow on a screen, an imitation of life, a narrative figure in a celluloid fantasy, a personality written up in feature articles or interviewed on television. When you are as famous as Jack Nicholson and your image is so firmly entrenched in the public mind, it might be difficult to disassociate the real self from the manufactured self.

As I write this, I have just finished listening to a radio interview Nicholson has given to a radio programme called *Woman's Hour* as part of a promotional tour for his latest movie, *As Good As It Gets*. The interviewer prefaces the recording with an allusion to Nicholson's reputation as a seducer and a 'wild man'; during the interview Nicholson plays the seducer role to the hilt. He refers to his own seductiveness and uses his most seductive drawl. The interviewer mentions his notorious short fuse and he explains, in that way that self-fascinated actors

have, 'I'm not necessarily rude, but I can be brutal. I go from "Oh, really?" to "I'll break your neck!" missing out on the rude bit.' He describes how he was brought up by women in a beauty parlour and that his sister Lorraine has said that since the age of three, there hasn't been a woman he can't seduce. By quoting his sister, he is distancing himself from the claim, but implicit in the statement is his belief in its accuracy. He reinforces his worldly image by confessing 'I've always been a smart alec.' There is an unspoken collusion between the interviewer and Nicholson that these are the aspects of the star's personality they want to stress. Nicholson is entirely happy with this, he is used to it, he has courted it ever since he became a star, it's a game he knows well and which he profits from. It is an integral part of being the public Jack Nicholson. He is that old devil Jack and he loves playing it. The radio people are happy for him to play that part, and the radio audience have their perception of Jack Nicholson reinforced. The interview plays a small part in the continuing process of the creation of the Nicholson mythology.

Yet Nicholson is nobody's dope, he has read widely, and apparently has a weakness for parading his learning by allusions to Camus, Nietzsche and other intellectual heavyweights, which is sometimes a characteristic of people who have missed out on a formal education but who have educated themselves later. The intelligence is there in spades, however, so he need not be so insecure. Intelligence shines through his best performances – he doesn't need to prove to us he's bright, though clearly he thinks he does. So why does this bright guy act the Nicholson fool so often, going along with these clichéd interviews where he plays the rogue to some prurient interviewer? Why does he act so crassly as to expose his bottom at Golden Globe ceremonies, as he did in 1998, or make chauvinist and unconsidered comments in *Playboy* interviews? There is a dichotomy here, but the answer probably is quite simple. These antics grab people's attention, and especially the attention of women. By his own testimony he was brought up among women. He had no male siblings and an absent father figure. Indeed, the man whom he thought was his father turned out to be his grandfather and to this day there seems to be some doubt about who his real father was. So the young Nicholson learned early how to get women's attention and he has been doing the same thing all his life, on and off the screen, playing basically the same part, the rascal, the grinning rogue with bedroom eyes, the scamp with an undercurrent of anger that threatens to erupt at any time, the demon who will have his wicked way. Earlier in his career, Nicholson went out of his way to outrage feminists, a bit like the writer Norman Mailer, who used to say outrageously chauvinist things to provoke feminist reactions – that way he got a lot of female attention. Nicholson has done the same thing for a long time and will continue to do so. Perhaps he's still trying to prove to himself that he is attractive to women, despite all his fame and his reputation for charm. All this corny 'old devil Jack' stuff comes out of a deep insecurity. Am I really attractive, he is asking. Can I still grab your attention?

TO BEGIN AT THE BEGINNING...

Jack Nicholson's life has been documented in numerous biographies and the purpose of this book is not to add another tome to that particular pile, but to examine his professional career. Naturally, that career, his style, what he brings to acting on screen, is partly shaped by where he came from and his formative years before he tried for stardom. Born in 1937, the same year as two other superstars of his generation, Robert Redford and Warren Beatty, Nicholson grew up in New Jersey coastal towns in what eventually turned out to be fairly comfortable middle-class circumstances. He was under the impression that his parents were John J. and Ethel May Nicholson, but his real mother was the woman whom he was told was his sister June. He only learned for sure that he had been an illegitimate child and that his sister was in fact his mother much later in life, after, indeed, his mother had died. He has stated that he felt an overwhelming sense of gratitude to the women in his family for having the courage to keep the secret for so long and for sparing him, through their subterfuge, the inevitable gibes from other youngsters if they had known he had been born out of wedlock. But can this really be the whole truth about his feelings on this central fact of his life?

John J. Nicholson was an alcoholic and away from home a lot of the time. Ethel May ran a successful beauty parlour and Nicholson has described how fascinated he was as a boy watching all these women being primped and fussed over while looking their worst. June had been a minor performer as singer and dancer on the stage, but had married a test pilot and moved in upper-class circles in Buffalo and Connecticut. Jack saw his married 'sister' from time to time, but he may felt out of place among the 'toffs' she and her husband knew. The couple had two children, but the marriage ended in divorce. June took her two children with her to Los Angeles in 1953. June encouraged Jack to visit her in 1954. The young Nicholson, by now a high school graduate, took to LA and soon became a permanent resident. He got a job in the mail room at the MGM studios in Culver City with the cartoon division. After failing a screen test by producer Joe Pasternak, he took some acting lessons, acquired his first agent and began to hang round Hollywood and Sunset Boulevards mixing with other wannabes. Crucially he joined actor Jeff Corey's acting classes where he met individuals who were to be important to him: Robert Towne (later to script *Chinatown*), Robert Evans (producer on *Chinatown*) and Roger Corman, who would give Nicholson his first screen roles that supplied the launching pad for his career. He also attended acting classes organized by Martin Landau, who was deeply influenced by the teachings of Stanislavsky, often referred to as the father of the Method school of acting. Yet Nicholson, although he has sometimes been described as a Method actor, belongs to no discernible school of acting and, indeed, his formal training as an actor, by British standards, was minimal indeed. He did some minor theatre acting in Los Angeles before breaking into movies, but even after he became a star, he was never tempted to return to the stage. As a hungry young actor in LA, he appeared in numerous bread-and-butter television series in small roles and he was glad to earn money in this way, but, similarly, he has never returned to television. The movies were to be the medium he was to shine in and the people who were to give him his first opportunities at acting on screen were the people he had worked with in the acting classes in which he learned some of his craft.

The rest, as they say, is screen history. Jack Nicholson's 'private life' has been lived in the full glare of publicity, and for a man who says he values his privacy, he has been curiously unreluctant to bare his soul and talk about his many love affairs to assorted scribes and media hacks. The whole world knows about his long-standing relationship with Anjelica Huston, his numerous affairs and his present partner, Rebecca Broussard, who was his daughter Jennifer's best friend before she became her fathers lover. In 1962 Nicholson had married actress Sandra Knight, with whom he appeared in the Corman quickie *The Terror*, but that marriage had ended in divorce. Down through the years Nicholson's name has seldom been absent from the gossip columns and his 'confessions' about his philandering and experimentation with drugs are well-known. His friendships with such figures as Roman Polanski and Marlon Brando, both of whom are surrounded by scandal of one kind or another, have stoked the legend of Nicholson as a star inhabiting the wilder fringes of Tinseltown, but the fact is that, for all his playboy antics, his hell-raising and his womanizing, he has found time to make a multitude of movies and work at being a serious actor in an industry that at times seems to do everything it can to discourage such aspirations. In essence, Jack Nicholson would not be worth writing about unless he had accomplished what he has done, at his best, on film. All the rest of it, the scandal, the laddish behaviour, his penchant for shocking the bourgeoisie, the playing out of his chosen image, would be of little or no interest unless he had created a body of work that was worth analysing.

NICHOLSON, THE ACTOR

When Jack is good, he is very, very good, but when Jack is bad, he is very, very bad. That is one of the arguments that I will make in this book as I write about his movies one by one. I can think of no other screen actor who has been so consistently brilliant in his roles, but who, in the course of his career, has also been so frequently bad and hammy. The name of Laurence Olivier perhaps comes to mind: Olivier was a brilliant actor on stage and on film; not only was he a great classical actor (*Richard III*, *Henry V*), but he could play non-classical roles (*Sister Carrie*, *The Entertainer*, *Spartacus*) with conviction. Nevertheless, despite this indisputable brilliance, at times Olivier was embarrassingly bad, as when playing Othello or when he blacked up again as the Mahdi in *Khartoum*. The gulf between the majestic Olivier, the leading actor of his

generation, and the hammy Olivier was immense. I would contend that a similar gulf exists in Nicholson's acting oeuvre, not that I am making any comparisons between Olivier and him. A more relevant comparison might be between Marlon Brando and Nicholson. Nicholson always admired Brando (whether that admiration stuck after they made *The Missouri Breaks* together is an open question), and he has often been referred to as Brando's natural successor in Hollywood. Yet Brando, for all his towering performances in movies such as *On the Waterfront*, *A Streetcar Named Desire*, *Julius Caesar* and *The Godfather*, was also incredibly bad in a succession of movies such as *Désirée*, *Sayonara*, *Bedtime Story*, *Candy* and numerous other turkeys. Nicholson's career is too often littered with comparable failures, where he has been bad in terrible movies, and occasionally bad in good movies. That's another one of those dichotomies that are a feature of the man: how can there be such a wide divide between the Nicholson of talent, intelligence and intuition, and the Nicholson of tastelessness, misjudgement and sheer over-the-top ham? Perhaps it is a result of being such a superstar: you become so important and egotistical that no one has the nerve to say in this one you're lousy, Jack, let's do it differently.

But this book would not be in existence if the brilliant performances did not outnumber the poor ones by a margin. Nevertheless, this is not hagiography. Where I think our hero has fallen short, I say so. I admire Nicholson as an actor, but I have not brought a fan's mentality to the task of writing about his career. That way lies fawning and uncritical acceptance. And, of course, it is all a matter of personal judgement. Readers will have their own views on Nicholson's performances. Some will rate his roles in *The Shining* or *Goin' South*, whereas I am critical of them. You may think I am too indulgent in my praise of his participation in movies such as *The Postman Always Rings Twice* or *Reds*, for example, but finally we are dealing in personal response here, and Nicholson is an actor who at least provokes strong reactions one way or another. He has style and he has presence. He is almost always worth watching. There are not that many Hollywood stars you can say that about.

2

STARTING OUT

STARTING OUT

The Cry Baby Killer (1958)

Allied Artists: Director, Jus Addis; Producers, David Kramarsky and David March; Screenplay, Leo Gordon and Melvin Levy, from a story by Leo Gordon; Cinematography, Floyd Crosby; Editor, Irene Morra; Music, Gerald Fried

Cast: Jack Nicholson (Jimmy Walker); Harry Lauter (Porter); Carolyn Mitchell (Carole); Brett Halsey (Manny); Lynn Cartwright (Julie); Ralph Reed (Joey)

Running time 62 minutes

Not many Hollywood actors play the lead in their very first movie: Jack Nicholson has that distinction, but perhaps it is a dubious claim to fame, given the quality of his first flick. *The Cry Baby Killer* was a teenage exploitation movie destined to play second feature to *Hot Rod Girl*, which is better known. Roger Corman backed the project financially, though it was not actually made by his company. Corman has claimed that it was his decision to cast Nicholson, but other versions have it that the producers Kramarsky and March, the director Addis and screenwriter Leo Gordon (a familiar sadistic heavy in fifties movies) decided to take a chance on the twenty-year-old unknown because his looks suited their concept of the role ('good-looking, but not too good-looking') and because Nicholson did a terrific reading when they interviewed him. Whatever the actual facts, this movie would launch Nicholson's screen career and establish a relationship with Corman, which had started

when they met at Jeff Corey's acting class and which would prove very important in the next decade.

Blackboard Jungle and *Rebel Without A Cause* had established that teenage delinquency could sell at the box office. In Eisenhower's America, there was a rising tide of concern about the increasing crime statistics and especially violent crime by the young. In addition, Hollywood had discovered that most of its remaining audience (movie audiences shrank by a half between 1946 and 1956) were under twenty-five. Thus, opportunist filmmakers climbed on the bandwagon of the James Dean phenomenon and produced third-rate imitations of *Rebel* for the late-night movie circuit in the States. These films also found an audience in Europe, where they were linked in the perceptions of young audiences with rock 'n roll and rebellion against the values of their staid elders.

Cry Baby lifts its plot almost straight from *Rebel Without A Cause*. Nicholson plays sensitive Jimmy Walker (Jimmy Dean, geddit?) who is trying to repair his high-school relationship with Carole (Carolyn Mitchell) and is hassled by some toughs. In his panic, he shoots two of them. Thinking that he has killed them, he takes three hostages. When the cops close in on him, Carole persuades him to surrender. He accepts a self-defence plea and things end fairly happily. In other words, this is routine teenage flick stuff and Nicholson is given little chance to shine. Whatever the faults of *Rebel Without A Cause* (and there are many), the movie had a director (Nicholas Ray) and a writer (Stuart Stern) who were trying to explore in some depth the alienation many teenage

Cry Baby Killer. Jack Nicholson(Jimmy Walker) looks sceptically at his screen love Carolyn Mitchell.

Americans were experiencing at that time from the suburban cosiness of Eisenhower's mainly affluent America. *Cry Baby* picks up on those themes, but they are never allowed to be represented in a 'serious' way, perhaps not surprising when the short duration of the movie is considered.

This early opportunity to play a lead role could have made Nicholson a star overnight. But the movie's generally tepid reviews (when it was reviewed at all), and its lowly status as a programme filler to *Hot Rod Girl*, ensured that overnight success was not to occur. Indeed, Nicholson's performance is at times gauche and unconvincing, so even if the film had garnered more attention, it is unlikely that many people would have tipped him for major stardom. Still, it was a start in the movie acting business, although it would be another two years before another screen part came his way.

Little Shop of Horrors (1960)

A Film Group Release: Director, Roger Corman; Producer, Roger Corman; Screenplay, Charles B. Girth; Cinematography, Arch Dalzell; Editor, Marshall Nelia Jar; Music, Fred Kate; Art Director, Daniel Hailer

Cast: Jonathan Haze (Seymour Krelboind); Jackie Joseph (Audrey); Mel Welles (Gravis Mushnick); Dick Miller (Fouch); Myrtle Vail (Winifred); Leola Wendorff (Mrs Shiva); Jack Nicholson (Wilbur Force)

Running time 70 minutes

Why any movie achieves cult status is difficult to assess, but that *Little Shop of Horrors* managed it is quite disorientating. Almost unbelievably, this movie, shot by Roger Corman and his merry band in a few days and on a budget that was not so much minuscule as non-existent, became a favourite of American college students on late-night television or at drive-in movies. I stress almost unbelievably because, after all, no filmmaker from Poverty Row ever went broke by underestimating the taste of the average American college kid on the trail of tripe entertainment. But *Little Shop*'s success is still puzzling: it isn't gross, or violent, obscene or even blasphemous like many other campus favourites. It is merely remorselessly juvenile, and therein probably lies the secret. It resembles a high school drama class improvisation when the teacher, as an end-of-term treat, tells the kids: 'Do me a horror movie spoof!'

And that's what the 'kids' serve up: a shallow, off-the-top-of-our-heads send-up of a horror movie that looks like it's the product of a combination of a script written at the last moment, or on a wet afternoon on the back of an envelope, and instant front-of-camera improvisation with a very lenient and undemanding director (Corman) decidedly not managing the proceedings. According to the legends surrounding the Corman factory, the small group of technicians and actors Corman had gathered round him had set out to make a 'serious' horror movie about a flesh-eating plant and had come up against the buffers of the

ludicrousness of their special effects and the inanity of the script. Faced with the prospect of producing a straight-faced turkey, even by the elastic standards of the market Corman was producing for, they decided to start again to make a spoof of the horror genre. Unfortunately, the satire is woefully unfunny and leaden in its realization. Corman might have got more laughs if he had persisted with his straight version and the movie might have yet achieved cult status.

The story concerns one Seymour Krelboind (Jonathan Haze), a put-upon shop assistant in a flower shop run by Gravis Mushnick (Mel Welles). Seymour develops a special hybrid plant that has, for no explicable reason, the desire to eat human flesh and blood ('Feed me!') and it also has the ability to speak English. The ghoulish plant is called Little Audrey after Seymour's bimbo girl friend, which may or may not be significant. Seymour accidentally kills a railway detective and a sadistic dentist and feeds both to the demanding plant. Mushnick (played by Welles as a stereotype Jewish shopkeeper) kills a thief in his shop and this unfortunate too becomes chopped liver for the highly unconvincing voracious growth, which increases in size so much that it soon attracts the neighbourhood gawpers.

The movie opens with a voice-over narration by Joe Fink, a detective in the Joe Friday-Dragnet tradition of tough guy cop spouting cryptic dialogue and he and his partner Frank Stoolie begin to investigate the disappearances, tracing them to the flower shop. At the end of the movie, Seymour offers himself as a sacrifice to Little Audrey, and his face, and the faces of the other victims, show up on the huge petals of the monster plant. Frankenstein devoured by his own creation?

Nicholson's brief role consists of a cameo part as a clean-cut, preppie but masochistic young man who comes to the sadistic dentist's clinic intent on having a pleasurable time by suffering as much pain as possible. His character (Wilbur Force) refuses dulling Novocain and revels in the painful pulling and drilling of his teeth. 'Don't stop now!' he screams. At the end of the cameo, there is a shot of the back of Nicholson's head, then he turns round and we see his teeth filed down and gap-ridden: 'I've never enjoyed myself so much!'. The humour, to put it mildly, is unsubtle and Nicholson's acting style matches. If there are no small parts, only small actors, then we have to assume that Nicholson was intent on making an impression in his few minutes on screen by hamming it up. An indulgent director gives him his head.

However, in terms of Nicholson's career, *Little Shop of Horrors* was another movie of sorts. At the time, it would not add to Nicholson's reputation as an actor one jot, but it certainly would pay dividends for the owners of the property when it was turned into a highly successful Broadway musical. What had started out as a frantic attempt to churn out something passable for the late-night movie circuits ended up by making big bucks when its ultimate cult status ensured its resurrection as suitable fodder for mainstream Broadway audiences partly made up of the middle-aged versions of those same college kids who had liked the movie when it was first released.

Too Soon To Love (1960)

Universal/Dynasty: Director, Richard Rush; Producer, Mark Lipsky; Screenplay, Lazlo Gorog and Richard Rush; Cinematography, William Thompson; Editor, Stephen Arnsten; Music, Ronald Stein

Cast: Jennifer West (Cathy); Richard Evans (Jim); Warren Parker (Mr Taylor); Jack Nicholson (Buddy)

Running time 85 minutes

Richard Rush would direct four of Nicholson's 'apprenticeship' films, including *Too Soon To Love*, yet another cheapie teenage problem movie, which was released by Universal. It is only noteworthy because it was one of the first times that abortion was dealt with directly in a Hollywood movie. The teenage lovers of the movie face hostility from parents about their relationship, they make love and the girl becomes pregnant. Cue social issue: to abort or not to abort. They go for the former and Jim (Richard Evans) is involved in a robbery to pay for the abortion; Cathy (Jennifer West) tries to kill herself. The resolution is they

decide to get married, hoping to avoid the mistakes of their parents.

Nicholson plays the hero's sidekick and is only briefly involved in a fight scene. The movie's agenda is to paint all adults and parents as out-of-touch with teenage realities and generally unsympathetic. As the flick is aimed exclusively at a teen audience, it was clearly meant to manipulate the emotions of millions of disgruntled, misunderstood American teenagers. This simplification of complex social questions, and the limited production values, allied to the fairly amateurish acting, condemns the movie to the junkyard.

Studs Lonigan (1960)

United Artists: Director, Irving Lerner; Producer, Philip Yordan; Screenplay, Philip Yordan from the trilogy of novels by James T. Farrell; Cinematography, Arthur Feindel; Editor, Verna Fields; Music, Gerald Goldsmith

Cast: Christopher Knight (Studs Lonigan); Frank Gorshin (Kenny Killarney); Venetia Stevenson (Lucy Scanlon); Carolyn Craig (Catherine Banahan); Jack Nicholson (Weary Reilly); Robert Casper (Paulie Haggerty); Dick Foran (Patrick Lonigan); Jay C. Flippen (Father Gilhooey)

Running time 95 minutes

To adapt James T. Farrell's sprawling trilogy of novels for a movie of 95 minutes duration was a tall order and a problem that the screenwriter Philip Yordan and the director Irving Lerner never solved. Farrell's trilogy had acquired a literary reputation, since diminished, of being a tough, authentic representation of working-class life in a slum district of Chicago in the inter-war years. The movie coalesced the time so that most of the action takes place in 1925, which was one of the reasons that Farrell himself disassociated himself completely from the project, that and the fact the movie version was 'a bit more cheerful and moral than the book'.

The commercial reasoning behind filming *Studs Lonigan* must have made sense: most of the remaining film audience out there were under twenty-five, Farrell's trilogy was well-

Studs Lonigan. Nicholson has a night on the town with Studs (Christopher Knight).

known and had a certain respectability that might draw in older customers, and other movies about alienated teenagers were doing well at the box office. But the movie turned out to be a dud, both artistically and commercially, and Jack Nicholson, appearing in a mainstream studio movie for the first time, was not to achieve his great breakthrough by being cast as Weary Reilly, a tough and amoral member of the street gang that the hero hangs out with.

Casting is crucial in any film, and by using the wooden and distinctly uncharismatic Christopher Knight as Studs, the filmmakers were stacking the deck against themselves. But he had conventional good looks and that must have been the reason why they chose him.

Nicholson did not possess conventional handsomeness and that is why he was cast in the minor role of Weary. He has said the only reason he won that part was because he was one of the few Hollywood actors willing to plough their way through the trilogy of novels, a stipulation that director Lerner made to his cast. Thus, his literacy, his intelligence, won him the role, but the deadness of the movie let him down. His performance, convincing as it is, goes for very little in the surrounding context. When it was released, *Studs Lonigan* aroused practically no interest, not even rabid reviews. It was simply a non-event and it remains so to this day, because it is very seldom revived, even by obscure cable stations. Jack Nicholson's elevation to star status was to be delayed for quite a few years yet.

Studs Lonigan. Jack finds himself in a compromising situation on the dance floor.

The Wild Ride (1960)

Filmgroup: Director, Harvey Berman;
Producer, Harvey Berman; Screenplay,
Ann Porter and Marion Rothman; Cinematography,
Tayler Sloan; Editor, William Mayor

Cast: Jack Nicholson (Johnny Varron); Georgiana
Carter (Nancy); Robert Dean (Dave)

Running time 63 minutes

Nicholson's cameo role in *Little Shop of Horrors* led directly to his being cast as the lead in this Corman-backed quickie, shot in two weeks. It features Nicholson in the first of his biker roles, though not as a fully fledged Hell's Angel type. Johnny is modelled on Marlon Brando's character in *The Wild One*, though, unlike Brando, he plays a vicious killer, the leader of a teen gang. As in *Rebel Without A Cause* and *The Wild One*, the gang play 'chicken' games on the highway. Johnny's best mate is Dave (Robert Bean) who wants to leave the gang, partly because he fancies Johnny's girl, Nancy (played by Nicholson's then paramour, Georgianna Carter).

By calling the movie *The Wild Ride*, the makers clearly wanted to associate it in the potential audience's mind with Brando's earlier biker

The Broken Land. Jack (Will) thinks about the clichés of the script, while Dianna Darrin tries to remember her next line.

flick. That kind of catchpenny thinking just about sums up this extremely modest effort. The only importance it has in Nicholson's career is that it was the first movie he and Monte Hellman worked on together, Hellman having been drafted in by Corman to help with the filming.

The Broken Land (1962)

20th Century Fox Release: Director, John Bushelman; Producer, Leonard Schwartz; Screenplay, Edward Lakso; Cinematography, Floyd Crosby; Editor; Carl Pierson; Music, Richard LaSalle

Cast: Kent Taylor (Jim Kogan); Dianna Darrin (Mavra Aikens); Jody McCrea (Ed Flynn); Robert Sampson (Gabe Dunson); Jack Nicholson (Will Broicous); Gary Snead (Billy Bell)

Running time 60 minutes

Two facts about the casting of this movie are of note: Nicholson's rival for the part of Will was Burt Reynolds, and the young good guy, Ed, was played by Joel McCrea's son, Jody. McCrea had made his name in westerns, but his son was not destined to emulate his pop. Indeed, the leads disappeared almost without trace and only Nicholson was destined for fame. Although *The Broken Land* was shot in Cinemascope and in colour, it was meant as a brief programme filler, hence its running time of sixty minutes.

Nicholson plays the son of a famous gunfighter and finds that the sins of the father are visited upon the son. The sheriff of a small Arizona town (Kent Taylor) rules by oppressive means and he seems to have it in for young men of Will's type in particular. *Broken Land* is not so much a western as a variation on teen flicks of the time, with the youngsters suffering at the hands of a cruel adult, who has to be vanquished in the end, although only after Ed, his deputy, is shot.

Nicholson got the part because he could ride a horse and because it was thought he could project a killer image. He succeeds in doing this, but the film, shot in ten days, is nothing more

than routine. In Nicholson's career, however, it marks his first role in a genre he would return to several times in the future.

The Raven (1963)

American-International: Director, Roger Corman; Producer, Roger Corman; Screenplay, Richard Matheson, based on the poem by Edgar Allan Poe; Cinematography, Floyd Crosby; Editor, Ronald Sinclair; Music, Les Baxter; Production Designer, Daniel Haller

Cast: Vincent Price (Dr Erasmus Craven); Peter Lorre (Dr Bedloe); Boris Karloff (Dr Scarabus); Hazel Court (Lenore Craven); Olive Sturgess (Estelle Craven); Jack Nicholson (Roxford Bedlo)

Running time 85 minutes

Corman had had successes with his previous Edgar Allan Poe adaptations (*The Fall of the House of Usher*, *The Pit and the Pendulum*, *The Premature Burial* and *The Masque of the Red Death*). Any reputation the films had depended on their visual impact because the normally frugal Corman had lashed out on spectacular sets and costumes, and those, allied with impressive colour photography and Vincent Price's hammy performances, had made this series of Corman movies cult favourites, which they remain to this very day. However, whereas the approach in these films had been basically serious, although imbued with a high camp sensibility, *The Raven* was set to be comic in intention, sending up the horror genre and utilizing the inherently risible aspects of the acting styles of Price, Peter Lorre and Boris Karloff, who constituted, along with Bela Lugosi, the most famous names in the horror canon. Nicholson must have relished the opportunity to act with these heavyweights of the classic Hollywood horror genre, but, unfortunately for him, he was cast as the straight man, Roxford Bedlo, a kind of foil to the excesses of the overripe trio. When Nicholson's later over-the-top performances in movies such as *The Shining* and *Goin' South* are considered, the suspicion cannot be avoided that this early contact with such over-the-top hams as Price, Lorre and Karloff may not have had a beneficial effect on his acting. The point is that

The Raven. Nicholson has the thankless task of playing it straight while old hams Price and Lorre chew the scenery.

this kind of Grand Guignol, fruity, exaggerated and corny performance was what you hired Price, Karloff and, to a lesser extent, Lorre for. It was their stock-in-trade, what they were known for, their stamp as actors. However, when in the future Nicholson would try hammy imitations of the style after he had established his acting reputation through a series of restrained and realistic portrayals, he would appear merely hammy without the surrounding charisma and 'fun' element that was associated with Price and the other two, which allowed them to get away with it.

The story of *The Raven* need not detain us for too long. Suffice it to say that it concerns the rivalry between mad magicians, played by the terrible trio. Nicholson plays Lorre's son and he demonstrates that, one, he is not suited to costume pictures, because he is a very contemporary actor and, two, he is not a conventional romantic lead. It is difficult for any actor to play the straight role when everybody else around you is camping it up for comic effect and when the screenplay is directed to emphasizing the ridiculous aspects of the story at the expense of the straightforward narrative. Apparently, Richard Matheson, the respected sci-fi writer, was tired of these serious Poe adaptations he had done for Corman and American-International, and decided that this effort would be a parody of the genre. Sadly for Nicholson, he wrote in a part for a routine male lead and that's what Jack got to play. The result is that Nicholson has to play it straight while the elder statesmen of the genre are having some fun with the material. It is a no-win situation for the actor and he makes little or no impression in the role.

However, there he was acting alongside some of Hollywood's most famous and receiving respectable billing. Some actors would die for such exposure, so I am sure that at the time he was very grateful for the chance. It was something to put on his CV, his list of credits. The danger was that the movie would only be remembered for the splendour of the sets and the colour, the hammy performances of the leads, and the special effects sequence representing the magicians' attempts to outdo one another in magical tricks. That turned out to be the case and yet again fame and fortune were to be postponed for the ambitious Nicholson.

The Terror (1963)

Grand National Pictures: Director, Roger Corman; Producer, Roger Corman; Screenplay, Leo Gordon and Jack Hill; Cinematography, John Nickolaus; Editor, Stuart O'Brien; Music, Ronald Stein

Cast: Boris Karloff (Baron von Leppe); Nicholson (André Duvalier); Sandra Knight (Hélène); Richard Miller (Stefan); Jack Dorothy Neumann (Old Woman); Jonathan Haze (Gustav)

Running time 81 minutes

Roger Corman has long revelled in his established status as 'King of the Quickies', postal address: Poverty Row, Hollywood, Los Angeles. The self-serving myth surrounding the shooting of *The Terror* has it that Corman and his merry band completed it in two days flat because Corman, never one to miss an opportunity, had suddenly realized that the hired sets he had used for *The Raven* were not

due back for a further forty-eight hours. In addition, Boris Karloff still owed Corman a few days work on his contract. However, other reports confirm that at least another two days were spent shooting the film with a week's exterior shooting on top of that. It is a curious aspect of the Corman phenomenon that his films and reputation seem to acquire more kudos the shorter the shooting schedules and smaller the budgets were. It is a kind of inverted cinematic snobbery. Corman himself claims he tried to out-Poe Poe and create a gothic tale from scratch. What certainly cannot be denied is that *The Terror* was indeed a quickie horror flick and that is confirmed in its every frame.

The Terror, then, is another example of Roger Corman's 'filming-on-the-hoof' and 'off-the-top-of-our-collective-heads' modus operandi. It's 'let's think up a story for a horror movie and see what we can get away with' time. The end result is that they don't get away with very much: the movie is sub-sub-Poe and it uses the oldest clichés of the horror genre to negligible effect. About the only redeeming features are the sets and the costumes, which had just been used for *The Raven*, and the Big Sur exterior shots, which a young Francis Coppola shot. Corman has admitted they had only a roughed-out storyline and that no one really knew what their characters' motivations were.

The game is given away in the pre-credits sequence in which Karloff, playing a Baron von Leppe, does a stereotyped Boris Karloff act wandering round the sets of *The Raven* for no discernible point. Well, the sequence eats up screen time, employs those hired sets and uses Karloff's contracted time. There follows a mightily unconvincing tale that was, if the myth is to be believed, made up as shooting progressed. We see André Duvalier (Jack Nicholson) riding along a shoreline in a country that is never identified but we can assume is Prussia. Francis Coppola almost certainly directed this sequence and he clearly tries to give it an arthouse look, probably influenced by the opening scene to Ingmar Bergman's *Seventh Seal*, in which the knight and the squire ride along the shore. Duvalier, a French lieutenant, is inexplicably 'resting' from the Napoleonic Wars and sees a young woman (Hélène/Ilse) in the sea and in a vision. She

23

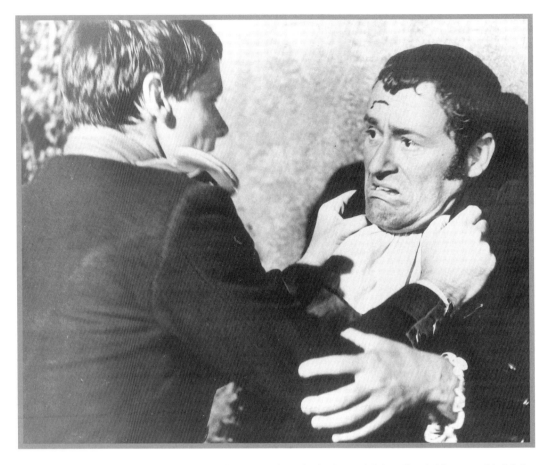

The Terror. Nicholson threatens Gustaff (Jonathan Haze) who is explaining 'Don't blame me! I didn't write your lines!'

saves him from drowning and he wakes up in a cottage; her face is above him but this vision dissolves into the face and form of a old woman (Dorothy Neumann). He quizzes her about the young woman and she tells him to look for her at the nearby palace of Baron von Leppe. Duvalier, obsessed by this visionary encounter, travels to the castle where Karloff tells him, 'What you see are the remains of a noble house, relics, ghosts of past glories.' (A Corman in-joke, perhaps, about reusing the sets from *The Raven*?) Duvalier sees a portrait of the Baron's deceased wife and surprise, surprise, she looks remarkably like the woman he is seeking. Equally unsurprisingly, the old woman from the cottage turns out to be a witch plotting the death of the Baron, whom

she says killed her son, Erik, for having had an affair with his wife twenty years previously. However, the Baron turns out to be the older version of the son who has killed the real Baron. Hélène, the young woman of Duvalier's vision, is the spirit of the dead wife, and she dissolves into a disgusting corpse in Duvalier's arms just as they are escaping from the palace and the Baron/Erik is busily flooding it. The spirit of Ilse flies away in the form of a bird.

The flooding of the castle is a visual metaphor for the actors drowning in a sea of horror flick clichés. We are not spared many: pounding waves, mysterious castles, banging windows, candles extinguishing, screams in the night, tombs, crypts, ghosts, witchcraft, bolts of lightning, gore, eyes that are plucked out by birds, eerie music – they are all there, folks, and if that's what you like, then there's plenty to keep you happy. Even by the undemanding standards of the genre, the plot makes no sense at all and it is not original enough in its realization to make us suspend our disbelief and leave logic and reality out of the equation.

In the midst of this mess, Jack Nicholson walks through his part as the hero delivering leaden lines such as 'What kind of woman are you?' and 'You mean she's possessed?' in wooden style. The nineteenth-century costumes may look good but not on Nicholson. He is the most contemporary of actors and it is difficult to think of any other movie actor less likely to convince in a period piece than him. A movie set in the 1920s or 1930s, yes, or in a western; as a French lieutenant in 1806 somewhere in Europe: no! He looks and sounds like a bemused 1960s American actor who somehow has found himself as the male lead in a gothic tale and with no directional aid to hand. One aspect of Nicholson's career is clear: when a director is uninterested in advising actors or incapable of doing it with insight, then his performance suffers. He was never destined to be a conventional leading man and this movie testifies to that. It was only when he started playing unstable 'off-the-wall' characters that his potential as an actor and as a star was realized.

Nonetheless, *The Terror* has some interesting aspects. As mentioned above, Francis Coppola directed some of it, as did Monte Hellman. Nicholson also directed himself in some scenes and certainly contributed to what there was of a screenplay. Corman says that Nicholson came to him saying that everybody 'in this whole damned town' had directed the picture so why couldn't he have a try? He was allowed to direct the last day's shooting. This multi-directorship of the movie was forced on Corman by his membership of the Hollywood Screen Directors Guild: only those who were at that time non-members of the Guild (Coppola et alia) could shoot with that small a non-regulation crew and with such a minuscule budget. The movie, then, could be seen as important in that it gave budding Hollywood luminaries the opportunity to cut their teeth on shooting footage for a feature film. Nicholson has described how he nearly drowned in the sea under the big arch in the Big Sur sequence and how Corman blamed him for going over budget when they got back to town.

In terms of Nicholson's career, it also gave him invaluable experience in several aspects of filmmaking: acting, writing and directing. *The Terror* crops up on late-night television and is included in serious retrospectives of Corman's oeuvre at film institutes. It has a certain historical interest, but other than that, it is without merit.

Thunder Island (1963)

20th Century Fox: Director, Jack Leewood; Producer, Jack Leewood; Screenplay, Jack Nicholson and Don Devlin; Cinematography, John Nickolaus

Cast: Gene Nelson (Billy Poole); Fay Spain (Helen Dodge); Brian Kelly (Vincent Dodge); Miriam Colon (Anita Chavez)

Running time 65 minutes

Thunder Island was co-scripted by Nicholson and his friend, Don Devlin. It was made for a 'quickie' unit headed by Robert Lippert operating within Fox. The plot concerned an attempted assassination of an exiled Caribbean dictator, who is threatening a coup and must be eliminated according to the political leaders who have taken over from them. They hire a hitman (Gene Nelson) and he embroils an expatriate American couple who operate a charter fishing boat business. The plot is foiled by the couple, so the evil ex-dictator lives on to plot a coup another day.

Political assassination was very much in the air at the time of the release of *Thunder Island* so Nicholson and Devlin, if nothing else, latched onto a very topical theme, but the movie is constricted by its brevity and its B-picture limitations, although it was praised in some quarters for its taut script that tried to deal with the ambiguities of performing an evil deed (assassination) for the greater good. Nicholson's writing career would soon be completely overtaken by his acting, but this movie shows that he had some talent as a screenwriter.

Ensign Pulver (1964)

Warner Brothers: Director, Joshua Logan; Producer, Joshua Logan; Screenplay, Joshua Logan and Peter S. Feibleman, from a play by Joshua Logan and Thomas Heggen, based on characters created by Thomas Heggen in his novel Mister Roberts; editor, William Reynolds; Cinematography, Charles Lawton; Music, George Duning

Cast: Robert Walker Jnr. (Ensign Pulver); Burl Ives (The Captain); Walter Matthau (The Doc); Tommy Sands (Bruno); Larry Hagman (Billings); Millie Perkins (Scotty); Kay Medford (Head Nurse); Al Freeman Jnr. (Taru); James Farentino (Insigna); James Coco (Skouras); Jack Nicholson (Dolan)

Running time 104 minutes

When an individual filmmaker directs a movie, acts as the producer and also co-writes the screenplay adapted from a stage play that he has also co-written, then, it could be argued, that such an individual has something close to auteur control over the finished film. Leaving the auteur theory out of the equation, you would at least have to say that such an individual bears a heavy responsibility for the finished film in question. As far as *Ensign Pulver* is concerned, the stage director Joshua Logan is the guilty party. He performed all those roles in the adapting and making of the movie. *Ensign Pulver* was such a stinker that he only made two films after that, *Camelot* and *Paint Your Wagon*, neither of any consequence. Logan's reputation was made on Broadway, but on the evidence of his track record in directing films, the rumours about his talents were much exaggerated. His best films are *Picnic* and *Bus Stop*, both of which were adapted from William Inge plays and both of which were close to being director-proof. Logan was also responsible for the distinctly awful *South Pacific*, *Sayonara* (Brando's worst film?) and *Fanny*, an outrageously bad remake of the famous Marcel Pagnol trilogy of movies set in Marseilles.

When Nicholson was cast as Dolan, one of the seamen in the US navy cargo ship captained by a humourless pedant (Burl Ives), he must have been quite hopeful that this might be his break into big-time studio filmmaking. If you can bear to watch the movie right through to the final credits (it seldom even crops up on cable or late-night television because it is so bad), you will see Nicholson's name and image as one of the featured players of the movie, which suggests he played a bigger role in the film that he actually does. I think we can assume that, either it was initially intended to build up his part and something changed in the shooting, or his part was mostly left on the cutting-room floor. In the event, Nicholson can count himself lucky that his part was trimmed because it means that people don't often remember he was ever in the film. Others not quite so lucky were Robert Walker Jnr., whose career zoomed after this starring role, Millie Perkins, who played Anne Frank in the 1959 movie, and Tommy Sands, a rock-and-roll singer whose acting career was definitely not enhanced by playing Bruno, the sailor whose domestic tragedy is the starting-point for what drama there is in the movie. However, a few individuals survived the experience and went on to better things: Nicholson, of course, Walter Matthau, who plays the wise old Doc on board, Al Freeman Jnr., James Farentino, Larry Hagman and James Coco.

Ensign Pulver is the sequel to the successful movie, *Mister Roberts*, that John Ford (nominally, at least) and Mervyn Leroy had directed in 1955; it had starred Henry Fonda, Jack Lemmon, James Cagney and William Powell, and had been a commercial success, as had been the Broadway stage play before it. It is not a film I warm to, because of its mixture of sentimentality, flag-waving, slapstick and tastelessness. Nevertheless, Logan and studio executives clearly thought a sequel would pay off in box-office terms. The character of Roberts had been killed off and none of the stars of the original film wanted to re-create their roles in this new film, including Lemmon as Pulver. Burl Ives took over Cagney's role, Walter Matthau Powell's and Robert Walker Jnr. Lemmon's. The action starts about a couple of months after the action of *Mister Roberts* had ended; references are made to Pulver's hero, the dead Roberts, and the crew and the cargo ship are still stuck in a backwater of the Pacific war. The Doc says, 'There hasn't been one gesture of virility or rebellion since Roberts left this ship', and describes the crew as having 'left their homes to fight but never got into the war'. In most Hollywood movies, ordinary GIs are always just dying to get their heads shot off. Pulver and the Doc's idea of rebellion is to fire a pellet into the 'bewtocks' (sic!) of the dictatorial captain as he forces the crew to watch a terrible horror flick he has shown time and time again. This is mainly in reprisal for the Captain's refusal to grant shore leave to Bruno, an ordinary seaman, whose 18-month old baby has just died. Pulver is most aggrieved that none of the crew think it possible he is the 'assassin' who played the trick on the Captain. During a hurricane, Bruno pulls a gun on his oppressor, Pulver intervenes and both are swept overboard, landing up in a lifeboat, on which they drift for days during which time the Captain unburdens himself about his unhappy childhood and why he is the ogre he is. The two reach a desert island where they are tended to by the islanders. The Captain has peritonitis and Pulver, who has ambitions to be a doctor, has to perform an appendectomy, being guided by the real Doc via shipboard radio. The Captain survives, but shows little gratitude: 'I'll never change!' Back on board, he resumes his tyrannical ways, even though the crew, unbelievably, have been rooting for Pulver to save the brute. Pulver has taken notes during the Captain's ramblings in the dinghy, apparently with a view to blackmailing him, but he tears the notes up in front of him. The Captain, now a commander, shows his gratitude in the only way he can by getting himself transferred to another ship. In an outrageously sentimental and incredible scene, the men give him a respectful goodbye.

Tasteless is the first word that comes to mind in describing this mess: the detail of the dead baby is tasteless, the pellet in the Captain's bum is tasteless, the scenes on the island are an insult to everyone concerned, especially all native Pacific islanders and the audience's sensibilities, and the crassness of the screenplay and the direction beggar description. These incredible plot manoeuvres are meant to be comical, but they are just embarrassing. The acting is on the same level. Robert Walker Jnr. is woeful as Pulver (he has the good grace to say in interviews that he finds the movie deeply embarrassing); Walter Matthau mugs and flails around in his desperation at finding himself in a movie this bad, Burl Ives is grotesquely awful, Tommy Sands is inadequate, and Millie Perkins, to put it kindly, is miscast. In the midst of this is Jack Nicholson, who crops up in numerous scenes with odd lines, but does not make any mark. Best not to be remembered for this one, Jack!

However, there were two and a half months of filming at the Screen Actors Guild minimum rate of $250 a day, and Nicholson also had a week's location work off Acapulco. *Ensign Pulver* ranks as among the worst movies Nicholson has appeared in, and that includes the quickest of Poverty Row quickies he made. He had found out, if he did not know it already, that working within the studio system with a name director, was no guarantee of quality.

Back Door To Hell (1964)

Medallion Pictures: Director, Monte Hellman; Producer, Fred Roos; Screenplay, Richard Guttmann and John Hackett; Photography, Mars Rasca; Editor, Fely Christomo; Music, Mike Velarde

Cast: Jimmie Rodgers (Lt. Craig); Jack Nicholson (Burnett); John Hackett (Jersey); Annabelle Higgins (Maria); Conrad Maga (Paco); Johnny Monteiro (Ramundo); Joe Sison (Japanese Captain)

Running time 68 minutes

Robert Lippert, who had an associate producer relationship with Fox, planned two low-budget movies to be shot back-to-back in the Philippines. Jack Nicholson was to appear in both of them, and was given the task of producing the screenplay for the second, *Flight To Fury*. Both films would cement his relationship with Monte Hellman and although neither would be artistically successful or specifically help Nicholson's career as an actor, they could be seen as rungs on a ladder that would eventually lead to higher things.

The cast and crew underwent severe privations while shooting the movies in the jungle heat of the Philippines. Monsoon rains were also a hazard, as were an army of insects, reptiles and all kinds of ravenous creatures. Living conditions were primitive and most people came down with some kind of illness. But it was some kind of adventure and the film team built up a strong feeling of camaraderie during the twin shoot.

Nicholson plays one of a trio of American soldiers during World War II who are ordered by

Back Door to Hell. Nicholson(Burnett)and John Hackett (Jersey) discuss military strategy.

their superiors to reconnoitre an island occupied by the Japanese. When the Japanese learn that the local inhabitants have been co-operating with the Americans, they threaten to kill the children in a village. Feeling a responsibility towards the villagers, the trio fight it out with the Japanese and succeed in getting the necessary information back to their commanders so that an invasion can be carried out.

Hellman tries his best to inject some 'serious' intent into this routine plot with its penchant towards conventional Hollywood heroics, but it is an uphill task and his efforts are largely sunk by the clichés of the script. Somewhere buried beneath the layers of clichés is an antiwar statement, but this is a programme filler of short duration and the demands of the actioner have to take priority. Hellman and Nicholson would have to wait only a short time till they could collaborate on a worthwhile project that would lend itself to personal statements.

Flight To Fury (1966)

A Lippert Picture: Director, Monte Hellman; Producer Fred Roos; Screenplay, Jack Nicholson from an original story by Monte Hellman and Fred Roos; Cinematography, Mike Accion

Cast: Dewey Martin (Joe Gaines); Fay Spain (Destiny Cooper); Jack Nicholson (Jay Wikham); Jacqueline Hellman (Gloria Walsh)

Running time 62 minutes cut from original print of 80 minutes

Flight To Fury received only a limited cinema release and it was destined to be sold years later to television in a cut version. Nicholson wrote the script on the voyage over to the Philippines to start shooting *Back Door To Hell*. Hellman and he intended the movie to be a homage to the John Huston-directed *Beat the Devil* (1953), which itself was a sort of parody of the kind of thriller (*The Maltese Falcon*, *The Treasure of Sierra Madre*) that had made Huston's name. Thus, *Flight To Fury* was an imitation of a parody, not a recipe for a coherent artistic point of view, and so it turns out. *Beat The Devil* itself divides opinion sharply between those who see it as a mordant, sharply observed black comedy and the rest of us who see it as a laboured in-joke that may have been fun for the director and the cast to make, but which is decidedly hard going for the audience. *Flight To Fury* is of the same ilk: Nicholson, Hellman and the rest of the cast had fun making it, but the joke falls flat when it reached the screen.

The plot concerns some stolen jewels in Manila with Nicholson as a psychotic smuggler. Along with his co-conspirators, he escapes from the island on a plane which crashes in the jungle. Predictably, the crooks turn on one another and the Nicholson character, realizing that all is lost, kills himself. The story, although the details are different, follows the outline of the plot of *Beat The Devil*, but instead of creating a homage, the makers managed only a damp squib of a flick, which hardly anyone at the time recognized as being connected with the earlier film. It must have been a severe disappointment to Nicholson and Hellman that the movie was more or less shelved by Robert Lippert, the producer, but that might have been a blessing in disguise: that way the damage to their reputations was limited and, anyway, just around the corner there was a much more worthwhile project awaiting their collaboration.

The Shooting (1966)

A Santa Clara Film: Director: Monte Hellman; Producers, Monte Hellman and Jack Nicholson; Screenplay, Adrien Joyce (Carol Eastman); Photography, Gregory Sandor; Editor: Monte Hellman; Music, Richard Markovitz

Cast: Warren Oates (Willet Gashade); Will Hutchins (Coley); Millie Perkins (The Woman); Jack Nicholson (Billy Spear); B. J. Merholz (Leland Drum)

Running time 82 minutes

When a film project entitled *Epitaph*, based

on a script written together by Monte Hellman and Nicholson and dealing, in part, with the issue of abortion, fell through because Roger Corman doubted its commercial appeal, Hellman and Jack Nicholson persuaded Corman to put up the money for a 'chamber western', *The Shooting*, based on a script by Carol Eastman, who eventually chose to use the name of Adrien Joyce in the film's credits. Indeed, Corman, ever one to go for economy of scale, agreed to a two-picture deal with Hellman and Nicholson, with Nicholson scheduled to write the script for a companion western after they had finished the first one. Corman did not want his name to appear as producer, so Hellman and Nicholson were also to be billed as co-producers.

Having scouted various western locations, including 'John Ford's' Monument Valley and the Alabama Hills near Lone Pine in northern California, Hellman and Nicholson finally chose a bleak desert landscape near to the Zion National Park in Utah for the location for *The Shooting*. This setting, and the style in which Hellman and his cinematographer shot the characters against the empty landscape, has much to do with any quality the movie has. If in this western Hellman wanted to make an existential statement about the essential meaninglessness of life, as it appears he did, then he could hardly have chosen a more appropriate background. It is greatly to the credit of Hellman and Nicholson that they did not give Corman what he seemingly wanted, 'a tomahawk and ketchup number', as Nicholson later described it, but went instead for a redefining of the western genre and the inscription of some philosophical meaning. Whether or not the resulting movie is artistically successful, a noble failure, or merely pretentious codswallop, is clearly a matter of personal judgement. I would not claim *The Shooting* is a masterpiece of film, but it is consistently interesting and several cuts above the usual western oater.

But what is the movie about? Well, the answer is the movie does not have one single meaning that was deliberately injected by the makers and which, we, the viewers, have somehow to discover. The film text is there for all of us to interpret as we wish and, indeed, most of us will arrive at different interpretations according to the route we take in getting into the movie. But what we can state is that the narrative is not transparent and the motivations of the figures within the narrative are, to say the very least, open to discussion. There is no clear-cut, linear story, and the resolution is ambiguous in the extreme. It is hardly surprising that the movie did not receive a wide release and that it garnered much praise in France as an existential western.

Warren Oates, excellent as usual, plays Willet Gashade, an ex-bounty hunter. Returning to an isolated mine that he owns with two partners, he realizes he is being tracked by a mysterious stranger. Back at the mine, he is told by the simpleton Coley (Will Hutchins) that his brother Coigne has vanished and that his friend Leland Drum has been shot dead and lies in a freshly dug grave. A woman (Millie Perkins) arrives at the mine and offers Gashade money to take her across the desert on a mission she refuses to talk about. Coley has mentioned that Coigne has probably been involved in an incident in a nearby town in which a man and a child had been killed. They set out on their meaningless trek, Coley being smitten with the woman, who sports a gun and acts in an imperious way. They are tracked by Billy Spears (Nicholson) who seems to be the woman's protector and takes against Coley in particular. Spears is a cold-blooded professional gunman (in his black hat and waistcoat and his chilling grin, Nicholson reminds us of the Jack Palance character, Wilson, in *Shane*). The woman resolutely refuses to discuss the object of the journey, although Gashade guesses that she

The Shooting. Nicholson as a latter-day Jack Palance with The Woman (Millie Perkins).

intends killing someone and that this is somehow connected with his missing brother and his involvement with the killings in the nearby town. As she is so intent in making good time, the woman rides her horse to death, and Spears forces Coley to give up his horse to her, leaving him in the desert to near certain death. Gashade seems unable to do anything for his buddy except leave him a water canteen. However, Coley catches up with the trio thanks to a horse he takes from a dead man he encounters in the desert, and, against Gashade's advice, he faces up to Spears who kills him. This forces Gashade to do something and in a struggle he overpowers Spears and uses a rock to break his gun hand. The woman, who is not named, has disappeared, but he finds her taking aim at a man on a ridge. He tries to stop her, perhaps because he realizes it is his brother Coigne, or because it is really himself. In a confusing ending, the woman and Gashade appear to die. Has Gashade been pursuing his own death and, by making the choice to accompany the woman, has he made the ultimate existential decision: the choice between life and death? The last moments of the film are long shots of Spears alone in the barren landscape clutching his broken hand, which could be interpreted as a metaphor for human existence: we are wounded isolated figures struggling to find some purpose in a hostile world.

Journeys are frequently used as allegories for existence and the landscape of wilderness is often a metaphor for the essential pointlessness of life, so there is nothing original about their use by Hellman, Eastman (the screenwriter) and Nicholson, but the movie is so tellingly shot by the director and lighting cameraman that the endless shots of the these figures against this bleak environment create a resonance that forces you to think in terms of deeper significance than the plot level or the motivation of individual characters. Indeed, it is clear that Hellman and his collaborators have eschewed making things easy for their audience in terms of narrative sequence and why the characters behave in the way they do. The movie is like an extended nightmare where nothing makes much sense and it ends in total confusion. Point of view shots remind us that all reality is subjective and that there is possibly no such definable thing as reality anyway. Indeed, struggling to make

logical sense out of it all is somewhat like trying to untangle the complexities of a dream. If you are to enjoy the film, let the images wash over you and do not get bogged down in what we might call the semantic meaning.

Nicholson's performance as Spears is evidence that as an actor he has advanced a great deal since his first faltering steps in the early Corman movies. It is not a part that gives him great opportunities for bravura acting, but he is convincing as the young, amoral and cold killer. His screen presence now has an authority that it had often lacked in the past. This role is an important steppingstone in the apprenticeship that will eventually see him play morally ambiguous characters in his major films. That he contributed to the movie not just in terms of his acting is also unarguable, and he must have been proud that, despite the hard fact that the movie made no money, he had been an essential member of a team that made one of the best westerns of the decade. Hellman and Nicholson had showed that low-budget movies within a popular and well-worn genre such as the western need not be totally conventional and anonymous. The statements about life that the movie appears to be making may be pretentious and hollow, but at the very least they were trying to make something serious. I like the movie and it has acquired more than a cult status, which is too often associated with campery. It is a pity that Hellman was not able to go on to be one of the major directors in Hollywood. Uncompromising talents like his are few and far between in Tinseltown.

Ride in the Whirlwind (1966)

A Proteus Film: Director, Monte Hellman; Producers, Monte Hellman and Jack Nicholson; Screenplay, Jack Nicholson; Cinematography, Gregory Sandor; Editor, Monte Hellman; Music, Robert Drasnin

Cast: Cameron Mitchell (Vern); Jack Nicholson (Wes); Millie Perkins (Abby); Tom Fuler (Otis); Katherine Squire (Catherine); George Mitchell (Evan); Brandon Caroll (The Sheriff)

Running time 82 minutes

This companion western to *The Shooting*, shot

back-to-back with that film by more or less the same team, handled similar themes and was suffused with the same pessimism. The film exists as a kind of counterpoint to westerns such as *Shane* which stress an optimistic view of the West and human nature in general and where the morality and resolution of the problems faced by the main characters are always neatly resolved. If *The Shooting* may be viewed as an existential western, so can *Ride in the Whirlwind* in the sense that it represents human beings adrift in a meaningless universe and subject to arbitrary acts of injustice and cruelty.

The plot, such as it is, has striking similarities to the storyline of *The Shooting*. Vern (Cameron Mitchell) and Wes (Nicholson) are forced to leave the small ranch they share because someone called Cain (whom we never see) is about to arrive to extract revenge or, perhaps, to arrest them. There is a deliberate vagueness of detail which adds to the film's general tone of paranoia. They start out on a journey seemingly without a destination. They fall in with a gang of outlaws (they do not know this initially), accepting their hospitality, but a posse catches up with the rustlers and they are assumed to be members of the gang. They are forced to run and to continue to run.

This time Nicholson is not playing a psychotic, but a young cowboy with a wanderlust. This is another side of the Nicholson screen persona, the aspect that is charming and rather naive in some ways. But the character's simplicity is no defence against a vengeful fate that has him branded an outlaw. Society gives him an identity that he cannot elude and he has to pay the price.

Thus, *Ride in the Whirlwind* has its pretensions to 'art', as did *The Shooting*. It shows the influences of the European art film in its bleakness of vision and its concentration on visual composition that emphasizes the characters' isolation and the constant threat they are under from a hostile world. Can a slight, low-budget western carry that much significance, or is this merely an example of Hollywood filmmakers getting in over their heads and aping the style of their European betters? Once more I would come down on the positive side and, while admitting that the film has its pretentious aspects, I would claim that it is a worthwhile addition to the western genre, which too often deals in clichés and well-worn narrative paths. At least, *Ride in the Whirlwind* has the courage not to spoon-feed its audience and not to spell out in capital letters what the movie is about. As a viewer, you are left to a large extent to make up your mind what it means, if anything. For such small Hollywood mercies, we should be eternally grateful.

Hell's Angels on Wheels (1967)

Fanfare Films: Director, Richard Rush; Producer, Joe Solomon; Screenplay, R. Wright Campbell; Cinematography, Lazlo Kovacs; Editor, William Martin; Music composed by Stu Phillips and performed by The Poor

Cast: Jack Nicholson (Poet); Adam Rourke (Buddy); Sabrina Scharf (Shill); Jana Taylor (Abigale); John Garwood (Jock); Richard Anders (Bull); Sonny Barger (Himself/Angels Leader)

Running time 85 minutes

Nicholson's next two films would both be cheap exploitation flicks. Roger Corman's *The Wild Angels* starring Peter Fonda had made big bucks at the box office and so further biker movies were bound to follow. Richard Rush had directed Nicholson in *Too Soon To Love* and now he cast him as a rebellious middle-class young man called Poet who throws in his temporary job as a grease monkey to tag along with a Hell's Angels gang led by Buddy (Adam Rourke). There is a rivalry between Poet and Buddy over Shill, the leader's woman, and this rivalry intensifies until there is a fight at the end of the movie in which Buddy is killed. Before that, we have witnessed the gang in fights with sailors, rednecks and other Hell's Angels, as well as indulging in mild orgies and initiation ceremonies, the chief purpose of which seems to be the humiliation of the prospective member. Poet's attitude to the wilder behaviour of the Angels is represented as ambivalent and the end of the movie leaves it in the air as to whether he will claim the leadership of the gang or whether he will abandon the neo-fascist lifestyle of the Angels for good.

The one outstanding feature of *Hell's Angels on Wheels*, apart from the banality of the dialogue and dramatic incident, is Lazlo Kovacs's

Hell's Angels on Wheels. Nicholson as Poet and Adam Rourke as Buddy act out quintessential sixties fantasy: bikes and chicks, man.

cinematography. He manages to invest the desert landscapes and highways along which the gang travel on their Harley-Davidsons with fresh interest. Perhaps Richard Rush, the director, deserves some credit for the visual impact of the movie, because it is clear that he did not waste much time directing his actors or perfecting the script. In these circumstances, Nicholson's performance is creditable. He manages to give some credibility to the part of the alienated Poet who, in his alienation from mainstream American life, desperately latches onto biker culture, which, as represented here, consists of mindless violence, reverence for leader figures and a generally fascist frame of mind.

The commercial rationale behind *Hell's Angels on Wheels* paid off as the movie became something of a cult success. The movie retains a certain passing interest because Nicholson is playing a character caught between two worlds and not fitting in comfortably with either. This could be said to reflect Nicholson's real-life situation in relation to mainstream Hollywood and

America in general. He is a rebel by nature, but he desperately wants to belong as well and to enjoy the fruits of the success that only the straight world can really offer. His incorporation into the Hollywood mainstream would not be long delayed.

Rebel Rousers (1967)

Paragon: Director, Martin B. Cohen; Producer, Martin B. Cohen; Screenplay, Abe Polsky, Michael Kars and Martin B. Cohen; Cinematography, Leslie Kouvacs (Lazlo Kovacs); Editor, Thor Brooks; Music, William Loose

Cast: Cameron Mitchell (Collier); Bruce Dern (J.J.); Jack Nicholson (Bunny); Diane Ladd (Karen); Dean Stanton, Neil Burstyn, Lou Procopio, Earl Finn, Phil Carey (The Rebels); Robert Dix (Miguel); some citizens of Chloride, Arizona

Running time 78 minutes

Nicholson had had a 'friendly' rivalry with Bruce

Hell's Angels on Wheels. Jack looks suitably cool in shades and biker gear in this location shot.

Dern ever since meeting him at Martin Landau's acting class in the fifties. Later, when Nicholson was a star, he remarked that Dern had been Roger Corman's favourite actor and hence he always lost out to his rival when the leading parts came up in Corman movies. Once more, then, in *Rebel Rousers* he was playing second string to Dern and their off-screen rivalry spills over into the narrative as Nicholson playing a would-be rapist, Bunny, challenges J.J.'s (Dern) authority over the biker gang. Dern is a very accomplished

actor and perhaps if he had possessed more conventionally handsome looks, he would have rivalled Nicholson's later superstar status, instead of largely 'disappearing' after initial successes. Some would argue that he is a subtler, more intelligent actor than Nicholson, and *Rebel Rousers* offers a chance to compare the styles of these two competitive buddies.

Dern and his small biker gang hit a small town in Arizona. There he meets Collier (Cameron

Mitchell), a high school buddy, who has since gone 'straight' and is in town on the trail of his partner, whom he has made pregnant. This lady, Karen (Diane Ladd), is determined to have the baby and has left Collier because he has tried to persuade her to have an abortion. They are arguing in their car on the nearby shoreline when they are terrorized by some members of the gang. J.J. tries to protect his former friend, but finds himself in a difficult position, open to charges from gang members that he is going soft by protecting these straights. Bunny/Nicholson leads the charge and is intent on having sex with Karen. J.J. explains to Karen that he is playing for time by suggesting a drag race to decide whether Bunny will have her or not. Collier, who has been badly beaten up, escapes to the town, where he is greeted with indifference by the townspeople when he begs for help to free Karen. However, a family of noble Mexicans living beside the beach eventually help and Karen is freed. Bunny/Nicholson, the villain of the piece, is killed in a knife struggle with J.J.

Nicholson may be playing second string to Dern, but he does his best to grab attention by wearing 'convict-style' striped trousers and a stocking cap. The trousers certainly ensure you can't miss him in the ensemble scenes. The arguments between Dern and him have a certain intensity, possibly arising from their off-screen rivalry, and this feature gives a certain edge to the movie it would not have had otherwise. Nicholson is convincingly nasty as Bunny and you can detect in this performance some of the characteristics that would define future Nicholson baddies: the grin, the flirtatiousness, the dangerous undertow of anger. As for Dern, he has a very individual way of delivering lines, even lines as dud as 'I can make it myself. I think that's what it's all about anyway.' He makes every line sound as though he were saying it for the first time and it is really emanating from the character he is playing. In the first scene of the movie when he encounters his former high school buddy, he subtly manages to convey some kind of regret that his life has not taken the same path as Collier's. Dern was a serious rival in the acting stakes for Nicholson and their rivalry was no doubt based on mutual respect and on the knowledge that they were both major players in the acting game.

The St Valentine Days Massacre (1967)

20th Century Fox: Director, Roger Corman; Producer, Roger Corman; Screenplay, Howard Browne; Cinematography, Milton Krasner; Editor, William B. Murphy; Music, Lionel Newman and Fred Steiner Cast: Jason Robards Jnr. (Al Capone); George Segal (George Gusenberg); Ralph Meeker (Bugs Moran); Clint Ritchie (Jack McGurn); Frank Silvero (Sorella); Joseph Campanella (Wienshank); Bruce Dern (May); Harold J. Stone (Frank Nitti); John Agar (Dion O'Bannion); Jack Nicholson (driver)

Running time 100 minutes

Nicholson's participation in Corman's big-budget gangster movie is minimal. He has one short speech and is on screen for a mere fraction of the running time of a hundred minutes. He was offered the part of the mechanic that Bruce Dern played, but turned it down for a smaller part that meant he was used in different scenes over a number of weeks and thereby guaranteed a big pay cheque. The Dern role would have meant a week-and-a-half's work; the role of the getaway driver for the killers ensured a seven week 'carry through', although he was only required for two days. Nicholson may have been serious about his acting, but he was still hungry and in this case he chose money over the size of the role.

At last, Corman's efforts on Poverty Row had won a contract with a big studio, 20th Century Fox. He had a good cast lead by Jason Robards, George Segal and Ralph Meeker. He was able to use the Chicago street sets, shoot in colour, have proper 1920s cars, lavish costumes and set decoration. For those who prefer Corman cheap and nasty, then this is one of the films he directed that they despise. There is a peculiar type of inverted snobbery among some cinema buffs that will laud movies done on a shoestring and shot in a few days, and denigrate the costlier films shot by the same director because somehow, it is thought, contact with the studio system corrupts the primitive talent of the auteur. *St Valentine Day's Massacre* is certainly no cinematic masterpiece and is definitely not the work of an auteur, but it is not that bad a movie. It is indisputably (except, of course, to a connoisseur of Corman schlock) superior to

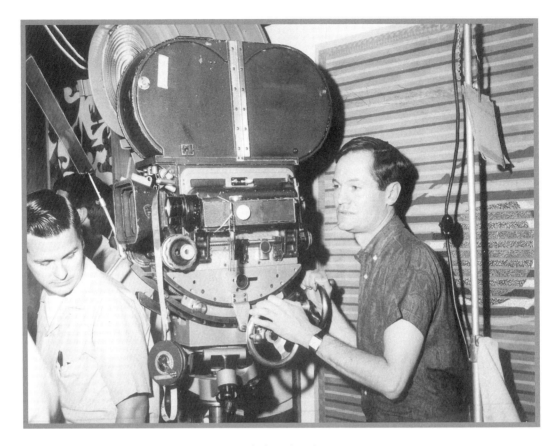

The Trip. Roger Corman behind the camera during shooting.

most of Corman's earlier films.

The movie's main faults are a rambling screenplay that remains unfocused and a corny *Untouchables* type narration that is intrusive and unnecessary. The use of the documentary-style voiceover is reminiscent of Kubrick's *The Killing*, but Corman's flick has none of the flair or the tension of the 1956 heist tale. The film too often seems like a pastiche of past gangster films and the performances from the normally talented leads are undistinguished. George Segal, in particular, is sadly miscast as a sadistic hood and suggests a slightly more sinister Sky Masterson from a touring production of *Guys and Dolls* rather than a psychotic. Surprisingly, that convincing actor, Jason Robards, finds no variation or depth in his playing of Al Capone, which perhaps is a fault of the screenplay. Ralph Meeker comes

out best of the principal actors. However, the movie is confusing and confused; at times, it is difficult to know why someone is bumping off someone else and there is no central protagonist for the audience to latch on to. There are extended scenes with no real point or attachment to the main narrative, notably a fight between Segal and his moll which is thrown in, it seems, as a parody of similar Cagney scenes in the old Warner Brothers gangster movies.

Nicholson delivers his lines in a high-pitched, throaty voice, in imitation of other gangster characters from the heyday of the genre. If an actor has three lines in a movie, then he has to make them count and that Nicholson assuredly tries to do. He explains why a gangster colleague is greasing bullets: 'It's garlic. The bullets don't kill you. You die of blood poisoning.' It is hardly the stuff of great acting and his role was not to get him noticed by critics or public, but there was a fat reward for very little work. For that, he had to thank his old pal, Roger Corman.

The Trip (1967)

American International: Director, Roger Corman; Producer, Roger Corman; Screenplay, Jack Nicholson; Cinematography, Arch Dalzell; Editor, Ronald Sinclair

Cast: Peter Fonda (Paul); Bruce Dern (John); Susan Strasberg (Sally); Dennis Hopper (Max); Salli Sachse (Glenn): Katherine Walsh (Lulu); Barboura Morris (Flo)

Running time 85 minutes

Nicholson wrote the part of John, Peter Fonda's 'minder' in this movie who sees him through an acid trip, with himself in mind, but Corman once more cast his 'favourite actor' Bruce Dern in the role. Nicholson need not have fretted too long about the loss of this part because *The Trip*, whatever else it is, is not an actors' picture, which is just as well because Peter Fonda has by far the largest part in it.

Nicholson's initial ambition to be a writer had somehow got sidelined by his acting jobs, but he wrote this screenplay for Corman based on his own experience of taking LSD under controlled laboratory conditions and also on his marriage break-up with first wife, Sandra Knight. *The Trip* was the first 'overground' American movie to try to represent the acid experience and it is little more than a Technicolor psychedelic roller-coaster of a film with minimal plot and characterization, not to mention dialogue. The imagery of the film is clearly influenced by European art movies, especially those by Ingmar Bergman and the Fellini who made phoney junk like *Juliet of the Spirits*. Viewed now, it has a certain historical interest but it does not add significantly to our knowledge of the drug experience or, for that matter, to the art of the motion picture.

The Trip, then, is replete with pop art imagery, derivative arthouse cinema sequences (hooded horsemen pursuing Fonda through a forest, for example), very fast editing and lots of conventional love scenes. If it is not an actors' movie, neither is it really a writer's film, so Nicholson's screenwriting credit was never likely to do much for his writing career. *The Trip* is a concoction aimed at the drive-in market and created by Corman as director and producer, Arch Dalzell, his cameraman, and Ronald Sinclair, his editor. Add a largely jarring score by The Electric Flag, and you have the sum of *The Trip*. The film hedges its bets about the effects of taking LSD. Is it life-enhancing or not? 'I'll think about that tomorrow,' says Fonda/Paul at the end of the film. It is a wholly dated film, a product of the drug and youth culture of the sixties, or, at least, an attempt to cash in on that phenomenon. Nicholson's participation in it reemphasized his connection with the counterculture, and his connections with Corman, Dennis Hopper (who plays a drug pusher in the movie) and Peter Fonda would lead to the big break that would make such cheapie exploiters as *The Trip* a feature of his past.

Psych-Out (1968)

American International: Director, Richard Rush; Producer, Dick Clark; Screenplay, E. Hunter Willett and Betty Ulius, from a story by E. Hunter Willett; Cinematography, Lazlo Kovacs; Editor, Ken Reynolds; Music, Kronald Stein

Cast: Susan Strasberg (Jennie); Dean Stockwell (Dave); Jack Nicholson (Stoney); Bruce Dern (Steve); Adam Roarke (Ben); Max Julien (Elwood); Henry Jaglom (Warren)

Running time 101 minutes

Just as *Ride in the Whirlwind* had been a companion piece to *The Shooting*, so *Psych-Out* was meant to perform the same function in relation to *The Trip*. Nicholson had written a script that director Richard Rush thought was too 'experimental' for mainstream cinema, so the concept of a 'youth' film based in San Francisco and dealing with flower power and drugs was taken over by other writers and Nicholson did not eventually receive a screen credit for his work, although he took what was essentially the male lead in the picture. *Psych-Out*'s main interest nowadays is as an

Psych-Out. Jack Nicholson (Stoney) slumbers while Susan Strasberg (Jennie) attempts to wake him.

interesting period piece and an exemplar of how Hollywood sought to cash in on the drugs and hippie phenomenon. The movie audience out there was mainly under twenty-five, so movies had to be churned out to draw them into the cinemas.

The story concerns a straight, but deaf, young woman, Jennie (Strasberg) who comes to San Francisco in search of her brother, Steve (Bruce Dern). The cops are looking for her as one of the many teenage runaways of the time and she is protected from them by three members of a folk rock band. She shares a communal house with them and gradually she and Stoney (Nicholson) become lovers. Stoney is ambitious to get on in the music world, even though another member of the band, Dave (Dean Stockwell) warns him about the dangers of selling out. Dave tries to make Jennie, giving her a hallucinatory drug. This engenders a bad trip, which is represented in

kaleidoscopic style on the screen. She finally locates Dave in a burning building. He is having a really heavy trip and his sister, still under the influence, wanders onto the Golden Gate Bridge, where she is saved by Stoney, who has come to realize he really loves her. Dave, however, is hit by a truck and dies with the immortal lines, 'Reality is a deadly place. I hope this trip was a good one.'

Hardly a cliché about drugs and flower power remains unused in this meretricious effort. The several attempts to recreate the nightmare visions induced by taking acid are less than convincing. Characters are given to saying things like 'It's all one plastic hassle' and the few 'straights' that are represented are shown to be either rednecks intent on teaching the hippies a lesson or outraged middle-class citizens offended by the way they dress and their long hair. On the one hand, the movie shows a cleaned-up version of San Francisco hippie life and on the other, it has an in-built conservatism that emphasizes the wholly negative sides of drug-taking. As is usual for this kind of exploitation movie, it tries to have its cake and eat it. It cannot be seen in any way to be condoning drugs or the lifestyle of the characters, but at the same time it represents the characters as having a good time and the straight world comes over as distinctly unattractive.

Another period interest is the soundtrack supplied by groups such as the Strawberry Alarm Clock and The Seeds. They remind us about how soft soft rock could be at times. The movie recreates the Haight-Ashbury of the time and undoubtedly it has some significance as a historical document. People fifty years from now will view this film and use it as evidence of a passing cultural phase in the 1960s, but for anyone who lived through the time, it is apparent that it never rises above the obvious, the clichéd and the superficial.

However, Jack Nicholson displays a continuing assuredness in his role as the selfish and somewhat callous Stoney. There is the arrogance, the intelligence, the bitterness and the charm. In some ways, it is a trial run for the role that would make him a star: George Hanson in *Easy Rider*. His character's part in the narrative could be read as a commentary on Nicholson's own career and his attitudes to the counterculture and success. Stoney is bumbling along playing gigs when he and his band get the chance to play a big San Francisco venue. Stoney is the member of the band who works the hardest and is focused on getting somewhere. After he has slept with Jennie, he is dismissive of her when she wants his attention and he is deep in rehearsal and preparing for his big break. He dismisses Dave's warnings about fantasizing about buying 'Continentals' as so much hippie bullshit, and it is clear he wants the money and success that the straight promoters, anxious to exploit the appeal an acid band has for the punters, offer. Nicholson wrote the part of Stoney for himself as part of the package. His co-star, Adam Rorke, has commented on how far ahead of the rest of them Nicholson was in thinking in these 'package' terms. Nicholson was intent on promoting himself and wanted to be a big

name in the movie business. His personal ambitions are paralleled in the movie by the desires of Stoney, his character.

Susan Strasberg is adequate as Jennie, and Dean Stockwell is convincingly repellent as the phoney Dave. However, Bruce Dern as the brother, known as 'The Seeker' has an unfortunate time running round in a shoulder-length wig. It is the only time I have ever seen this fine actor look silly on screen.

Head (1968)

A Raybert production for Columbia: Director, Bob Rafelson; Producers, Bob Rafelson and Jack Nicholson; Screenplay, Bob Rafelson and Jack Nicholson; Cinematography, Michael Hugo; Editor, Mike Pozen; Musical Director, Ken Thorne; Music Co-ordinator, Igo Cantor

Cast: Davey Jones, Mike Nesmith, Peter Tork, Micky Dolenz as The Monkees; Victor Mature (The Big Victor); Annette Funicello (Minnie); Timothy Carey, Logan Ramsey and Frank Zappa in cameo roles

Running time 86 minutes

Bob Rafelson and producer Bert Schneider 'owned' a part of the Monkees, having been asked by American television executives to create a homogenized version of the Beatles for a television series. The Monkees enjoyed a surprising popularity for a short period in the mid-sixties through the television show and even records, despite the fact that the music press exposed the fact that they did not play the guitars themselves in the recordings and had very limited vocal talents. The creation of the Monkees is a testimony to the cynicism pervading the exploitation of the teen market: it was all about selling ad time on television and shifting merchandise to naive teenagers desperate to buy anything associated with their new heroes. For Rafelson it had been a lucrative venture, but he undoubtedly felt guilty about it as well. There he was aiming to be a serious filmmaker and yet he had been instrumental in manufacturing the most plastic and talentless pop group of the era to milk the disposable 'incomes' of the young.

By 1968, everyone had had enough of The

Monkees, including the members of the group themselves, who were becoming increasingly sensitive to the criticisms levelled at them and tired of how they were being exploited by the record and television companies. Rafelson, despite the pangs of guilt he felt about the successful monster he had helped to create, persuaded Columbia to finance a movie to feature the less-than-fab four. But he was to use the project to expose the falseness that lay behind the manufacturing of such a phenomenon and, in the process, more or less kill off his creation: Frankenstein destroying the Creature.

Jack Nicholson was chosen to help write the screenplay, apparently on the back of his efforts for *Psych-Out*, because Rafelson wanted a freewheeling psychedelic script with little or no linear progression and certainly no narrative lines. In the event, Rafelson shared the screenwriting credit with Nicholson, which did not go down well with the Monkees themselves who claimed they had contributed to the script during a period spent in the desert with Rafelson and Nicholson when they had

Head. The less-than fab four think about those missing screenwriting credits.

'brainstormed' and come up with ideas for the movie, stoked, it is rumoured, by plentiful smoking of pot. But *Head* (the title refers to 'pot head' or what is going on in the collective head of The Monkees) is not a writers' movie; if it is anything, it belongs to the director, just as the Beatles' films, *A Hard Days Night* and *Help!* had belonged, to his credit or otherwise, to Richard Lester. Indeed, these two movies were clearly the model for Rafelson's film, but whereas the incorrigibly trivial Lester had been content to operate on the level of sight gags and a spurious brand of whimsical charm, Rafelson wanted to say something more weighty within the framework of what could have been a worthless and exploitative pop movie.

Nicholson has said that *Head* is about the suicide of The Monkees and that seems an apt description. It is their swan song, involving a tacit admission that they were a total fabrication and a con on the teenage public in particular. Nicholson wrote the lyric for the theme song of the movie, a parody of the television show's introductory music:

> *Hey, hey, we are the Monkees*
> *You know we love to please*
> *A manufactured image*
> *With no philosophy.*

The film opens with the Monkees disrupting an official occasion and a Mayor's speech. Mickey Dolenz jumps off a bridge and as he floats beneath the water, the Monkees are singing 'Goodbye, goodbye, goodbye…'. Images of a Monkees concert are intercut with gruesome images of the Vietnam conflict and the movie is clearly trying to say something about the manipulations of the communications industry. Crazy fans get to the Monkees and rip them apart, but they are tearing dummies asunder, not real people. There are montages of old movie clips from *Gilda*, *Golden Boy* to Bela Lugosi flicks. There are parodies of western and war movies, and every so often the audience are reminded that they are watching a film that has been made for their consumption. This is not reality, the filmmakers are saying, this is fiction. Rafelson, Nicholson and the film crew intrude into shot, conferring and reminding us that someone put all of this together. One of the Monkees walks off set angrily, telling Rafelson that he's through with it all. There are cameos by Victor Mature and Timothy Carey. In between the parodies, each Monkee does a 'turn'. There are old ads, more Vietnam footage, an Eastern guru figure and a Coca Cola machine that is blown up in the desert. The film is an assault on American consumerism, business and the war machine. At the end of the movie, we return to where it started with the Monkees being pursued and disrupting the official occasion. All four plunge from the bridge and the soundtrack plays 'Goodbye, goodbye...'.

Head is a brave attempt to make something meaningful out of dross. It is partially successful and the movie does manage to make some telling points about the control of the media by powerful forces in American society. The Monkees themselves are seen as part of that syndrome as well as being victims of it. The juxtapositioning of images, the fast editing, the kaleidoscopic, 'sixties' look, all add up to the statement 'style is meaning'. The Monkees were all about manufactured images and that phoney image, the filmmakers are saying, means nothing. The film was not a box-office success, probably because the Monkees craze was well on the wane by then, but possibly also because it was saying things well over the heads of its intended audience. It is possible to view *Head* as a rather cynical and belated apologia by Rafelson and others involved in the making of the Monkees, who, having made big bucks from their creation, then, when the group's popularity was on the wane, made an arty little film decrying the whole project. I prefer to give Rafelson the benefit of the doubt and applaud his talented attempt to make a statement about the kind of media manipulation he had been involved in himself. Nicholson also comes out with some credit for having helped to create a screenplay that supplied Rafelson with the launching-pad for this diverting movie, which has still some relevance for us today.

Easy Rider (1969)

Columbia: Director, Dennis Hopper; Producer, Peter Fonda; Screenplay, Peter Fonda, Dennis Hopper and Terry Southern; Cinematography, Lazlo Kovacs; Editor, Dawn Cambren; Music performed by Steppenwolf, The Byrds, The Band, The Holy Mondal Rounders, Fratenity of Man, The Jimi Hendrix Experience, Little Eva, The Electric Prunes, Electric Flag and Roger McGuin

Cast: Peter Fonda (Wyatt/Captain America); Dennis Hopper (Billy/Billy the Kid); Jack Nicholson (George Hanson); Antonio Mendoza (Jesus); Phil Spector (Connection); Robert walker (Hippie Leader); Sabrina Scharf (Hippie Girl); Luana Anders (Lisa); Karen Black (Karen); Warren Finnerty (Rancher)

Running time 94 minutes

You would need to be one of the Venusians Nicholson's character George Hanson talks about in one of the campfire scenes in *Easy Rider* not to know that this is the movie that transformed Nicholson from an actor stuck in small-budget movies to being a hot property in mainstream Hollywood. Yet it all came about by chance when the actor originally cast as Hanson, Rip Torn, walked out of the picture, reputedly more than somewhat disenchanted with director Dennis Hopper's meandering and incoherent ways. Nicholson, sent on location as a kind of minder by the producing company, Raybert Productions (Bob Rafelson and Bert Schneider), to try to influence the wayward and largely stoned Hopper to get on with things, was on hand to step into the role, after Torn stormed out a restaurant saying he wasn't going to do their bullshit picture. Nicholson got the part despite Hopper's objections, but with the full support of Rafelson and Schneider. It was to be the biggest break of his career and one of the reasons why Nicholson is now the subject of books like this one. It is ironic, too, that his energies were at that point in his career turning more towards screenwriting and directing than acting. But he had the good sense not to turn down such a juicy role and, not to be too uncharitable, he may have felt that with Fonda and Hopper in the two ostensible leading parts, he might be able to steal the picture from under their coke-stuffed noses. Of course, his big break might have come later in another film, but, then again, maybe not. From such twists of fate, and being in the right place at the right time, are great careers born.

Easy Rider can only usefully be viewed now within its social and historical context. Viewed as a historical film text, it has its own

Easy Rider. Nicholson as George Hanson gets Peter Fonda (Wyatt) and Dennis Hopper out of jail.

fascination. As a movie divorced from its context, it seems unbearably pretentious and phoney. Peter Fonda's role in the movie, and its making, is particularly hard to take. Here was this rich Hollywood movie star, the son of Hollywood royalty, playing at being a dropout and seemingly embracing hippiedom and the counterculture in general, whilst making sententious comments on contemporary American society, before retreating to his LA pad to count his money from the box-office proceeds. *Easy Rider* is an example of how Hollywood will incorporate almost anything to make a buck. Even if the principal players in the making of the movie did belong to the more unconventional and wilder shores of the film colony, none of them were in any danger of following the hippies they seem to admire so much in the movie and dropping out from the rat-race. They were all intent on furthering their Hollywood careers and

Easy Rider is as much an exploitation movie as any of Roger Corman's efforts.

Fonda plays Wyatt (Wyatt Earp – geddit?), who is also referred to as Captain America. Hopper plays Billy (yes, Billy the Kid!) and after setting up a lucrative drugs deal with a rich dealer (played by Phil Spector, the record producer), they take off on their Harley-Davidsons for the Mardi Gras in New Orleans. Wyatt/Fonda has the stars-and-stripes painted over his gas tank and helmet, while Billy/Hopper favours braided hide jackets, cowboy-style. Wyatt/Fonda, it is implied, may be a bit of a rebel, but he's basically a patriot at heart; he just has a different way of showing his patriotism from the rednecks. Wyatt and Billy are modern outlaws. Indeed, the characters' association with the old American West and its values is unsubtly stressed as they motor their way through the southwest

Easy Rider. Nicholson (Hanson) on back of Peter Fonda's bike as they follow the yellow brick road to New Orleans.

towards their destination. The endless shots of the staggering desert landscapes give the makers of the film ample opportunity to stuff the soundtrack with counterculture musical hits, including Hendrix, Steppenwolf and The Byrds. The name of this game is to sell records, of course, and the soundtrack of *Easy Rider* duly obliged, selling millions of copies.

One of their first stops, after being refused lodging at a motel, is on a ranch, whose simple but friendly owner invites the two heroes to share a meal with him and his large family. These people are clearly meant to symbolize something fine and enduring about the American West, a West that has largely disappeared at the hands of multi-corporations and oil interests. The parallel between the ranchers and the modern-day hippies is explicitly made through crosscutting between Hopper changing a tyre on his bike and the

rancher shoeing a horse. Fonda/Wyatt gives his royal seal of approval to the rancher: 'You do your own thing in your own time. You should be proud.' They pick up a hippie called Jesus (yes, I'm afraid so!), who tells them 'All cities are alike. That's why I'm out here now.' When they stop overnight in the desert, he informs them that 'The people this place belongs to are buried right under you,' this being a reference to the land having been stolen from Native Americans.

Jesus leads them to a hippie community in the wilderness. There are excruciating scenes where we see these 'city kids' planting seeds; these hippies are shot as though they are present-day Jesus disciples, but they look distinctly like stray extras from a fifties Hollywood biblical epic, a bunch of Jeffrey Hunter lookalikes from *King of Kings*. Fonda once more offers his saintly seal of approval: 'They're going to make it,' he says. It was desert hippie communities like these that a

Easy Rider. You see, Pete, here are these Venusians. Nicholson and Fonda around the camp fire.

few years later would produce Manson and his acolytes, who would murder Sharon Tate and others in Hollywood. When Billy gets restless about moving on, Fonda says, 'I'm hip about time, but I just gotta go.'

Wyatt and Billy are thrown into jail in a small, redneck town for parading without a permit when they drive behind a marching band and majorettes. There they meet a local lawyer and character, George Hanson, who is recovering from a alcoholic bender and who is well liked by the cops, whom he knows how to rub along with, even though most of his work is for the American Civil Liberties Union. Hanson says he can get them out of jail if they haven't killed anyone, 'anyone white, that is'. He has helped to free other long-haired counterculture types who have been victimized by 'scissor-happy beautify America' citizens. Invited to accompany our heroes to New Orleans, Hanson dons his

university sweater and his football helmet and hitches a lift on one of the bikes. He is introduced to the smoking of pot around the campfire and on one of these evenings under the stars he tells Wyatt and Billy about his belief in Venusians who live, work and mate with the rest of us without our knowing, because the government are engaged in a massive cover-up. He also gives us the benefit of his ruminations on the state of the nation: 'This used to be a helluva good country. I can't understand what's gone wrong with it…I mean, it's real hard to be free when you are bought and sold in the marketplace. 'Course don't ever tell anybody that they're not free, 'cause then they're going to get real busy killin' and maimin' to prove to you that they are…they see a free individual, it's gonna scare them.'

When they enter a cafe whose customers are a redneck sheriff and assorted equally prejudiced citizens who refer to 'Yankee queers', they leave because they feel menaced, but that night the rednecks attack them with clubs and Hanson is killed. Wyatt and Bill continue on to New Orleans where they visit a whorehouse that Hanson has enthused to them about. They enjoy the Mardi Gras with two of the girls and have a bad acid trip. On the road again, when Billy says, 'We're rich, man', Wyatt replies, 'You know, Billy, we blew it.' Shortly afterwards, they are shot dead by a redneck from a passing truck.

Undoubtedly, the best sections of the movie are the sequences where Hanson/Nicholson appears. Granted that Nicholson's Texan accent is not really authentic, he still manages to bring a style and a conviction to the part of the drunken lawyer that goes well beyond anything he had achieved on screen before. I remember seeing *Easy Rider* when it was first released in 1969. I was mostly bored by it and offended by the crass pseudo-philosophizing and posturing of Fonda in particular, but I wondered who the actor playing George Hanson was. And so did a lot of other people, because, despite the numerous films he had already made, Nicholson was unknown to the vast majority of movie-goers and to most film critics. Nicholson's playing of the role makes the character believable, whereas Fonda and Hopper are not playing characters as such, but embodiments of certain attitudes that the film wants to propagate. Amidst the Hollywood phoniness and the pretensions to significance and art, Nicholson's performance stands out as the genuine article. He walks away with the picture, his only rival being Lazlo Kovacs's cinematography. Indeed, one compelling reason for seeing *Easy Rider* is the magnificence of the scenery as shot by Kovacs's camera.

Yet *Easy Rider* cannot be dismissed out of hand, despite its essential silliness and hollowness. It does reflect something about America in the late sixties. There is no doubt that many young Americans felt totally alienated from mainstream society at that time and, of course, there was the horrible reality of Vietnam and the draft to contend with. In portraying the hippies in such a

po-faced and solemn way, the makers of *Easy Rider* were unconsciously representing what put so many people off about the sixties counterculture: it was exactly that solemnity, self-importance and self-righteousness that offended many people who were also equally alienated by mainstream America but who did not take the easy dropout route. The opposing political and philosophical camps as represented in *Easy Rider* are wholly stereotyped: the hippies and the rednecks are equally appalling. A mediating figure in the narrative is George Hanson, who is clearly alienated from his community, hence his heavy drinking, but who has not embraced the superficial rebellions of the counterculture before Wyatt and Billy come along. It is perhaps this mediating role in the narrative that Hanson plays that made his character so crucial to the movie, as well as the charisma and style that Jack Nicholson brings to the part. Only die-hard hippie phoneys could possibly identify with the incoherent Hopper, who intersperses 'man' in his speeches so often that it becomes a total parody of that kind of coke-head lingo, or with the bogus Fonda whose style and performance thirty years on only seem even more preposterous and shallow. One interesting aspect of the movie is how women are represented. They are either hippie mothers or whores. And the hippie girls are overwhelmed by the attractiveness of our two heroes. *Plus ça change.*

Nicholson was nominated for the Best Supporting Actor for his role of George Hanson. He lost out to Gig Young for his role in *They Shoot Horses, Don't They?*, but *Easy Rider* had changed his life and career forever. *Easy Rider* had been a massive hit at the box office and with its success, Hollywood finally realized that there was a huge audience out there for youth movies that embraced some of the rebellious attitudes of the counterculture. And Jack Nicholson was at the cusp of this revolution. He had been in the right place at the right time and his innate talents had enabled him to seize the opportunity. He was on his way to superstardom.

3

HARVEST TIME

HARVEST TIME

On A Clear Day You Can See Forever (1970)

Paramount: Director, Vincente Minnelli; Producer, Howard Koch; Screenplay, Alan Jay Lerner; Cinematography, Harry Stradling; Editor, David Bretherton; Musical Direction, Nelson Riddle

Cast: Barbra Streisand (Daisy Gamble); Yves Montand (Dr Marc Chabot); Bob Newhart (Dr Mason Hume); Larry Blyden (Warren Pratt); Jack Nicholson (Tad Pringle); Simon Oakland (Dr Conrad Fuller)

Running time 129 minutes

Actors sometimes make curious and perverse choices of roles. Nicholson did not get the part of Tad Pringle in *On A Clear Day* because of his sudden success in *Easy Rider* for the very good reason that that film was still in the editing stage when he was cast by director Vincente Minnelli. Robert Evans, a pal of Jack's, had asked Minnelli to view *Psych-Out* and the director had liked what he saw of Nicholson. He auditioned him and Nicholson sang a version of 'Don't Blame Me', which somehow got under Minnelli's aesthetic guard. Nicholson was signed for the role, which was initially meant to be a singing part. Minnelli was not only the director of the MGM musical classics *Meet Me in St Louis*, *The Pirate*, *An American in Paris* and *The Band Wagon*, but he had also at one time been married to Judy Garland, so he should have been able to recognize a musical performer when he saw one. The vogue of using 'non-singing, non-dancing'

actors in musicals had begun with Rex Harrison in *My Fair Lady*. These 'amateurs' in the musical field only underlined how talented the great MGM musical stars were, stars such as Gene Kelly, Fred Astaire and Judy Garland. Jack Nicholson was to prove no upstart rival to their reputations, indeed, wiser counsel prevailed and his one scene, which had included a singing duet between Nicholson and Barbra Streisand, was cut in such a way that audiences did not have the doubtful privilege of hearing Nicholson's singing voice. The song was entitled 'Who is there among us who knows?', which might well be a comment on the casting of Nicholson in the picture in the first place.

Nicholson has stated that he chose to be in the movie because of Minnelli. Vincente Minnelli had been undoubtedly one of the most talented of the MGM contracted directors during the great days at the studio, but by 1970, not only were his powers and talents on the wane, but the heyday of the musical were long gone. The great MGM musicals such as *Singin' in the Rain* and *Band Wagon* are essentially dancing musicals; even *Meet Me in St Louis* has a dancing feel to it, because of the movement Minnelli and his cameraman manage to inject into it. But that era had vanished and now we had the static musicals of Julie Andrews, Barbra Streisand and Lerner and Loewe, where people sang and any movement on screen had to be artificially injected through editing techniques. *Funny Girl*, Streisand's one big movie hit at this time, had even been directed by William Wyler, who was decidedly not a specialist director of musicals. *On A Clear Day* was to be the film version of a stage musical by Alan Jay Lerner and Burton Lane; the leads, Streisand and Yves Montand, were singers, not dancers, and so one thing the movie was not going to do was move in the style of the classic MGM musicals.

Minnelli was basically a designer-director, who adapted the style of high art to movie musicals. He was more interested in the visual and decorative aspects of film than anything else and he was notoriously uncommunicative with actors. Indeed, if Minnelli ever finished a sentence on set, or told actors exactly what he wanted, then that was considered a triumph. So if Nicholson had wanted to be in a Minnelli film, then he perhaps should have known that meant becoming an object within the decor, a human element in a visual composition that absorbed the director's interest above all. When Minnelli directed those great MGM musicals, he had been surrounded by many equally talented people, the entire Arthur Freed team, so his deficiencies could be more than adequately compensated for by extremely talented performers and specialists in every sphere of filmmaking. This Paramount production did not provide the same kind of safety-net for the director, and it shows.

Nicholson plays the ex-step brother of Daisy Gamble (Streisand), who lives in Brooklyn and is engaged to a very straight, uptight company executive who does not like her smoking habit. She visits psychiatrist Chabot (Yves Montand) in order to undergo hypnosis to cure her of the habit, but under the spell of the good doctor, she acquires strange psychic powers, including being able to make flowers grow and to relive a past reincarnation as Melinda in Regency England. As Melinda, Daisy is independent, beautiful and exciting. The doctor duly falls in love with this Melinda, while ignoring the charms of the rather less exciting Jewish girl from Brooklyn, who is, of course, smitten with him. True love, then, is thwarted, and the couple part at the end of the movie consoling themselves that in a hundred years from then they would be reincarnated again and will fall in love. This fantasy has strong resemblances to *Brigadoon*, the first success Alan J. Lerner had on stage way back in 1947, and the screen version of which, starring Gene Kelly, Minnelli had directed at MGM in 1954. The movie *Brigadoon*, however, can be seen as a masterpiece in comparison with *On A Clear Day You Can See Forever*.

Nicholson's character is supposed to be a sitar-playing hippie, but, man, Tad Pringle is the straightest counterculture representative you ever did see! Seemingly, Nicholson was even told by Minnelli to get a haircut for the part. Minnelli was hardly the type to understand or empathize with any aspect of counterculture and the representation of the so-called hippie is ludicrous. Indeed, in one of the melodramas Minnelli had directed at MGM, *The Sandpiper* (1964), starring Taylor and Burton, the director had already shown he had no idea of how to represent counterculture on screen. As the character of Tad Pringle had not existed in the original stage musical, it can only be assumed that the role was created to add some appeal to a younger audience. If so, it signally failed, as did the movie at the box office. Not even Streisand's pull could draw in the paying customers. Her scene with Nicholson on a rooftop patio is brief and pointless. Nicholson does not appear in the rest of the movie and we are left puzzled as to why the character exists in the scenario at all. Another reason why Nicholson had wanted to do the movie was because he was challenged by the idea of singing on screen. It seems that the challenge proved too much as the sequence was left on the cutting-room floor. Another complaint Nicholson had was that Minnelli did not allow him to move in the scene with Streisand, a fact that he complained directly to the director about. He also hinted that he would not have minded some direction from Minnelli and he clearly had no idea that the ex-MGM stalwart was decidedly not an actors' director, and that, indeed, he found it very difficult indeed to communicate his wishes to anyone connected with the project, not only the actors. Minnelli's talents, and they were considerable, lay elsewhere, but Nicholson clearly did not know that when he accepted the part. Is *On A Clear Day*, then, a total turkey? As is usual with a Minnelli-directed movie, it has a certain visual appeal: it is glossy and decorative, and if style is meaning, as it is, then the visual 'content' of the movie sends out its own message, over and above, and even despite the storyline, action and characters. The Regency sequences, shot in Brighton's Royal Pavilion, are pretty, and overall, it is the kind of movie where you think this is all very beautiful, but what tosh! The heavy hand of Alan J. Lerner is on the project and that means the audience is fed a large dose of whimsy, sentimentality and phoney romanticism. The songs by Burton Lane, except perhaps for the title number, are not that good, and your reaction to the performance of Streisand will depend on how you react to her particular style of performance, a mixture of Fanny Brice, Sophie Tucker and, as one American critic put it, the stage Jew. As for Yves Montand, he looks distinctly uncomfortable throughout, as well he might, because his English enunciation was never that clear, and as a singer he looks ill-at-ease surrounded by all this sumptuous Hollywood decor. As he also proved in *Let's Make Love*, the movie he did with Marilyn Monroe, Montand is not best suited to the indigenous American musical. His singing belongs in the French music-hall or smoky Parisian cellars.

However, running Montand very close in the ill-at-ease stakes is Nicholson, who clearly wrote off the experience as close to a disaster, although he was paid well for his work (twelve-and-a-half thousand dollars). One consolation for Jack is that the film is very seldom revived, even on cable television. At any rate, it would not harm his reputation as an actor, because *Easy Rider* was about to be released and his career was about to really take off.

Five Easy Pieces (1970)

Columbia: Director, Bob Rafelson; Producers, Bob Rafelson and Richard Wechsler; Screenplay, Adrien Joyce (aka Carol Eastman) based on an original story idea by Bob Rafelson and Adrien Joyce; Cinematography, Laszlo Kovacs; Editors, Christopher Holmes and Gerald Shepherd

Cast: Jack Nicholson (Robert 'Bobby' Dupea); Karen Black (Rayette Dipesto); Lois Smith (Partita Dupea); Susan Anspach (Catherine Van Ost); Billy 'Green' Bush (Elton); Fannie Flagg (Stoney); Ralph Waite (Carl Dupea); Helen Kallaniotes (Hitchhiker); Sally Struthers (Country Girl)

Running time 96 minutes

When an actor has a success like Nicholson had in *Easy Rider*, it is clearly very important that he build on that platform and that his next movie should stretch him and display his acting talents in a worthy 'vehicle', a movie that would

confirm his star status in the minds of those who matter in the film industry and with the paying customers. After all, George Hanson had been a supporting role; Nicholson now had to take on a leading role in a film that would establish his screen persona with the public and conform his marquee value. Nicholson found this role in *Five Easy Pieces*, playing Bobby Dupea. For this opportunity, he had to thank his success in *Easy Rider*, his own innate talent, and his buddies, Carol Eastman and Bob Rafelson, and the outstanding cinematography of Laszlo Kovacs. Eastman, accepting the screen credit under her pseudonym of Adrien Joyce, and Rafelson created a part for Nicholson that could scarcely have been better suited to his strengths as a an actor, a part that remains to this day a key role in this actor's career and in a movie that is not only one of the best he has ever appeared in, but also one of the most important films that Hollywood has produced in the last thirty years.

I am convinced that some movies are a kind of 'lucky accident', where the conjunction of the talents involved creates a work of art greater than anything that might have been expected of any of the individual artists participating. The great film noir movie, *Double Indemnity* is just such a case: Billy Wilder is a skilled Hollywood craftsman, but he has his limitations as a director; Raymond Chandler was a respected thriller writer but he had no track record for writing for the screen, nor even any particular skill at doing so; Barbara Stanwyck and Fred MacMurray were competent actors who had appeared in no great movies until *Indemnity*. But put those people together working within the film noir genre, on a story adapted from a James M. Cain pulp novel, add Miklos Rosza to compose the doom-laden score, get John Seitz to photograph it, and the result is a terrific film. Something of the same ilk happened with *Five Easy Pieces*.

Nicholson's career peak would come a few years later in *Chinatown*, but for Eastman and Rafelson, *Five Easy Pieces* would remain their most significant contribution to American cinema. Rafelson receives equal credit with Joyce/Eastman for the 'story concept', so we must assume that he has 'authorship' claims over the movie. Eastman apparently was none too happy with how Rafelson altered the representation of some of the characters (for

Five Easy Pieces. Nicholson grandstands it on the back of a truck.

example, Carl, Bobby's brother) and with the ending of the movie that Rafelson chose to impose. Inevitably, there would have been tensions among the leading participants as they wrote, filmed and edited the movie, but out of those tensions came a work of lasting worth.

Bobby Dupea (Nicholson) comes from an upper-middle-class and artistic family background, but as the movie opens we find him working on a Californian oil field as a rigger and living in a trailer with the mindless Rayette (Karen Black), who is completely untouched by the women's liberation movement and who has pathetic aspirations to be a country and western singer. She plays 'Stand By Your Man' on her record-player again and again, and is so needy and submissive to Bobby's whims that he treats her with near total contempt. His best friend at work is the redneck Elton (Billy 'Green' Bush), who has a wife who watches television all the time, and several kids. The four go bowling and Rayette annoys Bobby with her total incompetence at the game, because Dupea is competitive even in these unimportant matters.

Increasingly unhappy with the relationship, he spends his time playing poker with workmates, or having sex with a bimbo he picks up at the bowling alley. Ray announces she is pregnant and when, during one lunch break at the oil field, Elton tells him he should not be thinking of running out on her and of the delights of fatherhood, Bobby's self-disgust expresses itself: 'I can't believe I'm sitting here listening to some cracker asshole living in a trailer talking about the good life.' This provokes a quarrel with Elton, Bobby storms off, tells his boss he is quitting, then sees two men beating up Elton. It turns out that Elton has broken bail on a charge of robbing a filling station and he is hauled off to prison.

After finding out from his sympathetic sister, Partita (Lois Smith), that his father has had a stroke and is unlikely to live long, Bobby decides to return home and allows Ray to accompany him, although she is to stay in a nearby motel while he takes the ferry to an island in the Pacific Northwest, where his family live a sheltered but aesthetic life. The family are all accomplished musicians, including Bobby, we learn, but he has not played for years. The father is totally immobilized and has to be cared for permanently by a male nurse (John Ryan). 'He doesn't even know who I am,' Bobby says. 'I can't take much more of seeing him sit there like a stone.' The implication is that this sums up Bobby's former relationship with his undemonstrative and unemotional father. Dupea is attracted to Catherine (Susan Anspach), the lover and playing partner of Carl, Bobby's eccentric brother, with whom there is clearly a strong sibling rivalry. Catherine and Bobby have an uneasy relationship, although they become lovers, she despising his cynicism, his lack of 'inner feeling' and his decision to give up piano-playing when he had such a gift for it.

Five Easy Pieces. The famous diner scene when Nicholson cuts through all that have a nice day crap and demands his chicken sandwich.

Ray arrives at the house and she proceeds to embarrass Bobby with her mindless comments. After Catherine makes clear that she does not intend to have a lasting relationship with him, he decides to go, and after trying to express his feelings to his mute and uncomprehending father, he leaves with Ray. However, when they stop for petrol, he hands her his wallet, goes to the rest room and then hitches a lift in a lorry heading for Alaska. The last moments of the movie are of the petrol station forecourt in long shot with the lorry receding in the distance and the forlorn Ray moving towards the rest room to

see what is delaying her lover.

Eastman's original ending had Bobby being killed in a car crash, but that would have seemed too much of a traditional Hollywood cop-out resolution to Dupea's problems. Rafelson's 'imposed' ending is existentialist in its implications: Dupea is stripped of almost everything by a deliberate act of will. He divests himself of family, lover, identity, money and 'responsibilities'. He is reinventing himself, not in a mood of joyful liberation, but out of miserable desperation. Dupea, who has previously run away from his personal, family and emotional problems to live the redneck life, is now headed for the iciness of Alaska with no more hope of 'finding himself' than before.

It is a bleak ending to a film which is not uniformly bleak in its content. The central focus is on male inability to handle emotional commitments and to deal with interpersonal problems. Dupea escapes into 'mindlessness', symbolized by his redneck lifestyle and his relationship with Ray, because he does not want to confront his feelings towards his family, particularly his father, or, it is implied, undoubted sibling competition. Dupea is highly competitive, but he channels this competitiveness into meaningless games (poker, bowling). Bobby, as played by Nicholson, is brimming over with a frustration that threatens to spill over into violence at any time. There is the memorable scene in the roadside restaurant where he cannot get what he wants to eat because, as he is informed by a chilly, ungracious waitress, there are 'no substitutions' allowed. He sweeps the contents of the table to the floor and storms out of the restaurant. That is a famous Nicholson sequence and one based on an actual incident in Nicholson's life that Carol Eastman witnessed. Then there is the scene where Bobby and Elton are stuck in a traffic jam to Bobby's mounting anger. He climbs aboard a truck and discovers there is a piano which he proceeds to play joyfully as the traffic starts to move again. In addition, there is his attempt to free Elton by fighting with the cops who come to arrest him, or even the almost violent sex he has with the bimbo he picks up at the bowling alley. Or his aggressive glee in trouncing his brother Carl at table tennis and his struggle with the male nurse when he finds him in bed with his sister. All these scenes help to represent Dupea as a man

Five Easy Pieces. Nicholson (Bobby) the déclassé musician looks elsewhere while Karen Black as Rayette admires.

living on the edge of breakdown, so that the 'breakdown' of the conclusion seems inevitable. Even when he does show feelings, as when he plays the piano for Catherine and she is moved by it, he has to disown it: 'I didn't have any feeling. I faked a little Chopin and you faked a big response'.

The other famous scene in *Five Easy Pieces* is when Dupea, just before he departs, talks to his silent father on a hillside about his feelings and their relationship. He is moved to tears as he admits, 'We were never that comfortable with each other to begin with. The best I can do is apologise. I'm sorry it didn't work out.' Nicholson wrote this dialogue for himself, deciding against the original Eastman scene, and quickly writing the words down on paper just before the sequence was shot. It is highly probable that the actor was using his own feelings about his father, or who he thought was

his father at that time, to express his character's angst at the failure in his relationship with the dying patriarch. It is a moving moment in the movie and very well acted by Nicholson. He seemingly initially resisted Rafelson's request that he should cry on screen during this scene, but either he simply gave in or the emotion just came while the scene was being shot, because, unlike Bobby's fake Chopin, the feeling seems genuinely felt.

Indeed, Nicholson's performance throughout the movie is authentic. You can believe in him as the alienated black sheep of the too precious Dupea family as he tries to embrace the facile hedonism of redneck culture. He is absolutely convincing in his mixture of extreme irritation with, and feelings of guilt towards, the victim figure, Rayette, and we can understand his distance from the deadness of his family and their aestheticism and intellectualism. Eastman provides him with some 'grandstanding scenes' (for example, in the diner, or playing the piano on the truck, or when he describes exuberantly his Las Vegas piano accompaniment routine or when he castigates the intellectual friends of Carl and Catherine for being 'full of shit'). The movie falters only when it places 'straw characters' in front of Bobby for him to blow them away. The intellectuals are an example of this; it is interesting that the spokesperson for this group is a female celibate whom Dupea cannot resist berating. But they are too stereotyped, as is Carl, Bobby's brother, who is made to appear ridiculous, which makes it implausible that Catherine, a beautiful and talented woman, would become involved with him.

However, the movie has an unusually rich texture for an American film of this time. The contrast of the settings, the oil fields and trailer parks where these blue collar Americans try to get by, and the rural isolation enjoyed by the well-to-do but frozen Dupea family, is wonderfully observed. One of the most effective sequences in the movie is when Bobby and Ray pick up two lesbian hitchhikers, one of whom, played rivetingly by Helen Kallianiotes, launches into an extended diatribe about the filth and crap that is engulfing America. She is on her way to Alaska where it is 'clean' and where the pressures to buy more and more crap are fewer. This character is expressing her hatred of the 'uglification' of America through excessive consumerism, but she comes over as so obsessively neurotic that her complaints seem the ramblings of an alienated loony. However, she is linked to Bobby by the Alaska destination, which, it is suggested, is Bobby's goal when he runs away at the end of the movie.

Thus, following on his portrayal of George Hanson, the alcoholic lawyer who throws up everything to tag along with the hippies at the Mardi Gras, Nicholson once again was playing an alienated outsider, a man at odds with the two worlds he lives in, the milieu he was born into and the environment he has chosen as an escape. His new escape hatch, Alaska, symbolizes a last ditch chance to escape from the America of the time. Nicholson as Dupea represents the American male in flight from commitment, seeking to avoid facing up to himself and the emotions that undoubtedly shape his life but which are too painful for him to acknowledge. This role reinforced Nicholson's claim to be perceived as an actor who could stand for the eternal alienated outsider, the rebel without a real cause, the angry, frustrated American male unable to deal with his women or the demands that 'straight', mainstream America in all its crassness and materialism was making on him. *Five Easy Pieces* is a fascinating film, one of lasting value, and it provided Nicholson with one of his finest showcases.

Drive, He Said (1970)

Columbia: Director, Jack Nicholson; Producers, Jack Nicholson and Steve Blauner; Screenplay, Jack Nicholson and Jeremy Larner, adapted from the novel by Jeremy Larner; Cinematography, Bill Butler; Editors, Pat Somerset, Don Cambern, Chris Holmes and Robert Wolfe; Music, David Shire

Cast: William Tepper (Hector Bloom); Karen Black (Olive); Michael Margotta (Gabriel); Bruce Dern (Coach Bullion); Robert Towne (Richard Calvin); Henry Jaglom (Professor Conrad); June Fairchild (Sylvie Mertens)

Running time 90 minutes

Jack Nicholson's directorial debut was not a direct result of his new star status, because he had nourished hopes of making *Drive, He Said* from his own screenplay adaptation of a novel by Jeffrey Larner (who helped with the screenplay) for some time before *Easy Rider* and *Five Easy Pieces*. It would be easy to perceive *Drive, He Said* as an indulgence to the new star, a 'feed-the-star-ego' strategy to sweeten him up so he will appear in future films for you. Perhaps there was an element of that in this project, but the subject-matter of a student campus rebellion must have appeared potentially commercial material to Columbia, because other 'campus-on-fire' movies such as *The Strawberry Statement* and *Getting Straight* had done well at the box office. However, by the time *Drive, He Said* was made and released, American campuses had largely settled back into normal college life and the movie was to miss the boat and prove a total commercial failure.

Drive, He Said. Nicholson shows Karen Black (Olive) how he wants her to react.

Whether it is also a complete or only a partial artistic failure is a matter of personal judgement, but at least Nicholson managed to direct a movie that was not as glossy or simplistic as either of the two films mentioned above. Nicholson's sympathies are clearly with some kind of student protest, but it is at best a very ambivalent support he seems to give to the political causes they espouse. Nicholson is not a joiner of causes in real life, although he has been marginally involved in supporting some American Democrat candidates, and this movie appears to question whether anything in society can ever really be changed by direct political action. By taking this view, of course, Nicholson's movie would have undoubtedly endeared itself to mainstream Hollywood, because, whilst the American film industry was more than willing to incorporate the contemporary student unrest and represent it on screen in movies such as *The Strawberry Statement*, thereby reaching the youthful ticket-buyers it had identified as making up the

majority of its remaining audience, it much preferred to show revolutionary fervour as a passing phase or doomed to fail. Thus, when, at the end of the movie, the main protagonist representing student revolutionaries is carted off to the loony-bin, that must have salved their right-wing consciences and made them feel more comfortable with the project. But *Drive, He Said* is not only interesting as a document of its time, but also for how it reveals Nicholson's own position vis à vis 'the Establishment' and his ambivalent feelings towards rebelling against it or, indeed, joining it.

This dichotomy is represented in the two lead characters of the movie: Hector (William Tepper), a basketball star with no political conviction who is gradually radicalized by his friendship with Gabriel (Michael Margotta), a student revolutionary heavily into protests of a highly theatrical nature, particularly against the war in Vietnam. Gabriel avoids the draft by pumping himself full of drugs and acting crazy at the medical, while Hector acts the college hero on the basketball court who might win the college the championship, if he would only show more team spirit and adopt the values of the almost psychotic coach (Bruce Dern). The basketball scenes may have been one of the reasons why Nicholson wanted to direct this movie, because he is a fanatical Los Angeles Lakers fan. Another reason is the love affair between Hector and Olive (Karen Black), the wife of one of his teachers (Robert Towne); Black plays a depressed wife of an academic seeking some excitement in her life by this affair with one of her husband's students. The sex scenes are fairly explicit and Nicholson, almost with a naughty boy bravado, inserts scenes of female and male nudity at random. At the end of the movie, Gabriel is taken away to a mental institution, after some random acts of violence, including an attempted rape of Black and the releasing of poisonous snakes and reptiles from a university lab. Hector shouts powerlessly after the ambulance, 'Your mother called.' Hector's own future is left in the balance as to whether he becomes a professional basketball player or not, which would symbolize his wholesale embracing of the values of the college establishment, the crazy coach and society at large.

When the movie was shown at the Cannes Film Festival, it provoked strong reactions from critical audiences who almost booed it off the screen. There were even fist fights among the audience, which seems very odd from the vantage point of nearly thirty years later. Perhaps it was a case of a left-wing-orientated audience being offended by the defeatism and what could be perceived as the innate conservatism of the overall philosophy of the movie. The student revolutionaries, after all, are represented as unattractive losers griping from the sidelines, mouthing empty slogans and prone to useless gestures of rebellion. Gabriel's acts against the establishment seem to be no more than juvenile pranks and so the dice seems to be loaded against the rebels and in favour of the confused and ultimately pliable Hector, whose 'radicalization' is hardly discernible. He speaks back to his coach and refuses team discipline; he also pursues his teacher's wife, but these are not the acts of a person with a growing political consciousness. Perhaps

audiences wanted to see something more upbeat and optimistic about American student rebellion. Nicholson's own pessimism about the impossibility of changing anything in society would be seen by those who are politically committed as the classic cop-out, the excuse of a Hollywood star too involved in making it in the mainstream industry to show political action as potentially life-changing or effective in the long term. Nicholson has claimed it was merely a representation of how he felt at the time: 'That's the way I see it. Things just go on.'

The movie, by all accounts, remains very dear to Nicholson's heart and people criticize it in his presence at their peril. What is not in doubt is that it bombed at the box office and disappeared practically without trace. It crops up occasionally in the repertory of art cinemas, but is rarely seen on television. It must have been a major disappointment to Nicholson to realize the first movie he directed, which he also co-scripted, had been greeted with such indifference and, indeed, such hostility in some quarters. However, *Drive, He Said* has some interesting qualities: the inanities of college sport in America are well-observed (Bruce Dern is very effective as the Coach), the movie has a freedom from strict narrative conventions that, although it meanders somewhat, is refreshing in a Hollywood production, and it does represent some of the alienation that a significant portion of the American student body was feeling at this juncture in history. Nicholson came out of his first directorial effort in credit artistically, if not in financial terms.

Carnal Knowledge (1971)

Avco Embassy: Director, Mike Nichols; Producer, Mike Nichols; Screenplay, Jules Feiffer; Cinematography, Guiseppe Rotunno; Editor, Sam O'Steen;

Cast: Jack Nicholson (Jonathan Fuerst); Candice Bergen (Susan); Art Garfunkel (Sandy); Ann-Margret (Bobbie); Rita Moreno (Louise); Cynthia O'Neal (Cindy); Carol Kane (Jennifer)

Running time 96 minutes

Carnal Knowledge. Art Garfunkel (Sandy) and Nicholson (Jonathan) look unhappy with their male lot.

Mike Nichols had made his reputation in comedy acts, notably in a duo with Elaine May, in New York clubs and on records. From there he had graduated to directing Burton and Taylor in the screen version of Albee's *Who's Afraid of Virginia Woolf*, *The Graduate* and *Catch 22*. By 1970, he was definitely a golden boy of the so-called new American cinema. This was a director, it was thought, who could not only make adult movies that did not insult the intelligence of its audience, but also create box-office success at the same time. Nichols seemed to have taken the pulse of the times and was able to appeal to a wide cross-section of the cinema-going public. So when he and Jules Feiffer, the cartoonist and playwright, and something of a cult figure at that time, announced they were to work together on a new film about contemporary men–women relationships, the film was eagerly awaited and Hollywood actors stood in line to get parts in what was sure to be a real event in the film world.

Feiffer's cartoons and writings always sent up the 'aware' middle classes, those Americans with money, education and leisure, who were into self-knowledge and moral angst, city-dwellers (New York) who were surrounded by crime, injustice and gross inequalities and were guilty about it all. He was especially into examining the relationships between men and women in an altogether more acerbic style that, say, used by James Thurber, another New York cartoonist and writer, who had trod the same territory a generation earlier. He had, however, made his reputation with his cartoons rather than plays or screenplays (*Carnal Knowledge* was his first to be produced), and there is a world of difference between penning smart lines to a drawing and getting a laugh, and writing a screenplay that would develop through the course of a film of about a hundred minutes long and also creating believable characters with whom a mass audience would empathize.

Equally, although *Virginia Woolf* and *The Graduate* had been monster hits for Nichols, there was perhaps already the suspicion that there was something catchpenny about his approach to movies, something slick and superficial, a wish to pander to current prejudices and mores. If you re-view now the three movies that Nichols had directed before *Carnal Knowledge*, it is hard not to see something essentially hollow and false about all three. *Virginia Woolf* is given over to the star turn of Burton and Taylor, with the latter supposedly acting against type, but only succeeding in being strident and unconvincing. *The Graduate* was a popular success, but it is very much a movie of its time, with its compendium of folk-rock soundtrack, its tricksy photography and glossy look. *Catch 22* is a mess of a film and the madness of war that Joseph Heller communicated in the novel (which, in my opinion, is one of the overrated books of all time) comes over in the movie as mild eccentricities and it also is inflated with stars doing turns. Nichols, essentially, has a show-business sensibility. His main weakness is a superficial, pseudo-hip, New Yorker smartness and the ideas in his films are usually glibly represented.

Seemingly, there was never any doubt that he wanted to cast Nicholson as the extreme chauvinist Jonathan, claiming that the actor, after *Easy Rider*, was to be the most important star since Brando. For the part of the more gentle, but confused, Sandy, Nichols cast Art Garfunkel, who had featured in *Catch 22*. Garfunkel's acting credits had been limited; he had won fame as the songwriting and singing partner of Paul Simon, and Simon and Garfunkel songs had figured prominently on the soundtrack of *The Graduate*. The casting of Nicholson and Garfunkel opposite one another would affect the film, because there was a clear imbalance, not only in the acting talents of the two leads, but also in how the characters are perceived as a result of the actors playing them. As Susan, the young woman who both men fall in love with at college, there was Candice Bergen, at that time something like flavour of the month as far as actresses were concerned. Ann-Margret was cast as a silicone-injected bimbo, whom Jonathan disastrously marries on the basis that he likes her body a lot.

The ostensible, and one, theme of *Carnal Knowledge* is the pathological sexual attitudes of the American male. The action is spread over thirty-odd years, starting at Amherst College in the late forties and ending up in New York in the early seventies. Jonathan is always desperate to get laid by any available and attractive woman.

His attitude seems to be that they are only good for one thing, but in the mores of the late forties, he is not getting any. He meets and is attracted to the intelligent Susan, who returns the attraction, but will not sleep with him, pacifying him by masturbation. Sandy is equally interested in sex, but is looking for romantic love. He is also attracted to Susan, in fact, is in love with her, and is jealous when he hears about Susan's ministrations to Jonathan, who also loves Susan in as far as he can love any woman. But to Jonathan, women are traps, always trying to tie you down to home, babies and monogamy, and he cannot commit himself to her. There are a lot of scalps to be gathered before any woman is going to corral him. On the rebound from Jonathan and fond of Sandy as she is, Susan makes the mistake of marrying him, and then disappears from the movie entirely.

Having left college, Jonathan, settled in New York, indulges in endless affairs, which leave him feeling more and more cynical and misogynistic. Sandy's marriage, meanwhile, has broken up. Jonathan meets Bobbie, a mindless, 'fun-loving' beauty, whom he lusts after, shacks up with and ultimately, after she has attempted suicide because he has refused to make her his wife, marries. Later, the marriage breaks up when Bobbie leaves him. In the penultimate scene of the movie, Jonathan has Sandy (looking and sounding more alternative than in his college days) and his hippie-style, feminist girl friend round to his apartment. He presents them with a slide show of all the women he has slept with and one of his conquests is Susan, a fact which further alienates Sandy. Jonathan provides an acid and misogynistic commentary to the slide show, making clear his innate hatred of women.

Carnal Knowledge is a bleak film, but its intention to be consistently pessimistic is part of the problem with it. It takes one stance towards male sexual attitudes and it grinds it into the dust. Despite the supposed time span of the action, nothing moves on in the movie. Superficial changes are represented in the characters, but basically Jonathan is the same at the end of the movie as he is at the beginning. But that is the point, the filmmakers would say. Yes, but the point is too obviously made, and with suspicious relish by these supposedly pro-feminist and anti-male filmmakers, Feiffer and

Nichols. The character of Sandy is meant to be a kind of counterbalance to the crudities of the representation of Jonathan. He is more gentle and although he has some of the attitudes that Jonathan has in the first section of the movie, he never lets go of his romantic vision, which is of a female skater twirling on the ice at the Woolman Rink in New York: pure, beautiful, untrammelled by male desire. This image betrays the superficiality of the film's approach: there is nothing meaningful said about female sexuality or what kind of relationship men should be seeking with their women love partners. Sandy especially seems to settle on this corny romantic idea as his ideal, which is just as adolescent as Jonathan's libidinousness. The partner Sandy ends up with (played by Carol Kane) is represented as so drab, joyless and uninteresting that the question could well be asked why anyone would settle for her when Ann-Margret is around. In other words, there is no female protagonist on hand to represent a liberated, but non-man-hating woman, that is, apart from the Susan character who is, however, represented as too unassertive, feeble and pliable to be a serious alternative to the mindless women who are paraded as Jonathan's amours. And this is where the casting of Garfunkel against Nicholson seriously weakens the film. Jonathan is represented as deeply unhappy and cynical, but Sandy is no role model for any man: hangdog, rather pious, an early version of a wimp new man. Garfunkel is not much of an actor, but he is used to some effect to represent this kind of male drabbie.

Nicholson does bring a considerable degree of conviction to the part of Jonathan. Perhaps mischievously, he has given different readings of how he viewed the part. In an interview with *Playboy*, he said he found 'a certain heroism in Jonathan; it's tragic, but the man is after all, within his own limited perception, doing what he thinks is right, to the general disapproval of those around him; so maybe that's what an anti-hero is, someone who's behaving in all the ways that might produce heroic behaviour, but he's motivated differently.'

He went even further by saying, 'you could have a certain difficulty in separating my sexual stance from Jonathan's.' This is all calculated to stir up feminist opposition, which it predictably did. To counterbalance that, he has claimed to be 'a feminist long before women's rights became fashionable'. Leaving aside those public comments, which, as with most quotes from movie stars, should be taken with a large pinch of salt, Nicholson is highly successful in the role of Jonathan, that is, within the limits set by his screenwriter and his director. He manages to convey the character's cynicism, hatred and desperation. The scene with Rita Moreno at the end of the movie was a daring one for a star to undertake, but that is the kind of risks Nicholson has always taken in his career. *Carnal Knowledge* as a movie has not stood the test of time, although it certainly has historical interest and it is not without merit in its wit and sometime sophistication. But it is glossy (the photography is by the Italian cameraman Guiseppe Rotunno, who was a collaborator with both Fellini and Bertolucci in their glossier efforts) and one-note, wearing its cynicism and its commercial appeal on its sleeve. In this movie, the filmmakers are shouting we are going to be daring and cynical about male sexual attitudes and that is our selling-point. Not for the first or last time, however, Nicholson's performance would be the best thing in a movie he acted in.

A Safe Place (1971)

Columbia: Director, Henry Jaglom; Producer, Bert Schneider; Screenplay, Henry Jaglom; Cinematography, Dick Kratina; Editor, Peter Bergema

Cast: Tuesday Weld (Susan); Jack Nicholson (Mitch); Orson Welles (The Magician); Philip Proctor (Fred); Gwen Welles (Bari); Dov Lawrence (Larry)

Running time 94 minutes

Henry Jaglom had acted with Nicholson in *Psych-Out* and had helped to edit *Easy Rider*. He was a pal and close associate, so this perhaps explains why Nicholson chose as his next project a low-budget film written and directed by Jaglom. Jaglom had also managed to recruit Orson Welles to the cast, which may have been an additional motivation for Jack, although he never got to act in a scene with his hero.

Nicholson plays a bohemian, Mitch, who competes for the favours of Susan (Tuesday

Weld) with Fred (Philip Proctor) who more or less represents the straight world. Susan is trying to 'find herself'. Orson Welles plays The Magician, much given to pretentious sayings which are greeted by Susan as profound. Much of the action, such as it is, takes place in New York's Central Park and it is clearly meant as a rambling essay on personal growth and exploration. However, it is shapeless, trite and, yes, pretentious, and like Jaglom's later films such as *Sitting Ducks* and *Can She Bake A Cherry Pie?*, it soon ends up merely irritating you with its self-indulgent introspection and self-conscious eccentricity.

Nicholson claims to have improvised his entire part, which is quite believable because the whole movie smacks of improvisation. It was made around the time when Hollywood executives were prone to give big bucks to unknowns like Mike Sarne or prestigious directors like Antonioni in the hope that they would produce movies that would appeal to the kind of audiences that had made *Easy Rider* such a smash. It was not to be with *A Safe Place* and it is hardly surprising. It is phonily whimsical, gargantually self-indulgent and finally quite tedious. Nicholson's role in it does nothing to save the movie from being an embarrassing failure.

The King of Marvin Gardens (1972)

Columbia: Director, Bob Rafelson; Producer, Bob Rafelson; Screenplay, Jacob Brackman from a story by Brackman and Rafelson; Cinematography, Lazlo Kovacs; Editor, John F. Link II

Cast: Jack Nicholson (David Staebler); Bruce Dern (Jason Staebler); Ellen Burstyn (Sally); Julia Ann Robinson (Jessica); Scatman Crothers (Lewis); Charles Levene (Grandfather)

Running time 104 minutes

Jack Nicholson is a complex character. In some ways, he has been single-mindedly focused on making it as a star in Hollywood; in other ways, he has shown himself to be dedicated to doing challenging roles and developing his skills and range as an actor. Nothing exemplifies this

dichotomy in the man more than his decision to make *The King of Marvin Gardens* for Bob Rafelson instead of accepting one of the lead roles in the soon-to-be hugely successful *The Sting* or playing Michael in *The Godfather*, the part that elevated Al Pacino to stardom. The script for *The Sting* must have had all the hallmarks of a sure-fire popular success, and the prospects for *The Godfather* must have been only slightly less optimistic, yet Nicholson chose instead to play a downbeat part in a movie that was very unlikely to prove a hit with the general public. Nevertheless, Nicholson made the 'correct' decision because, however worthy *The Sting* and *The Godfather* proved to be in their own terms as entertainment, it is *The King of Marvin Gardens* that will have the more enduring artistic value and his performance as the repressed radio monologist in the movie will be seen in future years as one of his best.

The King of Marvin Gardens can be classed with *Five Easy Pieces* as companion movies, variations on the theme of the fruitless chase after the American Dream of happiness, success, money, love and community. David Staebler (Nicholson) at the start of the movie has indeed retreated from any kind of pursuit of happiness and has settled for his job as a late-night radio talk show host who talks to his listeners in a kind of confessional manner, intermingling memories of his past life with fantasies arising from his repressions. For example, he tells his radio audience that his brother, Jason (Bruce Dern), and he had in their boyhood stood by while their grandfather choked to death on a fish bone, but later we see the grandfather living in David's apartment. Is David confessing to repressed familial aggressions? Why is he telling such 'lies' to an anonymous radio audience? Staebler sees himself as a failed writer and his minor fame as oddball radio presenter is not much compensation, so when his brother Jason calls him from nearby Atlantic City and asks for his aid in pushing through a deal about developing a holiday resort on a Hawaiian island he intends to buy, he decides to tag along and see what happens. Jason (a brilliant performance by Dern) is unlike David in that he is not in retreat from the world. He is extrovert, brash and full of dreams of becoming rich through unlikely schemes such as the Hawaiian island resort. He is a gambler who owes money to Atlantic City gangsters who are uncompromising in their demands for payment. Jason, then, is living on the edge and veers from crisis to crisis looking for that one big break he thinks will transform his life. He lives with Sally (Ellen Burstyn), an ex-beauty queen terrified that she has lost her looks and therefore her commodity value in life. Sally is also scared that Jason will dump her in favour of her daughter, Jess. Indeed, it is this fear that drives her to shoot her lover dead near the end of the movie.

The King of Marvin Gardens is an uncomfortable movie to watch, because there is an inevitability about the ultimate failure of these characters to work out a reasonable way of living their lives that affords no respite. It is the very opposite of a feel-good movie. Several critics criticized the movie for being too self-consciously pessimistic, for parading its chic, existentialist gloom in imitation of European art movies. But if this had been a European art movie, would these critics have been saying this about it? 'Serious' filmmakers such as Rafelson working within mainstream American cinema often have to contend with the charge of pretentiousness and expressing fashionable ideas and attitudes, and sometimes these charges are entirely justifiable. Imitation of the European art-house movie is not a path many American filmmakers should follow. But *The King of Marvin Gardens* is so American in tone, milieu and theme that it can shrug off such criticisms. The setting of a wintertime Atlantic City with its empty, rainy and windswept boardwalks, brilliantly photographed by Lazlo Kovacs, the beauty queens, the casinos, the Mafia, the all-

The King of Marvin Gardens. Nicholson (David) in sombre contemplation as Ellen Burstyn (Sally) and Bruce Dern (Jason) face up to the reality of the gap between dreams and fulfillment.

The King of Marvin Gardens. Nicholson (David) in discussion with Scatman Crothers (Lewis) about his brother's sins and omissions.

pervading tawdriness, mark this film down as truly American. Later in the decade a French director, Louis Malle, would direct a movie about another loser in Atlantic City (*Atlantic City* with Burt Lancaster), and Malle too would use the tawdriness of the setting effectively.

Jason is the American hustler. His brother, David, is the kind of failed and ineffective intellectual who often finds a safe but depressing niche in academia. Jason's phone call brings David into contact with his brother's world of shady deals, debt, risky relationships, violence and duplicity. He is unable to help his brother because Jason is set on a path of self-destruction, but stands by trying to advise and intervene in his decent but repressed kind of way. Jason's death at the hands of Sally is almost arbitrary; his slayers could easily well have been the gangsters to whom he owes money. Sally is desperate; she has gambled that her beauty-queen looks will bring her what she wants in life, but her hopes are fading fast with her looks. Once again competition within the family is a strong theme in this movie, just as it was in *Five*

Easy Pieces. There is the sibling rivalry between Jason and David, although they are also tied to one another in an uneasy bonding because of the shared experience of their family misery. And there is the rivalry for Jason's admiration between mother and daughter, which ends with Sally killing Jason. The myth of the happy American family is blown away, as it was in the previous movie.

Bruce Dern has the showier part in this movie, whilst Nicholson largely has to react to narrative events and express things dug out from deep inside himself. There are no opportunities for Nicholson rages or bouts of crazy exuberance. Yet he is very convincing in the role. There are very few Hollywood stars who can convince as intellectuals. Nicholson is one of those few because he has an innate intelligence that permeates almost all of his work. He also is able to play characters from different class backgrounds. Here he is playing a middle-class man who is clearly well-educated. He is also playing a profoundly repressed character, a role that you might not associate with Nicholson, and yet he communicates David's repression without resorting to overt signals such as neurotic tics or some such facile mannerism. Just as in the scene with his mute father at the end of *Five Easy Pieces*, Nicholson partly wrote the monologue that he delivers at the end of the movie when he is telling his radio audience about the events that have just occurred in his life. Not only is the performance of the monologue brilliant, but the writing is of a high order: 'The goal didn't seem serious for moments, then certainly nothing more serious could happen. Maybe there would even be a trip to blue Hawaii. I certainly didn't want to stop it. At the funhouse, how do you know who's really crazy? How do you know if it's supposed to be you that stops it? Right now? And that you don't know how to stop it. The gun was always with the water pistols.'

The King of Marvin Gardens did not achieve the levels of commercial success that *Five Easy Pieces* had done. Soon after its release, it was treated as an arthouse commodity, and it is revived too seldom nowadays. Yet contemporary audiences should have the opportunity to see this fine movie, surely one of the key films of the decade. Nicholson's performance is up there among his finest and there is little doubt in my mind that the film will outlast all the popular successes that this star has been part of. *Marvin Gardens* and *Easy Pieces* are the high point of the collaboration between Bob Rafelson and Jack Nicholson.

The Last Detail (1974)

Paramount: Director, Hal Ashby; Producer, Gerald Ayres; Screenplay, Robert Towne, adapted from the novel by Darryl Ponicsan; Cinematography, Michael Chapman; Editor, Robert Jones; Music Johnny Mandel

Cast: Jack Nicholson (Bad-Ass Baddusky); Otis Young (Mule Mulhall); Randy Quaid (Larry Meadows); Clifton James (MAA); Carol Kane (whore); Michael Moriarty (Marine OD); Luana Anders (Donna)

Running time 105 minutes

Nicholson has always liked playing macho characters and, in so doing, inserting an implicit critique of extreme masculinity into his performance, either through deliberate satire or intuitive understanding of the uneasiness of the macho guise in the contemporary world. He understands macho, he can act it, he can empathize, but he is far too aware a man not to be critical at the same time, which shows in the bluster, false bravado and sheer unhappiness that he reflects in these characterizations.

Such a character is Bad-Ass Baddusky in *The Last Detail*. Baddusky is a brawler, a compulsive beer-drinker, a chaser after what he refers to as 'pussy', a grouch and, at times, a very insensitive fellow, but Nicholson manages to make him sympathetic and not just because of what the script calls upon to do in the movie. Nicholson is not a 'Method' actor in the strict sense of the word, but he does take an 'attitude' towards the characters he plays; he is not just playing a role, he is telling you in his performance what he thinks of the fictional human being he is supposed to be. At times, this can be very unsubtle; at other times, as in *The Last Detail*, he manages to be quite subtle in the portrayal.

Robert Towne, who had acted as 'special consultant' to Warren Beatty on the script of *Bonnie and Clyde*, had adapted the novel by Darryl Ponicsan, and Hal Ashby, who had had a critical success with the cult movie *Harold and Maude*, was slotted to direct. Ashby would go on to direct *Shampoo*, *Coming Home* and *Being There*. Robert Towne was destined to write the screenplay for one of the best films Hollywood has made in the last thirty years: *Chinatown*. Rupert Crosse, an actor friend of Nicholson's, was originally cast as Mulhall, the naval rating that pulls the 'shit detail' with Baddusky, but Crosse died of cancer before shooting began, so Otis Young was cast. As the unfortunate Meadows, who is sentenced to eight years in the 'brig' for attempting to steal forty dollars from the 'Polio contribution box' which happens to be the favourite charity of the wife of his commanding officer, Randy Quaid was chosen, which was fortunate casting indeed. The gangling, naive-looking Quaid caught exactly the essence of the natural victim, the born loser, to whom things just happen in life.

The title *The Last Detail* refers what happens in the novel at the end, but not in the film: in the source material, Baddusky, who has a heart condition, dies. Towne decided to cut that and substituted a bleak ending where the two ratings deliver Meadows to the naval prison in Portsmouth, New Hampshire, and stand by helplessly while he is whisked away from them into the not-so-tender care of the military policemen. They then have to stand still for a berating from an officer, who suspects wrongly that they have deliberately used violence towards Meadows. This is hard to stomach, as the only violence they have employed is to prevent Meadows from escaping, the rest of their time and energies having been devoted to showing the kid a good time. But this is just part of the overall injustice of the system whereby lower orders like themselves, 'lifers', are subject to the whims and indignities of the officer class and the crazy rules of an

inhumane organization like the navy.

Initially, the two sailors, Baddusky and Mulhall (a black American) are appalled when they land the 'shit detail' of escorting Meadows by public transport all the way from Norfolk, Virginia to Portsmouth, New Hampshire. But Baddusky suggests they run their prisoner all the way there in two days and then spend the rest of the time and unused navy expenses in having a good time. However, when Baddusky finds out the paltry nature of Meadows' crime and the incredible punishment that has been meted out, his instinctive anti- establishment feelings and an innate human sympathy are roused: 'They really stick it to you. Stick it in and break it off,' he complains. This is from a man who glories in the name and reputation of 'Bad-Ass', who likes to think of himself as a bad dude, with nothing soft or 'homo' about him. Baddusky has his limitations, however.

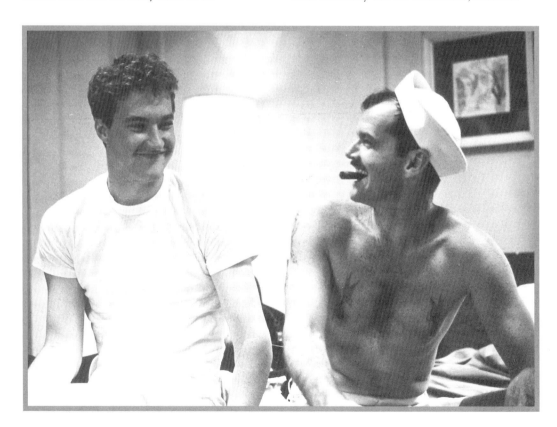

The Last Detail. Nicholson (Baddusky) tries to lighten the burdens of Meadows (Randy Quaid).

When on the first leg of their journey on a train, Meadows makes a bolt for it and starts crying when he is dragged back to his seat, Bad-Ass looks at him and says, 'He ought to see a fucking psychiatrist. Fucking mess.'

A subtle change has come over Baddusky, however. He adopts a fatherly attitude to Meadows. They stop off in Washington and are looking for something to eat. There is an understated scene where they look into a fairly fancy restaurant and Baddusky moves away, saying it is too crowded. He instinctively knows that three naval ratings in uniform would not be welcomed with open arms in such an establishment. Nicholson communicates perfectly that a man like Baddusky has felt ill-at-ease all his life in middle-class surroundings. For all his bravado, he doesn't feel himself good enough, so they find a lowly hamburger joint. Meadows has mentioned that he likes his cheese really melted on his cheeseburgers, but when he is served with his order and the cheese isn't melted at all, he passively accepts it, until Baddusky intervenes and tells the waiter to melt the cheese this time. Meadows learns from this and later on in the movie he sends back fried eggs that have not been done to his satisfaction. Baddusky tells him, 'Have it the way you want it,' which is ironic, because Baddusky's life is hemmed in by restrictions, but in the small territory where he feels secure, for example, hamburger joints, he knows how to operate.

When they are refused drinks in a bar, partly because Meadows is underage but also because the bartender does not want to serve a black, Baddusky explodes, brandishing a gun, after the thug has threatened them with a baseball bat and with calling the shore patrol. 'I am the mother-fucking shore patrol!' he boasts. Afterwards, he is as excited as a kid who has just come through his first test of masculinity: 'I am a bad-ass, ain't I?' He teaches Meadows to hand signal, navy-style, and on his suggestion, they take the prisoner to see his mother, who is unfortunately out for the day. 'I don't know what I would've said to her anyway,' Meadows says. Whatever they try to do for Meadows will never compensate for the dreariness of his life and the injustice of his fate. Baddusky's growing frustration with his role, and his seething anger at the authority that can impose such inhumane

treatment on a harmless individual like Meadows, leads him to start a brawl in a station toilet with some Marines. Somehow they wander into a meeting full of mantra-chanting alternative culture people and they are invited back to a party, where his benefactor, a middle-class woman, offers to help Meadows to escape to Canada. Meadows says he couldn't do that: 'It would be their ass. They're my best friends.' Meadows and his two escorts are expectant that he will get laid at the party, but his hostess makes another offer, saying 'I'm going to chant for you' instead.

Nevertheless, Badass is determined to introduce Meadows to 'the wonderful world of pussy' and takes him to a seedy brothel in Boston, where ultimately the virginal rating manages to make love to one of the prostitutes (Carol Kane). While waiting for the kid, Mulhall asks Badass whether he has ever been married: 'Not so you'd notice,' he says, and then describes how his wife had wanted him to go to trade school to learn to be a TV repairman, which he couldn't bring himself to do, so he had escaped to the security of being a lifer in the navy. When Meadows mentions that if it were summer, they could have a picnic, they try to meet his wishes and pathetically have a barbecue amidst the winter snow in the park. Meadows suddenly makes a bolt for it, and Baddusky and Mulhall run after him, realizing that it is their ass on the line. In subduing Meadows, Baddusky vents his frustration at his situation by hitting him more than he needs to. The time finally comes when they have to deliver the body to the prison. Meadows begins to weep as they enter the compound and, before they can even say a farewell, he disappears into the cells. The navy has won, they have fulfilled their function, they are as powerless as they have been from the start.

The Last Detail offers a discourse on class in American society. As is the case with many Hollywood movies, the class issue is disguised so that it is implicit rather than explicit. The navy lifers, and Meadows, who not only has been jailed for eight years but has also been dishonourably discharged, stand in for working men, the despised and disposable underlings of a system that values them only for the menial tasks they can undertake, in this case, the

The Last Detail. Nicholson (Baddusky) and Otis Young (Mulhall) grapple in the snow with their prisoner Randy Quaid (Meadows).

escorting of one of their own to a punitive establishment where he will be treated with cruelty and contempt. The only culture they seem to have revolves round boozing, whoring and fighting with other working-class men. And yet Baddusky and Mulhall reveal their sensitive side; they do care about Meadows and show kindliness towards him because they can see what the system is doing to him. Their methods are born of Baddusky's macho view of the world, but within those limitations, they do their best. Indeed, that is what they are doing in the totality of their lives: rubbing along, trying to keep their noses clean, avoiding 'shit details', squeezing as much pleasure out of life as they can, and being loyal to their buddies. Despite the way the navy treats them, they need the safety of the prison it has become for them. They can only afford to kick against the system to a small extent, and when the chips are down,

they have to obey orders, which is why they recapture Meadows. They are near the bottom of the pecking-order in society and they know this, although they cover it up with macho posing.

Although *The Last Detail* has its comic moments, ultimately it is a bleak film, a view of an unjust society in microcosm. Nicholson gives an aware, true performance as Baddusky. This is not the performance of a middle-class actor impersonating a working-class rating. It is obvious that Nicholson has known, observed and empathized with men like this in his own life. Again it is a risky performance for a star actor in Hollywood: Baddusky is not initially, or even ever, likeable, but by the end of the movie, you are forced to concede his innate humanity, his angry sense of injustice, his working-class hatred of arrogant and cruel authority. Some critics could not warm to the character at all. Vincent Canby in the *New York Times* wrote about Baddusky: 'I think we're ultimately supposed to find him and his sort worthy of pathos, though I can't.' It is that phrase 'him and his sort' that betrays the class attitudes of Canby and critics like him, attitudes that closely resemble the kind of prejudice that the characters face in the movie itself.

Ashby directs in an understated way, which is not the same thing at all as not directing at all. Nicholson's performance never gets out of hand, Quaid is remarkably good, and Otis Young in a part that gives him less opportunity to shine is just right as the black American who considers the navy has done a lot for him. Nicholson was nominated for the Best Actor Oscar, but lost out to Jack Lemmon in *Save The Tiger* in which he played a burnt-out small businessman, a role clearly closer to the hearts of Academy voters than a working-class navy rating with an obscene mouth.

Chinatown (1974)

Paramount: Director, Roman Polanski; Producer, Robert Evans; Screenplay, Robert Towne; Cinematography, John A. Alonzo; Editor, Sam O'Steen; Music, Jerry Goldsmith

Cast: Jack Nicholson (J.J. Gittes); Faye Dunaway (Evelyn Mulwray); John Huston (Noah Cross); Perry Lopez (Escobar); Dianne Ladd (Ida Sessions); Darrell Zwerling (Hollis Mulwray); John Hillerman (Yelburton); Roman Polanski (Knife-wielding punk)

Running time 131 minutes

Chinatown is one of the key American movies of the seventies, along with, arguably, *Five Easy Pieces*, *The King of Marvin Gardens*, the two *Godfather* films, *The Conversation*, *All the President's Men*, *The Deer Hunter* and *Apocalypse Now*. Other movies such as *ET* and *Star Wars* would make more money at the box office during this decade, but if we're talking serious movies, then these are the ones that count.

If any one movie thoroughly demolishes the auteur theory which accords the director full

authorship rights over his or her film, then *Chinatown* does. It is not a Roman Polanski film, nor is it a Robert Towne film (the screenwriter); it doesn't even belong to our hero nor Robert Evans, the producer. But for all these contributors and also for Richard Sylbert, the designer, Jerry Goldsmith, the composer, and Faye Dunaway, *Chinatown* marks a career peak that they will be unlikely to top. As happens on a few projects in Hollywood, the combination of talents involved ensures that the final product is greater than any single individual of the team could have produced on his or her own. *Chinatown* is a triumphant example of the collaborative nature of film-making within the Hollywood system. Polanski, for example, has never directed another movie that comes even close to the quality of *Chinatown*; Robert Towne has never scripted anything so fine, and as for our hero himself, I would say that this is the role he will be remembered for long after he has joined other Hollywood immortals in the Hollywood firmament.

Yet there is another crucial contributing factor to the quality of *Chinatown*: the traditions and style of the genre to which it belongs: film noir. Generic determinations shape and influence the movie in its story, philosophical content and visual style (although style should not be divorced from meaning because style is meaning). A Hollywood genre such as a western, a musical, a horror flick or social-issue movie, is like a palimpsest, a scroll on which you can detect under the top layer previous writings by other hands. These 'traces' are motifs, conventions, signs, storylines, characters, plot variations, structures and resolutions that are the key characteristics of movie genres and which filmmakers working within a particular generic framework employ either according to strict conventions and formulas or with some variations. Filmmakers may also work against generic conventions and create, for example, an anti-western as in the case of *Missouri Breaks* or, for that matter, *The Shooting*.

Chinatown is an example of late film noir. To the cinematic purist, film noir as a genre ended round the time of Welles's *Touch of Evil* in 1958, because the term 'film noir' may only be applied to movies shot in black-and-white in the 1940s or 1950s. How then, the purists say, can a

Chinatown. Roman Polanski looks angrily tense while his star wonders if this is for real. John Huston (in background) puffs on a cigar.

film shot in colour like *Chinatown* and made in 1974 be an example of film noir? The term 'film noir' was first used by critics of the French journal *Cahiers du Cinéma* in the immediate post-World War II years. There was a series of books published in France called *Série noire* which were translations of the work of Dashiell Hammett, Raymond Chandler, Cornell Woolrich, James M. Cain and other pulp American authors. Many of the movies the French began to see after the Liberation were adapted from these 'Série noire' authors so the intellectual critics took the *noir* tag and dubbed this body of films *film noir*. In addition, and this was probably the important factor in making this tag stick, the critics noted how dark in their visual style and in their general view of the world these movies were. During the German occupation, the French had been deprived of the new American films and so when they eventually saw films such as *The Maltese Falcon* and *Double Indemnity*, they were struck by how different they looked visually from the brightly lit movies Hollywood had been making just before the war. Not only that, they were much more pessimistic and doom-laden than the average pre-war Hollywood product. Hence, the term 'film noir' established a genre that was not really a genre like the western or war movie genre, but one that was identified by a visual style and philosophical stance.

In the forties and fifties, the heyday of film noir, the studio heads and the hired hands of the Hollywood system did not sit down round a table and decide to make some film noir as they might have done if they wanted to make some musicals or horror movies. However, by 1974, when *Chinatown* was made, film noir was an accepted genre among serious filmmakers so the movie is a self-conscious tribute to, and 'copy' of, the most memorable film noir of the forties. What, then, are the chief characteristics of film noir and how does *Chinatown* fit into the canon? The classic film noir storyline such as in *The Maltese Falcon* (1941) or *Out of the Past* (1948) (aka *Build My Gallows High*) has a

Chinatown. Nicholson as the sharp suited-private eye Jake Gittes.

central protagonist, invariably male and very often a private eye, engaged in untangling a mystery, which then turns out to be far more complicated and multi-layered than it initially seemed to be, and which involves a web of intrigues, double-crosses, crimes, murders and twists which the hero becomes increasingly obsessed with and personally involved in. There is invariably a femme fatale, a spider woman

Chinatown. Evelyn Mulwray (Faye Dunaway) confronts Escobar (Perry Lopez) while Gittes (Nicholson) looks elsewhere.

whom the hero falls in love with and who is at the centre of the mystery. He loves her almost against his will and distrusts her; often the hero is destroyed by this woman (the Robert Mitchum character in *Out of the Past*) and sometimes the male protagonist has to destroy her to save himself (the Humphrey Bogart character in *The Maltese Falcon*). The underlying tone of film noir is cynical and misanthropic, perhaps even misogynist, the one Hollywood genre, if genre it is, where an unhappy ending can be guaranteed.

The male protagonist's main defence in this untrustworthy world is a wisecracking worldliness, which is generally shown to be no real defence at all. If he survives, it is at a heavy price (Sam Spade shopping his love Brigid to the cops at the end of *Maltese Falcon*). Flashbacks and voiceovers are a staple convention of the

genre, a narrative device that adds to the doom-laden tone because it reinforces the idea of a fate that cannot be avoided and a sequence of events that cannot be altered. Film noir is in essence about an urban nightmare where less than saintly protagonists walk down the mean streets of shadowy and menacing cities and struggle against the forces of evil and their increasing doubts about their ability to untangle the mystery they have set out to solve. Nothing in film noir is as it initially appears. All is veneer, subterfuge, double-dealing and iniquitous.

Given the historical circumstances of World War II and the aftermath of the Cold War and the hysterical anti-Red atmosphere that gripped America in the decade following, it is perhaps not surprising that Hollywood and its more able filmmakers produced film noir when they did. It was inevitably a time of social disruption, of widespread distrust and paranoia, of fear and alienation, and all these aspects of American society during the war and the ten years that followed are represented in the body of film noir. *Chinatown*, released in 1974, equally reflects the unease of its time. It was the era of Richard Nixon's presidency, the Vietnam nightmare, Watergate and government hit lists. Americans were discovering how the highest elected and non-elected officials in the land could stoop to illegal acts involving burglaries, dirty tricks of all kinds, blackmail, assassination attempts and murder, in order to protect their power base. This stew of intrigue and cover-ups would culminate in the resignation of Tricky Dicky and further revelations of how the CIA and FBI were intrinsic to the operation of governmental and corporate criminality. The worst paranoiac fears of the opponents of the Nixon government were justified: yes, they were on a hit list, and, yes, government agencies were involved in plotting against those who were designated enemies. The corruption seemed to reach to the very heart of the American system of democratic government and there seemed scarcely a politician or government agency that was untouched by the cancer. *Chinatown*, although the action is supposed to take place in the Los Angeles of 1937 and the story is based on actual events that happened in 1908, is a direct reflection of what was happening in America in the early 1970s. It is a movie child born of Nixon and Watergate.

Jake Gittes (Nicholson) is a Los Angeles private eye in the mould of Sam Spade or Philip Marlowe, both played by Humphrey Bogart in forties film noir. The opening titles and score immediately take us back to that Hollywood era. The movie certainly wears its cinematic references and influences on its sleeve, but thankfully this is more than just an affectionate and nostalgic pastiche we are about to see. Gittes is sleazier than Spade or Marlowe was ever represented as being. When the film opens, one of Gittes's customers is looking at with horror photographs of his adulterous wife caught in flagrante delicto by Gittes's operatives. When the customer in his chagrin claws at the venetian blinds of Gittes's office, the sharply but vulgarly dressed private eye says dispassionately, 'That's enough, Curly, I only had the venetian blinds installed Wednesday.' Gittes is detached, the kind of man who appears to be unlikely to leave himself open to such betrayals and emotions. He has all the surface characteristics of the classic male protagonist of film noir: he is hard-bitten, worldly, cynical, apparently self-assured and wisecracking. He seems confident he can present reality to his clients through the lens of a camera. There you go, Curly, that's your wife, that's reality. But the character is being set up so that this knowingness, this veneer of self-assurance can be shattered. Even Gittes's attempts at immaculate grooming and showy camouflage will be destroyed as he gets deeper into the mire.

When a Mrs Mulwray asks him to find out who her husband is having an affair with, Gittes says, 'Do you know the expression let sleeping dogs lie? You're better off not knowing.' However, once he is involved in uncovering the intrigues set off by Mrs Mulwray's visit, it is Gittes who cannot let sleeping dogs lie, who becomes obsessed with knowing, by employing his hopelessly inadequate tools of investigation, covert surveillance, hidden cameras and all the stock-in-trade of a sleazy operator like himself. He thinks he knows what reality is, but a rude awakening is just around the corner. Firstly, he discovers Mrs Mulwray is not the real Mrs Mulwray, but an impostor used to set him up to expose Mulwray in the press as an adulterer with a very young girl as a mistress. Mulwray is the head of the Los Angeles water authority; the city is in the middle of a drought and he has uncovered a plot to divert the city's water to nearby locations, thereby hiking the price of the land which has recently been purchased by the plotters, lead by Noah Cross (John Huston), the father of the real Mrs Mulwray (Faye Dunaway). Gittes may be sleazy, but he does not like being made a fool of. When a customer in a barber shop criticizes him for making a buck out of public exposures of the private lives of people like Mulwray, Gittes explodes with righteous anger. The real Mrs Mulwray visits his office and threatens to sue. His sense of himself and his secure place in the LA universe has been disturbed. When Mrs Mulwray changes her mind and drops the law suit telling Gittes to forget the whole affair, he says, 'I don't want to drop it. I'm not supposed to be the one who's caught with his pants down.' He is hooked, because his raison d'être is involved, his view of his personal reality, and soon he is under the spell of Evelyn Mulwray, the femme fatale of this example of late film noir.

The *Chinatown* motif crops up throughout the movie; it becomes a symbol of evil and the unknowable, of corruption and the state of mind that knows there are no just solutions, no clear resolutions, no definable contours or limits to human wickedness. When Evelyn Mulwray first appears in Gittes's office, she overhears him telling a disreputable story about a man making love to his wife like a Chinaman. When he meets up with his former Los Angeles Police Department colleagues at the scene of Mulwray's murder, he says to Escobar, the lieutenant, 'Still putting Chinamen in jail for spitting in the laundry?' and Escobar replies 'I'm out of Chinatown.' We learn that Gittes has contributed to the death of a woman he once loved and whom, as a cop, he had been trying to protect when he was working in Chinatown: 'I was trying to keep someone from being hurt and I ended making sure she did get hurt.' His endeavours to protect Evelyn Mulwray and her daughter, the offspring of an incestuous relationship with her father, will again end in the death of the loved one and the tragic results of his actions will again find their culmination in Chinatown.

Noah Cross warns Gittes that he may think he knows what he's dealing with but that he doesn't. However, Gittes thinks he knows better, but only finds out he knows very little. He is scarcely a knight in shining armour but his efforts to save his maiden-in-distress end in her death, the result of a bullet fired in Chinatown by Escobar's assistant after Gittes had interfered with Escobar's aim as he shoots at the tyres of the car in which Evelyn and her daughter are escaping from Noah Cross and the police. All Gittes' well-intentioned interventions come to nought, he is adrift in an amoral world where the bad guys triumph (Cross goes off with the daughter), and where there are concentric circles of interweaving corruption (' My father owns the police'). No one seems to care about or even understand what is going on. All is moral chaos and confusion. The universe and the behaviour of the human beings in it are shrouded in mystery, resulting in a paranoia and a profound sense of existential anguish. Gittes walks away from the tragic debacle, perhaps a wiser man, but undoubtedly a destroyed human being. His partner's attempt at reassurance, 'Forget it, Jake, it's Chinatown' can scarcely be anything but the slightest consolation. If the whole world is like Chinatown, what consolation can there be?

From the perspective of the nineties, the use of Chinatown as a symbol of moral chaos and a hell ruled by the irredeemably corrupt may seem somewhat on the racist side, but the image is woven deliberately, sometimes too self-consciously, into the narrative. *Chinatown* is undoubtedly a dark, dark film; in addition to the larger historical circumstances that influenced its content, we could also cite the Manson killings that had recently shocked the Hollywood community. Those crazy, almost motiveless slayings had involved Roman Polanski himself in that his wife, Sharon Tate, had been one of the victims. It seems that the producer, Robert Evans, had wanted a less pessimistic ending to the film: Evelyn was to shoot her father to save her daughter from falling into his clutches, but Polanski insisted on the ending we now have, in which the victim of Cross's incestuous urges dies and Cross escapes with the prize of his daughter. Given Polanski's experience of losing his wife in such horrific circumstances, it is perhaps not surprising that the director held out for such an uncompromisingly bleak resolution. The movie is all the better for its tragic ending because there is a kind of tragic inevitability to it, which all the great film noir have.

What, then, of Nicholson's contribution to this movie, one of Hollywood's all-time greats? Jake Gittes is one of the roles that forces you to take Nicholson seriously as an actor. At times on screen, he can be shallow, irritating, slapdash and facile, but in *Chinatown* he is convincing as the cocky Gittes, as well as vulnerable, witty and shaken as the private eye in over his head and coming apart at the seams. Not many Hollywood superstars would agree to spend a large proportion of screen time sporting an enormous white bandage on his nose after it has been split open by a punk played by Polanski himself. When Nicholson is redefining the 'Bogart role' he delivers his smartass lines with just the right amount of superficial confidence. No actor can trade in male banter and insults with more style than Jack. Naturally there are echoes of Bogart in his playing of Gittes (deliberate echoes, like so much more in the film), but he makes the role his own. As the character's confidence unravels and his secure world is turned upside down, Nicholson communicates the desperation of a drowning man clinging to the wreckage of some knowable reality. This depends on Nicholson's intuitive and intellectual understanding of the man. All the evidence points to the fact that the actor was totally committed to the role and the film as a whole, and this is reinforced by the fact that he was to direct himself playing an older Jake sixteen years later in *The Two Jakes*. Some actors become identified with one great film role in their careers (Brando with Terry Malloy in *On the Waterfront*, George C. Scott in *Patton*, Olivier in *Richard III*); posterity will perhaps forever couple Jack Nicholson's name with the role of Jake Gittes in *Chinatown*.

The Passenger (1975)

MGM: Director, Michelangelo Antonioni; Producer, Carlo Ponti; Screenplay, Mark Peloe, Peter Wollen and Michelangelo Antonioni; Cinematography, Luciano Tovoli; Editors, Franco Arcalli and Michelangelo Antonioni; Musical adviser, Ivan Vardor

Cast: Jack Nicholson (David Locke); Maria Schneider (The Girl); Jenny Runacre (Rachel Locke); Ian Hendry (Martin Knight); Steven Berkoff (Stephen); James Campbell (Witch Doctor)

Running time 119 minutes

The Passenger. Maria Schneider and Nicholson in a very typical Antonioni shot.

A bizarre aspect of the search for new audiences and new talents by Hollywood studios in the sixties and early seventies was the deal MGM, that glossiest of glossy studios, made with the austere Italian director Michelangelo Antonioni. It was a three-picture deal and MGM had struck it lucky with Antonioni's first effort for them, the 1966 *Blow-Up* set in the mythical London of the mythical swinging sixties, which had proved a surprising box-office success, although the movie had not been uniformly admired in serious critical circles. Antonioni had followed that up by making *Zabriskie Point*, which not only bombed at the box office but seemed to advocate violent revolution and mass love-ins in the desert. Louis B. Mayer must have been revolving in his grave, which is certainly one justification for the movie having been made. Now Antonioni was proposing a kind of 'thriller' involving arms-dealing and set in the Sahara, London and Munich. When Jack Nicholson shook hands with Antonioni and agreed to appear in the movie, and Maria Schneider, who had achieved notoriety from her role with Marlon Brando in *Last Tango in Paris*, was also signed up, MGM gave the go-ahead,

The Passenger. David Locke vents his frustration as he realises there is no escaping the identity others give you.

although by that time they were reportedly anxious to rid themselves of the tiresome Italian 'genius'.

Nicholson had always professed to admire Antonioni and it must have fed his ego that the leading exponent of avant-garde cinema wanted him to star in his latest movie. However, he must have also been aware that Antonioni expected a minimalist acting style from his actors. There would be no 'personality' acting in *The Passenger*, no tantrums, tirades, grandstanding or pyrotechnics. Antonioni purportedly usually told his actors to say the lines and make the movements, and that was it. He also did not usually welcome suggestions from his cast. This was not at all what Nicholson was used to and it is a tribute to Antonioni's stature and the respect Nicholson held him in that he apparently accepted these conditions and gave the director what he wanted.

Antonioni's most widely respected film was *L'Aventurra* (1960), a movie supposedly about the mysterious disappearance of a rich young woman while on a cruising holiday near the Italian coast. Antonioni uses this slight storyline to paint a picture of the emptiness and boredom of the lifestyle of the Italian bourgeoisie. Their pampered leisure activities and sexual adventures only seem to emphasize the pointlessness of their existence. The leading male character (Gabrielle Ferzetti) has been a talented architect, but has given himself over to meaningless sensuality and 'high society'. Dialogue is sparse and there are many lingering shots and sequences that for many people are over-prolonged, where the visual composition within the frame conveys meaning to the audience, visual signs that are the essence of 'pure' cinema for Antonioni's admirers, of whom I am one, although frequently, as in *Zabriskie Point*, his camera style slips over into portentousness and longeurs.

The Passenger has a 'rambling' narrative style similar to *L'Aventurra*. Audiences have to grasp what the story is from elusive clues supplied by the director. There is little in the way of exposition or explanation. Nicholson plays the role of David Locke, a television reporter who is in Africa trying to set up an interview with some guerrilla fighters in a war-torn country. He is not having much success in his task. Locke feels a failure and almost a non-person. At his hotel, he has befriended an English 'businessman' called Robertson, but returning one day from another abortive attempt to make contact with the freedom fighters, he finds Robertson dead, apparently from a heart attack. On an impulse, and because he has more than a passing physical resemblance to Robertson, Locke changes identity with the Englishman by wearing his clothes, switching photographs in their respective passports and convincing the hotel manager that it is he, David Locke, who has died. Locke has reinvented himself and he heads off to London to find out about who he is now.

He tracks down Robertson's wife and adopted child and watches the television reports of 'his' (Locke's) death. Then he moves on to Munich and Barcelona as per Robertson's schedule and gradually he discovers that Robertson has been involved in arms deals, supplying the same guerrillas that Locke had been trying to contact. Meanwhile, Locke/Robertson has picked up a bohemian young woman (Maria Schneider), who now travels round with him. Eventually Locke/Robetson is murdered in a hotel room and it is left ambiguous as to whether the Schneider character has set him up and has been working for his pursuers all the time.

The last sequence of the movie is a seven-minute, unedited tour de force which starts in the hotel room where the couple have just made love and then moves into the hotel courtyard, where the camera follows the movement of the various characters until it returns to the room again and we discover that Locke has been murdered. It is an impressive sequence and one that took eleven days to shoot. These were the days before the Steadicam camera that allows cinematographers to film with a hand-held camera without the normal shakiness

The Passenger. Nicholson with Maria Schneider, the woman who possibly sets him up to be killed.

associated with that technique. Thus, Antonioni must have worked out a way of moving his camera out of the hotel room into the courtyard and panning to follow the characters' movements and then moving it back into the room again without one editing cut. Such technical virtuosity would be merely an interesting aspect for movie buffs to chew over if it were not used to some thematic purpose. In other words, technical brilliance for the sake of it is largely meaningless. However, in this sequence, Antonioni condenses what *The Passenger* has been about: the random nature of human existence, the inability of human beings to understand what is happening to them, the myth of personal identity, the impenetrability of individual motivation and the impossibility of escaping from the identity that society ordains for you. *The Passenger* explores existentialist themes in a slow-moving, elliptical narrative where the conventions of the movie thriller are only employed in minor ways and where few concessions are made to the mass audience. It is one of those films that could be claimed as the work of an auteur; Antonioni, after all, not only directed but helped to shape the screenplay. Certainly, it is one of the films Antonioni will be remembered for, along with *L'Aventurra*, *La Notte*, *L'Eclisse* and possibly *Blow-Up*.

So what about our hero's participation in this highbrow enterprise? Nicholson has said that his performance is exactly what Antonioni wanted from him, and indeed, the star is restrained and seemingly does what he was told to do by the director. There are no Nicholson grins, leers or grimaces, no extravagant show of temper, few emotional outbursts and no improvisation in the style of Method actors. Yet he is curiously convincing in the part, just as Ferzetti had been in *L'Aventurra*. He is playing an alienated character, a man at odds with his own existence, a man desperate to escape from the confines of the observer role he has made for himself. He plunges into an adventure of reinventing himself and finds that there is no escape from himself or the role that the world has given him under his new identity. It is a bleak view of human life that Antonioni represents and Nicholson is in sympathy with that view. The dark side of the famous Nicholson exuberance is the doom-laden, self-destructive persona, the man who strikes powerlessly out at an all-encompassing fate. Nicholson knows how to embody that and

he is effective in the movie, although some would see his talents as having been wasted in a part that many other actors could have performed with ease. That would be a mistaken notion. Nicholson brings understanding and empathy to the role and, for once, commendable self-restraint. With *Five Easy Pieces*, *The King of Marvin Gardens* and *Chinatown* and now *The Passenger* on his track record, Nicholson could now claim to be a serious movie actor who had been involved in some of the most powerful films of the decade.

Tommy (1975)

Columbia: Director, Ken Russell; Producers, Ken Russell and Robert Stigwood; Screenplay, Ken Russell from the rock opera by The Who; Cinematography, Dick Bush and Ronnie Taylor; Editor, Stuart Bird; Musical Direction, Pete Townshend

Cast: Ann-Margret (Nora Walker); Roger Daltry (Tommy); Oliver Reed (Frank Hobbs); Elton John (The Pinball Wizard); Keith Moon (Uncle Ernie); Jack Nicholson (The Doctor); Eric Clapton (Bizarre Character); The Who (Themselves)

Running time 111 minutes

Nicholson had admired some of British director Ken Russell's work, whilst disliking some of his movies as well. That is a familiar enough reaction to Russell's films: the man undoubtedly has some talent for creating striking visuals on screen and pumping up the melodrama with the use of powerful musical underscoring, but his juvenile obsession with playing the enfant terrible of the movie industry and with shocking the bourgeoisie is very wearing. For a long time now, whatever innate talent the director once had, has disappeared down the plug-hole of his own immense ego. In 1975, when Nicholson agreed to play the cameo part of The Doctor in the film version of The Who's ludicrously pretentious rock opera, *Tommy*, Russell's reputation was still riding high after *Women in Love* and *The Music Lovers*. *Tommy* was not to add one iota to Nicholson's reputation as an actor, and it would signal that Russell was a director with nothing much to say but who would insist in saying it in a bombastic and childish manner.

Tommy (Roger Daltry) is a deaf, dumb and blind lad whom, we are expected to believe, is traumatized when he sees his stepfather (Oliver Reed) making love to his mother (Ann-Margret). Tommy lives in an isolated world, although he endlessly cries out 'See me…feel me…touch me….heal me'. He defeats the Pinball Wizard (the grotesque Elton John) and becomes a teenage idol, Christ-like in his meekness and the adoration he inspires. I think we are meant to think that the movie is commenting ironically on the adulation that pop icons like The Who themselves receive from the adoring, unthinking masses, but as the film itself is in the business of marketing The Who and the rock music industry in general in a movie aimed straight at the teen market, then its so-called message about the dangers of mass manipulation through contemporary idols can safely be dismissed as humbug. The movie becomes a concerted assault on the eardrums, the eyes, the emotions and the guts of the audience, only the mind is left untouched.

Nicholson plays a Harley Street doctor brought in to treat Tommy's mother and her son. He has some words to sing 'Go to the mirror, boy' and his later boast that at least he sang better than Oliver Reed is faint self-praise indeed. As an afterthought, has there ever been a worse actor on screen than Roger Daltry? Well, I guess anything's possible.

The Fortune (1975)

Director, Mike Nichols; Producer, Hank Moonjean; Screenplay, Adrien Joyce (Carol Eastman); Cinematography, John Alonzo; Editor, Stu Linder; Music, David Shire

Cast: Jack Nicholson (Oscar); Warren Beatty (Nicky); Stockard Channing (Freddie); Florence Stanley (Mrs Gould); Richard Shull (Head Detective); Tom Newman (John the Barber)

Running time 88 minutes

Apart from *Tommy*, Nicholson's career had been on a high since *King of Marvin Gardens*, but now there was another turkey on the horizon. *The Fortune* can be seen as a seventies version of *Ishtar* in that it is another movie where Beatty gets together with one of his Hollywood buddies to make a wacky comedy that is meant to be endearing and displays the star's (Beatty) willingness to send up his own image. *Ishtar*, the 1987 mammoth flop co-starring Beatty and his pal, Dustin Hoffman, would enter Hollywood history because of the profligate expense of the production and because it was universally trashed by the critics as an example of what happens when superstars are indulged. It was ignored by the public. *Ishtar* is definitely not as bad as it was made out to be at the time and indeed, compared with *The Fortune*, it is almost a masterpiece. But it is difficult not to see *The Fortune* in the same light: the movie is an indulgent mess.

It can be imagined how *The Fortune* came to be made: Beatty and Nicholson, chums and probably rivals at the same time, want to work together and there is this crazy script by Carol Eastman which their co-pal Mike Nichols wants to direct. It must have seemed such a great idea in the initial discussion stages and everybody was bound to have a great time making the movie. The stars almost certainly had more fun making it than audiences have in watching it. It is that kind of comedy where the players seem to see the joke but the spectators don't. It also has a tasteless quality that seems to have passed Nichols and the two male leads by, but then Nichols has never had faultless taste and he isn't really much of a film director at all. Nicholson is on record as saying he likes working with this director because his attention is on the actors, but, because Nichols is good at flattering and listening to actors, that does not make him a talented director.

Beatty plays Nicky, a fortune hunter with greased-back hair and a pencil-thin moustache; Nicholson is Oscar, a dim ex-bank teller with a shady past, whom Beatty is blackmailing into helping him with a scheme to run off with a sanitary napkin heiress, Freddie (Stockard Channing). However, Nicky is married already so because of the Mann Act (the action is set in America in the twenties), he cannot travel with a woman across state lines for immoral purposes. Oscar has to marry Freddy so that Nicky can travel with them. From this unlikely premise, the plot develops to the point where the two anti-heroes decide they will have to bump Freddy off because she has threatened to give all her money

The Fortune. Nicholson as Oscar and Beatty as Nicky are arrested for their attempts to bump off Freddie.

away as she has realized they are only after her wealth. Thereafter, the movie shows their bumbling attempts to kill her, including throwing a rattlesnake at her which is eaten by the pet chicken Oscar has given her, and by dropping her from a bridge. Does this sound funny? No? You would be right because it is no funnier up there on the screen. In the end, after Oscar has confessed to everything, the heiress forgives them and the trio walk off together to continue their ménage à trois.

Stockard Channing as the heiress does her best with the role as she is a talented actor and she knows how to be funny without trying too hard. Beatty, however, is not naturally a comic actor and he simply tries too hard to be funny. He is not 'funny in his bones' and so he resorts to putting his comic performance within exclamation marks: 'Gee, folks, here is Warren Beatty being funny!' Nicholson scarcely comes

off any better, although he can perform comedy better than Beatty. Nicholson can be funny, but he is only really effective when the comedy emerges from a character he is fully immersed in and he can display his intelligence. Oscar is meant to be a dope, a variation on Stan Laurel, and so here we see a bright, intuitive actor pretending to be dumb and it doesn't work. The technique, or lack of it, shows through and Nicholson is almost as guilty of acting 'funny' as Beatty is. If, as Nicholson says, Nichols listens to actors, in this case he listened too much and was far too indulgent towards them. The movie is a sort of actors' jape and the chief victims are the audiences who watch it. There is scarcely anything worse in the theatre or the cinema than a farce that goes flat and that is what happens with *The Fortune*. It is a damp squib of a movie and one that does not add to the stature of either Beatty or Nicholson.

One Flew Over The Cuckoo's Nest (1975)

United Artists: Director, Milos Forman; Producers, Saul Zaentz and Michael Douglas; Screenplay, Lawrence Hauben and Bo Golden from the novel by Ken Kesey; Cinematography: Bill Butler and William Fraker; Editors, Lynzee Klingman and Sheldon Kahn; Music, Jack Nitzsche

Cast: Jack Nicholson (Randall McMurphy); Louise Fletcher (Nurse Ratched); William Redfield (Dale Harding); Will Sampson (Chief Bromden); Brad Dourif (Billy Bibbit); Marya Small (Candy); Louisa Moritz (Second Hooker); Sydney Lassick (Cheswick); Scatman Crothers (Turkle); Danny DeVito (inmate); Dr Dean Brooks (Dr Spivey)

Running time 129 minutes

Ken Kesey had become a cult writer and 'personality' of the druggy sixties, and his novel *One Flew Over The Cuckoo's Nest* had been a best-seller since it was published in 1962. Kirk Douglas had starred in a Broadway version in 1963 and when, with the passing years, a movie version could not find financial backers, he passed on the rights to his son, Michael Douglas, at that time best known for his role in the television series *The Streets of San Francisco*, who went into partnership with Saul Zaentz, the head of San Francisco's Fantasy Records, to get the movie made. By the seventies, Kesey's novel was perceived as too sexist by half in its portrayal of the chief villain of the piece, The Big Nurse of the mental institution, and it was decided to tone down the caricature and make Ratched more human and to try to stress that the struggle between the male free spirit, Randall McMurphy, and the female controller of the patients in the mental ward was not a straightforward example of the gender war, but a conflict between libertarianism and oppressive institutional values. This, I think, was wishful thinking on the part of the scriptwriters and producers, because, although Nurse Ratched may be less of a monster in the movie than she is in the book, nevertheless she is still represented as quite a monster and the movie, therefore, offers a very slanted discourse on man–woman relations and

indeed on contemporary treatment of mental distress. Some highly esteemed novels and movies fall in stature with the passing of time, and both Kesey's original novel and this movie version seem much less admirable from the vantage point of the late nineties.

Most Hollywood movies are emotionally manipulative. We are instructed how to feel by a battery of signals, usually involving the particular actors who are chosen to play particular parts, their role in the narrative, musical underscoring, cutting, camera angles and all kinds of other visual and aural signs. *One Flew Over The Cuckoo's Nest* is as manipulative as they come, and that is not to say that it isn't emotionally overwhelming at times, but it is one of those films that, having distanced yourself from it, you realize just how slanted it is in its representation of the narrative figures and the issues about mental illness and its treatment in institutions.

However, Randall McMurphy, the symbol of rebellion against institutional repression in the movie, was a part tailor-made for Nicholson. McMurphy is a product of the sixties, a macho figure who is a total hedonist, rejecting all kinds of control in his life. He has been convicted of statutory rape, and feigns insanity to get out of the work detail at the prison he is sent to. Arriving at the mental institution he is referred to, he is shown striking up a friendly relationship with Dr Spivey, the nominal head of the hospital, and he comes over a charming, probably irresponsible and possibly self-destructive man. As far as McMurphy is concerned, he has been victimized by society because he 'fights and fucks too much'. He joins the ward ruled over by the quietly spoken but vindictive and controlling Nurse Ratched (Louise Fletcher). They lock horns almost immediately, he realizing that she is an enemy of free spirits like him and that under the guise of doing good to her patients, she operates an entirely oppressive regime, which keeps the patients, some of whom are there voluntarily, powerless and imprisoned in their worlds of fear and guilt.

'Medication time' is when the patients get their sedation to keep them passive, but McMurphy, after initially refusing to swallow his on the grounds it might be a saltpetre that would

One Flew Over the Cuckoo's Nest. McMurphy gets overly exuberant in the ward in order to wind up Nurse Ratched.

impair his libido, fakes taking his pills by putting them under his tongue and spitting them out later. He asks Ratched to tone down the Mantovani-type music that is meant to soothe so that the patients can talk to each other without shouting. Ratched calmly refuses, although it is obvious that she recognizes the growing challenge to her authority posed by McMurphy. This rebellion culminates in a vote about the patients watching the baseball World Series on television, which Ratched opposes because it would upset the daily schedule. McMurphy persuades over half the patients to vote for seeing the baseball, but Ratched vetoes it on the grounds that she had adjourned the meeting before enough votes had been garnered by McMurphy. Ratched's regime of 'democracy' is revealed for what it is: a total sham.

Ratched also uses the patients' therapy sessions

to increase her control, playing on her knowledge of what presses their buttons, especially in the case of one stuttering inmate, Billy (Brad Dourif), who has a fear of his mother and inhibitions about sex. McMurphy tries to break out of the ward to go to town to see the series, but fails, saying, 'I tried, didn't I, goddam it, at least I did that.' He then conjures up the baseball games for himself and the other patients by making up a fictional commentary on the games. When he is interviewed by three psychiatrists, he says of Ratched, 'She likes a rigged game, know what I mean.' He then cons his way onto a fishing boat with a group of the patients and they have a joyful day of release. This jape leads the medics to dub him 'not crazy but dangerous'; Ratched argues for keeping him on the ward because she thinks she can help him. The implication is that she wants him there so she can finally break him. After he smuggles

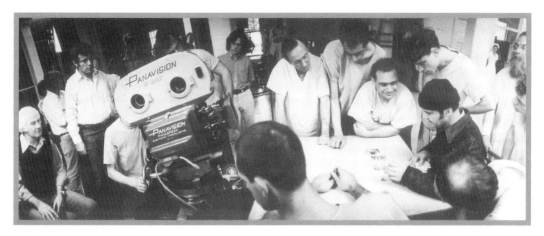

One Flew Over the Cuckoo's Nest. Milos Forman (with white hair, extreme left) sits behind the camera as his cast enact the card scene.

two prostitutes into the ward and Billy sleeps with one of them, the ward and the medical records are left in a total mess. Ratched cruelly and knowingly tells Billy she is going to tell his mother what he has done, whereupon Billy slits his throat. McMurphy, who has been on the point of escaping from the institution, chooses instead to avenge himself on Ratched, and tries to strangle her. As punishment for this, he is lobotomized. When the Chief, a giant native American who is pretending to be mute, but who has opened out to McMurphy, sees the vegetable that McMurphy has become, he smothers him and makes his own escape. McMurphy's free spirit lives on in the Chief.

Milos Forman, the director chosen by Zaentz and Douglas, was a Czech who had made an art-house reputation through quirky social comedies such as *A Blonde in Love* and *The Fireman's Ball*, before becoming an exile from his homeland when the Soviet Union invaded in 1968. He had made one American film before *Cuckoo's Nest*, *Taking Off*, a quite acerbic comedy about sixties teenage runaways and their ineffectual suburban parents. Forman allowed a fair amount of improvisation during the therapy sessions sequences and in the first scene we see McMurphy in the film, when Nicholson shares a scene with a non-professional actor, Dr Dean Brooks, who was head of the institution in Oregon where the movie was shot. These scenes have an authenticity within the 'comic realist' parameters the movie sets for itself, but the

psychological problems of the characters are represented in rather a superficial, simplified way in order to make the controllers look bad and the patients largely the victims of an oppressive regime, out to make sure no one at all has a good time. Even the medical orderlies are shown to be sadistic, while the psychiatrists on show seem to be as much in need of help as the patients. There is an impressive performance from Louise Fletcher as Ratched, who realizes the best way to play opposite McMurphy's/Nicholson's exuberance is to be still, unemotional and only to let feelings rise to the surface on rare occasions. Her first appearance in long shot as she walks down the ward's corridor, dressed in ominous black and with a shapeless hair style and scrubbed features, is meant to tell us all. The representation of Ratched never gets beyond this limited level. We are never allowed to see matters from her point of view, indeed, the point of view supplied is almost entirely McMurphy's, and as he is the individual who makes the other patients feel better about themselves, then we are manipulated into taking his side. When McMurphy springs at Ratched's throat at the end of the movie, then it appears that we are being encouraged to cheer him on.

Yet McMurphy himself is shown to be equally manipulative in his own way. He takes on a bet with the other patients that he can put 'a bug up Ratched's ass' and then uses them in confrontations with her designed to challenge

her authority. His 'medicine' for curing the patients consists of booze, sex with prostitutes and having wild days out fishing on a boat that they steal from the harbour. There is no critical dimension in the movie in relation to McMurphy. The whores he uses are all amenable and appear to love him, although he is clearly exploiting them and cares little about them as individuals. He is shown to care about Billy and the Chief, but his rage about Billy's death seems to be more about revenging himself on Ratched than anything else. One interpretation of the character's psychology could be that he perceives Ratched as a mother ogre figure, or as representing controlling and judgmental women in general who have tried to tie him down in his life, and so that is why he makes her an enemy from the start. Nurse Ratched is only seen through his eyes and we, the audience, are invited to share that vision completely.

Jack Nicholson received his first Oscar for his performance in *Cuckoo's Nest* at the next year's Oscars ceremony. Indeed, the movie won in all the five top categories, the first time that had happened since *It Happened One Night* in 1934. It won Best Actor, Best Supporting Actress (Fletcher), Best Picture, Best Screenplay and Best Director. The evening was clearly a crowning night in Nicholson's career. The film had not only won him an Oscar and had been generally lauded by the critics, but had also been a box-office hit, which firmly established him as the leading movie star of his time. He plays a lecherous, macho, rebellious, immature and anti-establishment anti-hero, wearing a woolly hat and grubby jeans. It is a star performance for all the talk of ensemble playing. *Cuckoo's Nest* can hardly help being a star vehicle because the character of McMurphy is allowed centre stage for almost all the movie and his point of view is privileged, especially since the only movie star in the picture is the actor playing that role. And, of course, Nicholson grabs his opportunities with both hands producing a charismatic, energetic performance that only rarely goes over the top, but he has done better things and been in better films. It is very likely, however, that this will be one of the five or six movies he will be remembered for, although I would be willing to bet that the movie will be seen more and more of as a product of its particular time. It represents attitudes that were in the air round the time when the action of the movie is meant

to take place (1963). For all its pro-life stance and its anti-repression message, it leaves something of a nasty taste in the mouth. If the original novel was misogynist, then the movie version cannot escape that charge either. It is interesting to speculate why it was such a popular hit in the mid-seventies and why the members of the Motion Picture Academy awarded it so many Oscars. Perhaps there are a lot of men out there who with scores to settle with Mummy.

The Missouri Breaks (1976)

United Artists: Director, Arthur Penn; Producer, Robert M. Sherman; Screenplay, Thomas McGuane; Cinematography, Michael Butler; Editors, Jerry Greenberg, Stephen Rotter and Dede Allen; Music, John Williams

Cast: Marlon Brando (Robert E. Lee Clayton); Jack Nicholson (Tom Logan); Randy Quaid (Little Tod); Kathleen Lloyd (Jane Braxton); Frederick Forrest (Cary); Harry Dean Stanton (Calvin); John McLiam (David Braxton)

Running time 126 minutes

Perhaps you should never meet your heroes in person, whether they be movie stars, writers, film directors or whoever. The gap between your notion of the idealized individual and the person in reality can lead to disenchantment. If you admire an actor or a writer, then admire the work they do and keep your distance.

Maybe Jack Nicholson learnt that lesson after starring with Marlon Brando in *The Missouri Breaks*, which, by all known accounts, he found less than an enchanting experience, not just because of his disappointment with his personal hero, Brando, but because of his general lack of faith in the movie. James Dean had been an earlier fan of Brando's, treating the older man as a kind of god, an admiration which Brando had repaid with scorn. Brando, for all his ego and for all his stature as an actor, clearly has a problem with self-esteem, because for most of his life he has chipped away at his own worth and reputation, constantly telling the world that he thinks the awe he is held in is bullshit and that what he does professionally is practically worthless, so anyone who approaches him with a touch of hero-worship is bound to be treated with less than respect. A man who does not like himself, like Brando, or what he does, will scarcely accept veneration from another actor or a fan without showing some kind of contempt for the acolyte.

Nicholson was a strong admirer of Brando's (he is actually Brando's near neighbour in Los Angeles where they share a driveway) and clearly the opportunity to act with his hero in a western directed by Arthur Penn and scripted by the well-known novelist, Thomas McGuane, was too good to pass by. Arthur Penn at this time was still something of a golden boy of the new American cinema. He had directed *Bonnie and Clyde* and *Little Big Man*, and he could be identified as being on the liberal wing in terms of Hollywood politics. Certainly, his films seem to take the side of the outsider against corporate America: the gangsters in *Bonnie and Clyde*, the hippies in *Alice's Restaurant*, a convict in *The Chase* and the Indians in *Little Big Man*. Penn had directed Brando in *The Chase* and had a reputation for 'being good with actors'. However, *The Chase* might have sounded a warning bell to Nicholson, if he saw what Brando got away with in that movie. For much of the time, the actor cannot be understood, he mumbles his lines so badly, and that is not say that he is not quite powerful in the role of the southern sheriff who stands up to mob rule. But it is an indulgent performance and the film, though it has a certain power, is something of a mess. These faults, Brando's performance, and the overall lack of control over the script, were to be magnified in *Missouri Breaks*.

Thomas McGuane was, and is, a highly regarded novelist. He writes about self-destructive characters in Montana, struggling to come to terms with the fact that the macho kind of western life that is part of American mythology of the frontier has difficulty in being accommodated or even surviving in the present-day west. A constant subtext in his novels is a mourning for the old west when men could be men. However, McGuane can write seriously and much of his observation of his macho heroes is ironic and not uncritical. Yet he had only scripted two movies before *Missouri Breaks* (*Rancho Deluxe* and *92 in the Shade*, two films destined for obscurity), and writing novels is

certainly not the same thing as writing a screenplay.

Yet it is completely understandable why Nicholson would agree to participate in the project. Such a talented team rarely came together for a Hollywood movie and all the principal players were on the liberal side in terms of politics, so there was a fair chance that something significant would come out of the collaboration. In addition, Nicholson was to be paid $1.25 million plus ten per cent of the gross in excess of $12.5 million. However, for the 'smaller' part of the two, (five weeks work as compared to Nicholson's ten), Brando was to be paid a million and a half, plus 10 per cent of gross in excess of $10 million, so the diffident Brando was still exercising his muscle in the marketplace. He may have despised being a movie star, but he never lost interest in squeezing the last drop out of the money men, so that he could finance his hare-brained schemes in Tahiti and support his growing family.

The action is set in McGuane's beloved Montana where the Missouri River breaks over the hills in that underpopulated state. A rancher, Braxton (John McLiam), symbolizing rampant and ruthless capitalism, is losing too much to cattle rustlers and hires a 'regulator', a euphemism for a killer, to track down the rustlers and eliminate them. Clayton, the regulator, as played by Brando, is very eccentric: he speaks in a variety of accents, but predominantly Irish, or at least, stage Irish, and dresses in bizarre outfits, including at one time, a woman's dress and bonnet. The 'hero', or anti-hero, is Logan (Nicholson), who doubles as a farmer and part-time rustler. He gets involved with Jane Braxton (Kathleen Lloyd), an independent woman who despises what her father stands for and takes the initiative in her affair with Logan. One by one, Clayton kills the members of Logan's gang, until Logan, using the methods of the oppressors, shoots the rancher dead and slits Clayton's throat.

The social critique that *Missouri Breaks* encapsulates is not particularly subtle. Like the Penn-directed *Bonnie and Clyde* and *Alice's Restaurant*, it has a knee-jerk support for the outsider against the wicked establishment, but this attitude does not seem to come out of any thought-out political stance but is more a modish, soft liberal and romantic expression of discontent. *Bonnie and Clyde* had romanticized two gangsters as folk heroes of the Depression, forced into crime because of the deficiencies of an uncaring, capitalist society. Similarly, Logan is forced to adopt the ruthless ways of the regulator to defend himself and there is no doubt where the sympathies of the film lie, however clouded the differences between the good and bad guys may be in the movie. An early Penn film about Billy the Kid, *The Left-handed Gun*, has the same kind of romanticism running through it. American movies have consistently romanticized gangsters of one kind or another from the early Warner Brothers movies to present-day Scorsese and Coppola epics. In reality, almost all gangsters and outlaws were not left-wing folk heroes out to redress the inequalities in the distribution of wealth in the cause of the greater good, but neo-fascist thugs who were trying to seize a part of the capitalist cake for themselves by methods that usually involved killing off ordinary people who were

employed to protect the wealth of the property-owning class. Liberal American directors and screenwriters have always been half in love with the notion of criminals as rebels, whilst steering clear of representing politically motivated individuals who were seriously interested in changing society.

Clearly, Penn had the intention of demythologizing the west and creating a kind of 'anti-western'. There are no heroics in this western: the regulator dispatches his victims cruelly and with a mordant sense of twisted humour: he shoots one of the gang while he is sitting on the toilet. Equally, Logan does not go in for traditional shoot-outs where the faster gun wins fairly and squarely, but shoots the wheelchair-bound rancher and creeps up behind Clayton to slit his throat. This is the antithesis of the traditional western hero: can you imagine Gary Cooper being asked to carry out actions like these? Yet all this demythologizing is overdone and one of the most excessive scenes is

The Missouri Breaks. Nicholson shares a relaxed moment off-set with co-star Marlon Brando, who, however, irritated Jack because he seldom knew his lines and kept changing his accent.

where Clayton/Brando is in a bathtub and covered in soap suds. The regulator (and, therefore, Brando) are meant to appear ridiculous and it can be imagined what pleasure Brando had in playing these scenes. He has been such a vocal critic of westerns and particularly how the genre has traditionally portrayed Native Americans. In many scenes, it appears Penn and Brando are more interested in an 'in-your-face' debunking of western conventions than anything else. There is lots of mud, the characters look 'real' (Nicholson sports a beard throughout), and even the love sub-plot has a hard-edged grittiness to it, as though the makers had decided to eschew any romantic representation of the west through any traditional love interest. Despite this, however, the movie falls into the trap of a false romanticism of its own, and the question is bound to be asked: why should we feel any more sympathy for Logan and his gang than for the regulator and the rancher, except that the gang are played by sympathetic actors such as Nicholson, Harry Dean Stanton, Frederick Forrest and Randy Quaid and they are represented as being poor?

But your reaction to the movie may revolve round what you think of Brando's performance as the regulator. On the evidence of this movie, the legend of Penn being good with actors can be interpreted as Penn being indulgent with actors. There is no rhyme nor reason to the way Brando plays Clayton. He seems to be acting on whims, adopting this or that accent, dressing in this or that bizarre outfit, improvising in this or that scene. Nicholson, that most professional of actors, was seemingly astonished that Brando used so many cue cards to remember his lines, that is, when he actually bothered saying those in the script. He must have become increasingly disenchanted with Brando's wayward ways of working, because in Brando's performance there shines through a subtext of contempt for the movie and perhaps for the profession of acting itself. It is transparently true that many actors take themselves and their profession far too solemnly, but there is a difference between not taking yourself or your craft too seriously and just simply horsing around. In *Missouri Breaks* Brando is guilty of just that and it seriously harms the movie and Nicholson, by comparison, suffers. He is playing the main protagonist, but he is not stretched in the role. In too many of his scenes with Brando, he is reacting to some outlandish ploy on the part of his co-star. Another way of interpreting Brando's performance in the movie is to see it as a not-so-subtle scene-stealing exercise at the expense of his younger rival. All actors, even Brando at this stage of his career, are competitive and think about how they are coming over and how significant their role is in whatever they are involved in. Brando may have been acting as though all this was just a lark for him, but his unconscious motivation may have been to steal the picture from Nicholson.

Yet much of the critical reaction to the movie was too harsh. The Brando-haters, and they are numerous, had a field day, calling him excessive and self-indulgent, and making that the movie. The movie still has some power, however, and is in its own way, superbly photographed by Michael Butler. Despite its excesses, it does have the look of Montana a hundred years ago. It portrays the corporate rancher as aspiring to high culture and a level of sophistication whilst acting like a Mafia boss to protect his property. Compared to most westerns that Hollywood has produced, there is a depth of characterization and wealth of social observation well beyond the average example of the genre. Yet it does fail to hang together and Penn had already shown in earlier films that he

The Missouri Breaks. You got me, you sonuvabitch! Fate catches up with Logan (Nicholson).

is not an efficient script-doctor, like Hitchcock, for example, was; even though he himself was not a writer as such, Hitchcock knew what to include and what to cut from a script. Penn has never shown that talent. McGuane was also unhappy with the film. Robert Towne was brought in at the end to add the scene where Nicholson shoots the rancher, a scene which McGuane hated. The novelist complained that changes had been made without consulting him. The romantic interest in the movie might as well not have been there; certainly, there is no screen spark between Nicholson and Kathleen Lloyd. He complained to friends that he didn't even like her, so he found it difficult to make screen love to her. At any rate, Ms Lloyd's movie career did not flourish as a result of *Missouri Breaks*, but it has to be said, in all fairness, that it could not have been easy working with two male stars with the clout of Nicholson and Brando.

To add insult to injury, Brando was later to be less complimentary about Nicholson, saying he wasn't that bright and comparing him unfavourably with Robert De Niro, which is not exactly a friendly and neighbourly thing to do. The men's friendship did survive, however, and Nicholson was around to help out his Hollywood neighbour when, in the early nineties, Brando's son shot his daughter's boy friend. Nicholson himself managed to alienate his director, Arthur Penn, by stating in a *Cosmopolitan* interview that the film was unbalanced and that it should have been cut differently. Penn, seemingly, stopped talking to Nicholson. So with Nicholson out of tune with Brando, his female co-star and his director, it could be said that *Missouri Breaks* had not been the most rewarding experience of Nicholson's career. However, the most that could be said for it as far as his track record was concerned is that most people saw that he was up against it and did the best he could. Most of the blame for the movie's comparative failure artistically (it failed commercially) was attributed to Brando, Penn and, to a certain, extent, McGuane. Despite the strictures I have expressed, the movie remains an interesting oddity and certainly a film of its time in that it attempts to present a view of immediate post-Watergate America through a representation of corporate barbarity in the Montana of a hundred years previously.

The Last Tycoon (1976)

Paramount: Director, Elia Kazan; Producer, Sam Spiegel; Screenplay, Harold Pinter from the novel by Scott Fitzgerald; Cinematography, Victor Kemper; Editor, Richard Marks; Music, Maurice Jarre

Cast: Robert De Niro (Monroe Stahr); Ingrid Boulting (Kathleen Moore); Robert Mitchum (Pat Brady); Jeanne Moreau (Didi); Jack Nicholson (Brimmer); Tony Curtis (Rodriguez); Donald Pleasance (Boxley); Ray Milland (Fleischacher); Dana Andrews (Red Riding Hood); Theresa Russell (Cecilia Brady)

Running time 125 minutes

Scott Fitzgerald's unfinished novel *The Last Tycoon* was a fictional study of a top movie executive with unmistakable resemblances to Irving Thalberg, who had been Louis B. Mayer's head of production at MGM until his (Thalberg's) premature death in 1936. Thalberg had the reputation for being a man of culture and taste in the aesthetic wasteland of Hollywood and MGM in the thirties. Here, the legend goes, was a studio executive who actually wanted to make art out of the motion picture. In fact, if Thalberg's record as a producer is analysed, what he seemed to be interested in was making glossy and respectable screen adaptations of literary works such as *The Barretts of Wimpole Street*, *Mutiny on the Bounty*, *Romeo and Juliet*, *The Painted Veil*, *Strange Interlude* and *Idiots Delight*. In a very real sense, he was not innovative producer, but an entrepreneur who wanted to give his studio's product something called 'class'. Thalberg, it was, who was credited with establishing MGM's credo of 'Make it big, make it good, give it class.'

The Last Tycoon had emerged from Fitzgerald's largely unproductive spell as a screenwriter at MGM. The revered novelist died before he could complete his tale and the fragment has acquired a kind of 'unfinished masterpiece' status. Fitzgerald was fashionable in Hollywood at this time, even though the 1974 *The Great Gatsby* starring Robert Redford

The Last Tycoon. Nicholson seems to be saying 'It'll be all right, trust me!' to veteran director Elia Kazan, but, as it turned out, all would not end happily.

and Mia Farrow, and directed by British director Jack Clayton, had been critically flayed on its release. Jack Nicholson had been passed over for the part of Gatsby in favour of Redford, a major mistake, because the latter was miscast, as was Mia Farrow, and the whole film had suffered perhaps from an over-reverential approach to the Fitzgerald classic and certainly from its overly glossy production values. The loss of the Gatsby part obviously rankled with Nicholson; he has been quoted as saying, 'I was righter for it than Redford. He looks like a privileged person. He wouldn't worry about chopping his way up.' This criticism is right on the button, because one of the faults of the movie is Redford's inability to suggest the drive and dreams of someone like the shady gangster Gatsby. Nicholson, with his

outsider and rebel image, would have been much more believable.

Ironically, producer Sam Spiegel had wanted Nicholson for the part of Monroe Stahr in *Tycoon*, but Elia Kazan, the veteran director, had opted for Robert De Niro. De Niro and Nicholson were now being paired in people's minds as the two leading movie actors of their generation, and that 'rivalry' perhaps continues to this day. Nicholson, in the event, was offered the cameo part of Brimmer, the Communist union leader who comes to Hollywood to negotiate with Stahr over a writers' strike. Once again, Nicholson can congratulate himself on his good luck in missing out on a lead part in a movie: De Niro did not add to his reputation by playing Stahr and it is doubtful whether Nicholson would have fared any better, given the weaknesses of the script and the anonymity of the direction. Doubtless, Nicholson accepted the smaller part on the basis of the combined reputations of Kazan, Pinter and Spiegel, and for the chance to act opposite De Niro.

On the face of if, it was a very talented team who came together to make *The Last Tycoon*. Screenwriter Harold Pinter was not only an established big name in the theatre with plays such as *The Caretaker* and *The Homecoming*, but he had been responsible for the screenplays of several Joseph Losey-directed British movies such as *Accident* and *The Go-Between*. Director Elia Kazan was the famous director of *On the Waterfront*, *East of Eden* and *A Streetcar Named Desire*. Kazan had emerged from the left-wing Group Theatre which, in the thirties, had tried to inject some social realism and radical socialist attitudes into American theatre. Many of those involved in the Group Theatre had gone on to work in Hollywood, including actors John Garfield, Lee J. Cobb, Frances Farmer and Karl Malden. Most of them would fall foul of the McCarthyite House Un-American Activities Committee (HUAC) investigating alleged Communist infiltration into Hollywood. During this appalling period in the fifties, Kazan had ensured his own safety and career by naming names to the committee and had brought down on himself the opprobrium of many of his former colleagues on the left and many of those working in Hollywood then. Numerous of Kazan's films from that time on can be seen as a justification for his actions (for example, the Brando character in *On the Waterfront* who snitches on his waterfront pals to the crime commission and is ostracized by the community).

However, Kazan's talents lay in the emotional intensity he brought to his films. Most of his successful films are high on emotionalism and melodrama, and he had a reputation, quite justifiably, as an actors' director. Both Brando and James Dean had given their best performances under his direction. But Kazan's triumphs belonged to the relatively distant past and he was approaching seventy by this time. More importantly, was he really the director to bring an unfinished novel by Scott Fitzgerald to

the screen? Fitzgerald's style is poetic, full of echoes, regrets and uncertainties. Kazan's great films had been characterized by the opposite: certainties, realism and raw feelings. In addition, Pinter is a writer whose talent, if that is what he has, lies in resonances, silences, subtexts and subtleties. Personally, I find most of Pinter's writing hollow and pretentious. He is not a skilled screenwriter at any rate; his work, if it belongs anywhere, belongs in the theatre.

Indeed, *The Last Tycoon* is testimony to the fact that gathering 'names' together to make a prestigious movie is no guarantee of success. The 'name' talents have to be suited to the project in hand. Kazan was demonstrably not the right director for this material and so it proved. Pinter delivered a badly constructed screenplay (it can only be assumed so, unless his script was butchered and redrafted along the way), adapted from a half-finished novel. Robert De Niro had one of his few failures as Stahr. He employs his usual repertoire of De Niro 'tricks': his grins, his quirky delivery of lines, the sense of improvisation he brings to his roles, the impression of a volcano lying just below the surface, the attention to detail of appearance and manner. But there is no 'character' there and he is acting in a sequence of scenes that seem at times to have little connection. The opposing values of Stahr (standing for taste and discrimination in picture-making) and the other studio executives as played by Robert Mitchum and Ray Milland are never represented in a clear enough manner, so it is difficult to hang onto anything in the movie. Increasingly opposed by the philistines at the studio, Stahr finds solace in his love for, and idealization of, a young woman whom he has first seen on the studio set when filming goes disastrously wrong and people lose their lives. This sequence is typical of the film in that you are left wondering what is the point of this, other than to provide a bit of minor spectacle in an otherwise static movie.

Stahr's love for Kathleen is akin to Gatsby's obsession with Daisy. Both men are ruined by this love, which they cling to as compensation for the tawdriness and emptiness of much of the rest of their lives. If Mia Farrow had been miscast as Daisy in the recent version of

Gatsby (made by the same studio, Paramount), how can one describe the casting of Ingrid Boulting as Kathleen? 'Unbelievable' should cover it. Perhaps some American moviemakers have a blind spot about English actresses with posh accents. They may think that stands for real class and some kind of mystery. Ms Boulting comes over as a Home Counties young lady with as much charisma and mystery about her as a Wimbledon ladies singles player. At the core of the picture, then, there is this vacuum. We have to be able to share some of Stahr's romantic vision, but it is quite impossible to do that. The lack of chemistry between De Niro and his co-star is palpable and for a so-called actors' director, Kazan singularly fails to elicit any kind of excitement between the screen lovers.

In the midst of this confusion and tepidness, Nicholson shines out like a bright light. He does not need to overact in this cameo to be noticed, and in his scenes with De Niro, there is a sense of his standing back a bit and allowing the power of his screen personality to steal the show. He convincingly communicates the hard-nosed, cynical union leader, sceptical of the good intentions of studio moguls. If their scenes together are seen as a fencing match between the two stars, it is as if De Niro is prancing around trying to score points with showy darts and feints, whilst Nicholson is waiting for his 'opponent' to attack in order to pick him off without doing that much. Nicholson has the advantage: his role is fairly clear-cut, whilst De Niro's is nebulous and unrealized. Nicholson is well-cast, De Niro is not. On this occasion, it is no contest.

The rest of the cast mostly flounder in the inadequacies of the script and the direction. Robert Mitchum is not suited to the part of Pat Brady, the movie executive scheming to oust Stahr. Ray Milland is cast more appropriately, but has little to do. Tony Curtis as a superstar of the time, worried about his declining sexual powers, seems entirely extraneous to the proceedings. The participation of Jeanne Moreau as a Garbo-type star, and Theresa Russell as Brady's daughter, who is intent on seducing Stahr, largely goes for nothing. The film was mostly panned on its release, although Nicholson attracted some favourable comments for his role. It is no bad thing for an actor to be

remembered as one of the few good things in a turkey of a movie. He may have missed out on the lead role, but he walked away with the acting honours.

Goin' South (1979)

Paramount: Director, Jack Nicholson; Producers, Harry Gittes and Harold Schneider; Screenplay, John Herman Shaner, Al Ramus, Charles Shyer and Alan Mandel; Cinematography, Nestor Almendros; Editors, Richard Chew and John Fitzgerald Beck; Music, Van Dyke Parks and Perry Botkin, with additional music written and performed by Ry Coorder

Cast: Jack Nicholson (Henry Moon); Mary Steenburgen (Julia Tate); Christopher Lloyd (Frank Towfield); John Belushi (Hector); Veronica Cartwright (Hermine); Richard Bradford (Sheriff); Jeff Morris (Big Abe)

Running time 109 minutes

For some time, Nicholson had been contemplating directing a western called *Moon Trap* from a novel by Don Berry, but suddenly he dropped that project and turned to another western script which would also give him a 'Gabby Hayes' type role and allow him to direct as well. The movies that film stars direct themselves naturally have a special place in their affections and seemingly Nicholson can be touchy when *Goin' South* is mentioned disparagingly, but only the most die-hard of Nicholson fans could find anything memorable about this slight addition to the western genre. One of the main problems with the film, apart from the script, is that Nicholson directs as well as stars in the movie. As I have stressed, he is an actor who needs directing, otherwise he can get out of control. When the restraining hand behind the camera is Jack himself, or an indulgent other, then there are real problems.

The westerns Nicholson had acted in before he became a star had basically been 'debunking' examples of the genre with an underlying compulsion to undercut the myths of the pioneering days and the use that Hollywood had made of those myths ever since filmmaking had started amidst the orange groves of LA. *The Missouri Breaks* had been a very flawed example

Goin' South. An authentic-looking picture of frontier folk with a bearded Nicholson and Mary Steenburgen sitting in front of him.

of this kind of anti-western, but that had not put Nicholson off this approach to filmland's most famous genre and he was clearly keen to direct again, the failure of *Drive, He Said* obviously still smarting. Indeed, he was not keen to star in the movie himself, but United Artists insisted the movie needed his name on the marquee before they would give him $6 million for the budget.

The script was by long-time Nicholson friend and associate, John Herman Shaner and his writing partner Al Ramus, but they were ultimately dismissed by the producers and replaced by Charles Shyer and Al Mandel, who eventually shared the screenwriting credit. This may be a case of too many cooks spoiling the broth and it is impossible to gauge whether the movie would have turned out any better if the original script had remained intact. As an

incidental to the whole mess that *Goin' South* became, it should be noted that Nicholson had to stand by as his old pal Shaner was sacked from the project. Nicholson was now a big-time movie player and he had to come to terms with the suits, even if it meant sacrificing old pals in the process.

The casting of 'unknown' Mary Steenburgen reads like a legend from the old days of Hollywood when stars were, according to the legends, discovered sitting on a stool at Schwab's. Nicholson by chance met Steenburgen at the Gulf and Western office in New York. By this time Jane Fonda had turned down the part of the female lead, and Nicholson had considered Jessica Lange and Meryl Streep. Steenburgen was at that time working as a waitress, had very little track record and none in movies, but Nicholson was so taken with her,

Goin' South. Director Nicholson sets up the next shot.

especially after she read for the part, that he took a gamble on her. Steenburgen emerges from *Goin' South* with considerable merit, because while Nicholson is mugging his way through a dismal performance, she is restrained and carries some real presence in a role that is not dissimilar to the spinster Katherine Hepburn played in *The African Queen*.

The story concerns one Henry Moon (Nicholson), a bank, horse and cattle thief, who is due to be hanged in Longhorn, Texas to the great glee of the local populace and especially of the deputy sheriff, Frank (Christopher Lloyd). Moon comes under especially close scrutiny from some women in the town, which turns out to be because of a local ordinance, dating back to Civil War days, that allowed a condemned man to be saved from the gallows if an unmarried lady would agree to marry him and be responsible for his good behaviour. Julia Tate (Steenburgen) steps forward at the last moment to save the rogue, because she wants someone to help her mine the gold mine situated on her ranch outside town, an area that the railway company is threatening to swallow up. Moon finds that his hopes for marital bliss with Julia are to be dashed: she wants him strictly for his muscle and labour. However, gradually he wears her resistance down and they become lovers. They strike gold, but Julia is jealous of his former lover, Hermine, a member of the gang that Moon used to be part of. When the gang decide to rob the bank and, in doing do, steal the gold that Moon thinks Julia and he have deposited there, he forestalls that by robbing it himself. He then discovers that the trunk is full of rocks instead of gold. Julia, stung by jealousy, has lit out with the gold, having sold the land to the railway company. Moon chases after the coach and when the couple change their minds about shooting each other, they head off for Mexico: *Goin' South*.

The movie is played for broad comedy, the broadest of broad. Nicholson leers, pulls faces, sticks his tongue out, rolls his eyes, winces, and most bizarrely of all, employs a 'glottal' type of nasal delivery that makes him sound as though he has a permanent cold and which led some American critics to hint that it was the result of too much cocaine-sniffing during the shoot. It is a performance totally out of control and presumably there was no one around who was

strong or perceptive enough to tell him that. He acts like a parody of himself. Unfortunately, it is contagious and everybody else, with the honourable exceptions of Steenburgen and Richard Bradford as the sheriff, overacts like crazy. Christopher Lloyd is one of the worst offenders, while John Belushi, whose part seemingly shrunk the longer filming lasted, is simply offensive as a Mexican stereotype. Other guilty parties included Danny DeVito, Jeff Morris and, to a lesser extent, Veronica Cartwright as Hermine. Presumably they were acting under orders from the director who showed a monumental lack of judgement all-round.

Nicholson had the good sense to employ cinematographer Nestor Almendros, who had shot several Truffaut movies. The opening sequences of *Goin' South* promise far more that is ultimately delivered: a solitary figure in a desert landscape who mounts and gallops towards the distant horizon. Then a pursuing posse sweeps into the frame. Moon crosses the Rio Grande into Mexico and stands on the opposite river bank taunting his pursuers. But they ignore the time-honoured rule that they cannot enter Mexico to apprehend a horse thief, and when Moon tries to mount his horse, Speed, she is unwilling to get up from her prone position. He is arrested and led away, as he complains 'It ain't fair!' The debunking agenda is set and followed through on, but the rest is so grotesquely caricatured that all subtlety goes out of the window, so that the over-the-top nature of the antics on screen become an insult to the intelligence of any discerning viewer. It is in questionable taste anyway to extract comedy from capital punishment, but when it is laid on with a trowel, then it crosses boundaries of taste into sheer loutishness. Nicholson's pleading speech from the gallows sets the tone: it is overacted and robs the scene of any impact at all. Nicholson is once again, as in *The Fortune*, acting funny instead of allowing the comedy to emerge from the character and the situation. It is a nudge-nudge performance telling the audience all the time that is meant to be funny. Audiences all over the world refused to be convinced and stayed away in droves.

Very few movie stars have managed to combine the roles of director and star in the same movie. Orson Welles immediately springs to mind, but he was an immensely talented director; Olivier in the trilogy *Henry V*, *Hamlet* and *Richard III* was another. Kenneth Branagh in his *Hamlet* was a notable failure and Nicholson certainly belongs to this group. But the nature of stardom is such that the money men want the star's name for its marquee value as an acting commodity and are willing to indulge an actor's whim to direct if they can have his name above the title. In the case of *Goin' South*, this policy clearly failed. The movie was neither a critical nor commercial success and constituted something of a setback to the ongoing Nicholson success story.

The Shining (1980)

Director, Stanley Kubrick; Producer, Stanley Kubrick; Screenplay, Stanley Kubrick and Diane Johnson adapted from the novel by Stephen King; Cinematography, John Alcott; Editor, Ray Lovejoy;

Cast: Jack Nicholson (Jack Torrance); Shelley Duvall (Wendy Torrance); Danny Lloyd (Danny Torrance); Scvatman Crothers (Dick Halorann); Barry Nelson (Stuart Ullmann); Philip Stone (Delbert Grady); Joe Turkel (Lloyd)

Running time 142 minutes

The Shining. A grim-faced Jack Torrance goes more than slightly crazy and more than slightly over the top.

The Shining is one of Jack Nicholson's movies that usually splits opinion down the middle between those who hate the picture, and his performance, and those who admire the film greatly and like him in it. I come somewhere in the middle: I like the movie, but I have severe doubts about Jack's performance. In fact, I think the movie works despite his performance.

Stanley Kubrick, the director of the movie, had by this time in his career made a number of commercially successful and critically admired movies, from the heist movie *The Killing* (1956), to the anti-war classic *Paths of Glory* (1958), the epic *Spartacus* (1960), the bleakly satirical *Dr Strangelove* (1963), the space flick *2001* (1969), the violent *A Clockwork Orange* (1971) to his previous effort *Barry Lyndon* (1975). Every Kubrick movie was an event and usually controversial, like *A Clockwork Orange*. He has as many detractors as admirers. The latter see him as a fully fledged auteur with something to say about contemporary life, whilst his detractors claim he makes showy, pretentious movies that have much more to do with style than content. For example, Andrew Sarris, the American critic and a confirmed auteurist, is a detractor: 'He has chosen to exploit the giddiness of middlebrow audiences on the satiric level of Mad magazine.' Kubrick himself certainly believes his movies say something about the modern world: 'Man in the twentieth century has been cast adrift in a rudderless boat on an uncharted sea. The very meaninglessness of life forces man to create his own meaning. If it can be written or thought, it can be filmed.'

Kubrick, an ex-Life magazine photographer, is notorious for the number of shooting days he requires and the number of takes he insists on at times. Any actor signing on for a Kubrick movie must have been aware that the schedule would very likely be drastically overshot and the director would be a hard taskmaster. Kubrick has not acquired a reputation, however, for being an actors' director; indeed, that is one of the accusations his detractors hurl at him: that he is not interested in characters or performances, and his actors become almost anonymous against a visual background that he has meticulously created. That is certainly true of *2001*, *A Clockwork*

The Shining. This shot from the ballroom sequence gives some idea of how overripe Nicholson's performance was.

Orange and *Barry Lyndon*, but is it really accurate about *Paths of Glory* or *Dr Strangelove*? Kubrick may not be an actors' director, but Kirk Douglas, Peter Sellers, Sterling Hayden and George C. Scott gave their most memorable performances under his direction. As for the charge that his films are cold and unfeeling, surely there is a very strong sense of outrage at the injustice meted out to the ordinary soldiers in *Paths of Glory* by the army generals, and in *Strangelove*, *2001*, *Orange* and *Barry Lyndon*, there is an implicit humanism that does not screech out at you as in most Hollywood films. The style of the movies invites audiences to distance themselves and not to wallow in sentimentality or a facile sympathy for the characters. What is sometimes called the heartlessness of Kubrick's films is, in fact, a director treating audiences as though they had intelligence and the ability to

stand back from a movie and not be manipulated to feel what the makers want them to feel in the traditional Hollywood manner. Kubrick had admired Nicholson's acting since he saw him in *Easy Rider* and he had been looking for opportunities to work with the actor. When he read Stephen King's novel *The Shining* at galley stage, he was impressed by the writer's reworking of the horror genre. King, by then, was a major writer in the genre with millions of fans all over the world. Kubrick, in choosing to film one of his books, would come under close scrutiny from horror-movie fundamentalists and fanatical King fans. But Kubrick saw something in the novel that he could work with. Nicholson was clearly just as attracted to the idea of working with Kubrick as the director was with him. Additionally, he would have the chance to play a deranged character in a film that, basically, said something, under the trappings of its horror narrative, about the family and its capacity to repress and breed murderous resentments. I am convinced that one of the reasons some people hated this film so much was because of what it implicitly said about the institution of the family.

The narrative is set in an isolated snowbound Colorado resort hotel (the hotel used is actually in Oregon), where Jack Torrance, a ex-teacher and aspiring novelist, has been employed during the winter months as caretaker of the vast, sprawling building. The general manager tells Torrance that a previous caretaker had gone crazy because of the isolation and had murdered his two daughters with an axe. The hotel had been built over an ancient Indian burial ground and rumour has it that the ghosts of native Americans haunt the hotel. Torrance is anxious to have the time and solitude to write a novel, so he brings his wife (Shelley Duvall) and his small son Danny to Colorado to spend the winter. Jack starts writing, his son whizzes down the long corridors on his tricycle, and Mrs Torrance attends to her husband's needs; indeed, they seem an almost perfect nuclear family unit. However, weird things begin to happen. All three are subject to frightening visions of corpse-like creatures and two young girls, who are obviously the ghosts of the two murdered daughters. Torrance wanders into the hotel's vast bar, which has been transformed back into the twenties; elegant people swan around and there is a bartender whom Torrance has conversations with. Danny has the power of 'shining', the ability to see through space and time, which the cook at the hotel (Scatman Crothers) recognizes and fears. Torrance is becoming crazier by the day; his wife discovers that his frenzied writing amounts to no more than typing over and over 'All work and no play makes Jack a dull boy'. He has become increasingly dictatorial towards his family and his young son, who realizes (because of his special powers) that his father has been overtaken by the evil inherent in the place. Torrance kills the cook with an axe and then attacks his family. They manage to escape the deranged father.

Style is meaning, and that maxim is one that many film critics who took against *The Shining* refuse to accept or choose to ignore. The semantic meaning of the movie is not overemphasized, indeed, you have to be alert to pick up the information about the former caretaker and the Indian burial grounds, but any meaning the movie communicates is in the way it is shot, which is true of most of the films Kubrick has directed. When Kubrick tracks the kid travelling at speed down the long, empty and ominous corridors of the hotel, he is not just interested in exploring the possibilities of the Steadicam, but he is saying something implicitly about the mounting craziness of the situation they find themselves in. Isolated as a family unit, thrown back on their own devices and forced into each other's company, the family unit begins to fray at the joins. The husband becomes more and more frustrated at his inability to create something worthwhile and his frustrations are directed at his wife and ultimately his child. The ghosts and the corpse-like creatures that are staple elements of the horror genre are used to represent the madness that is about to envelop this family as all civilized restraints are severed and the deep resentments that have been repressed break through and murderous mayhem ensues. The ghastly visions, and these are convincingly and revoltingly created, also remind us of the injustices imposed on native Americans in American history. These are ghosts from America's past that have come to haunt present-day Americans. Sometimes the movie could be accused of an uncertain tone, as when Torrance is using an axe to break down a door to get at his wife and child and he shouts 'Heeeeere's Johnny', which mimics the introduction that was used to introduce the star of the long-running and hugely popular chat show of Johnny Carson. Using this icon of middle American popular culture in association with a potential axe murderer reflects the movie's intentions. Kubrick is intent on revealing the fissures beneath the surface of American life. Torrance and his family have only to be isolated from 'normal' life for the reality of their family situation and its dysfunctional nature to be revealed. Kubrick has used satire in previous films to make serious points (*Dr Strangelove*, *A Clockwork Orange*) and there is a good deal of dark humour in *The Shining*.

The story has it that Nicholson, while he was shooting the film, was concerned that his performance was too 'broad'. He was right to be concerned, because it is too broad, far too much so. At times, it is a parody of the characteristic Nicholson madness and raging. He pulls demonic faces, grins crazily, delivers his lines bizarrely, sounds like Richard Nixon occasionally and generally does a 'mad' act. It is indeed well over the top and his performance at the core of the film sets up that uncertain tone I have already mentioned. Is *The Shining* a 'serious' horror movie, or is its intention to send up the genre while delivering some conventional elements of this type of flick? No red-blooded male movie critic should perhaps admit this, but I actually find the movie quite scary at times whether it is meant to be satirical of the genre or not. It is just that Nicholson's performance keeps getting in the way. It is not long into the movie before he is acting crazy and then there is nowhere for him to go. It is not represented as a gradual progression into madness, but a sudden descent, that undermines the idea of his craziness and his animosity to his family being partly the product of the isolation in which they are living and the 'ghosts' that haunt them. We are given some hints at the job interview that perhaps Torrance is not exactly a stable individual, but thereafter the onset of weirdness is very rapid.

Nicholson generally chooses his directors with care, but in working with Kubrick, he was working with a director who was likely to be more interested in the visual composition of the movie than his performance. As Kubrick was a Nicholson admirer, he probably mentally calculated that he could trust him to deliver the performance he wanted, but even talented actors need a guiding hand. They need to be told if it is too much or too little, for example. According to reports, Shelley Duvall had a hard time during the shoot, Kubrick demanding a lot from her and even being accused of bullying his female lead. No doubt there are different stories about what actually happened during the shoot, everyone will have their own version, but even Nicholson must have tired of the sometimes forty takes that Kubrick would demand, including the scene where Torrance attacks the hotel cook with an axe, and the sequence where he has a conversation with the ghost of a barman in the ballroom scene. The shoot predictably took much longer than scheduled (over a year), which is a long time to spend on one movie, even one directed by someone as perfectionist as Kubrick. But it appears that

Nicholson was in tune with Kubrick's stylistic intentions. He has said about the role of Torrance that he tried 'to find someplace where the style merges with the reality of the piece, some kind of symbolic design'. Kubrick surely could not have said it better himself. Symbolic design was exactly what Kubrick was trying to build in the filming of *The Shining*. The details of the plot and all the motifs of the horror genre are much less important than this unifying design that he tried to give the film. On balance, I think he succeeded, and the film has recovered from the critical mauling it was given in some quarters to become, if not a classic, certainly one of the most imaginative reworkings of the horror film ever made.

For once, in a film of some worth, Nicholson was not one of its major assets, although that may seem a strange thing to write in a book about an actor the author admires. However, all talented actors give performances that are inadequate or hammy, and I happen to think that Nicholson's performance in *The Shining* falls into the latter category. The movie, nevertheless, survives the hamminess of the central performance.

The Postman Always Rings Twice (1981)

Paramount: Director, Bob Rafelson; Producers, Bob Rafelson and Charles Mulvehill; Screenplay, David Mamet, adapted from the novel by James M. Cain; Cinematography, Sven Nykvist; Editor, Graeme Clifford; Music, Michael Small

Cast: Jack Nicholson (Frank Chambers); Jessica Lange (Cora Papadakis); John Colicos (Nick Papadakis); Michael Lerner (Katz); John Ryan (Kennedy); Anjelica Huston (Madge); Jon Van Ness (Motorcycle Cop)

Running time 123 minutes

Remakes of old, 'classic' Hollywood movies are, by received wisdom, inevitably inferior to the originals. Thus, when the 1981 *The Postman Always Rings Twice* was released, the critical consensus was that it was not half as good as the 1947 version starring Lana Turner and John Garfield. I have to say I find that an

The Postman Always Rings Twice. Bob Rafelson (left) sets up a shot with distinguished Swedish cameraman Sven Nykvist.

extraordinary verdict and one that stems from that peculiar kind of snobbery that affects many cineastes about the innate superiority of Hollywood in its golden age. In this case, however, the 'classic' Hollywood movie is, if not exactly a turkey, so flawed that I cannot understand why it attracts much critical attention. Lana Turner, who could not act, is totally miscast as Cora, the wife of the owner of a roadside diner; she looks and sounds like a plastic Hollywood glamour goddess and the casting of this star signals the intentions of the production: to produce a glamorized, cleaned-up and 'acceptable' film version of James M. Cain's pulp novel. John Garfield was a powerful actor and he could have been effective as Frank Chambers, the itinerant who falls in love with Cora and helps her to plan the murder of her Greek husband, Nick, but the glossy production values almost sink him as well. Luchino Visconti,

the Italian director, had also made a version of Cain's novel in 1942, *Ossessione*, and that is vastly superior to the 1947 Hollywood movie. Nicholson had, in fact, wanted to film a remake of *Postman* for some time, but, when in the mid-seventies, studio executives had mooted Raquel Welch as his co-star, he had backed off. Almost certainly he had seen what the casting of one Hollywood glamour girl with very limited acting talents had done to the earlier version and he did not want to scupper the remake from its very beginnings. Casting is a very important part of a movie's success and most often you can tell what the makers' intentions are by the leading actors they use. The casting of Raquel Welch would have sent a very clear signal of intent.

Because of his determination to get it right, Nicholson was eventually to be blessed with the bounty of Jessica Lange as his co-star. Lange is not only beautiful, but is willing to tone down her glamour for a role, and she can act as well. It was the casting of equals; both are intelligent, intuitive and charismatic actors. In addition, his friend, and the director whom he had done his best work with, Bob Rafelson, was to direct. David Mamet, the most interesting playwright in America of the time, was to write the screenplay, and, an exceptional bonus, Sven Nykvist, Ingmar Bergman's cinematographer, was to photograph the movie. Add to those, Michael Small, who wrote an excellent score, supporting actors John Colicos (Nick), Michael Lerner (the lawyer Katz), John Ryan (the blackmailer) and Anjelica Huston (the circus lady whom Frank has an affair with), and an exceptionally talented team had been assembled for the movie.

The action is set in the Depression years in Nowheresville close to Los Angeles. Frank Chambers (Nicholson), an itinerant bum, after conning his way into a free meal at Nick's roadside diner, accepts Nick's offer of a job as handyman, mainly, it is implied, because he lusts after Cora (Lange), Nick's 'young' wife. The movie implies a submerged racism in the couple's attitude to the Greek husband, who is proud of his roots. When Nick gets drunk, he speaks of America as the land of opportunity, but where there is no happiness and foreigners are cheated and spurned. Frank and Cora are clearly attracted to one another, but it is a resentful, distrustful attraction, and their first coupling starts off as a kind of rape, which turns into violent, explosive lovemaking. These scenes are explicit, but there is no nudity as such, so the film cannot be accused of being exploitative. Almost all of the sex scenes, however, reflect the violent nature of their love affair, full of conflicting urges of lust, love and hate. We learn that Frank has a criminal record for armed robbery and assault. Cora half-explains her motivations: 'You don't know what it's like to be a woman trapped in this kind of…I have to have you, Frank. Just you and me. I'm tired of what's right and wrong.' The movie successfully manipulates the audience into hoping the lovers get away with the murder of Nick, which they finally succeed in doing after a botched attempt. They fake a car crash after Frank has hit Nick over the head and in the immediate aftermath of the killing, Cora seduces Frank into making love

to her. The violence of their murderous actions finds a metaphor in the violence of their lovemaking. But the cops do not buy their story of Nick having died in the crash; there is the evidence of the blow on the back of Nick's head and inevitably they find out about Frank's criminal record. In addition, they look at Cora and guess that the two are lovers. There is the additional motive of an insurance policy on Nick's life, which Cora has been unaware of, but which the prosecution use as another reason for the couple to murder the husband. Eventually, Katz, a smart but unethical lawyer, arranges a deal between two interested insurance companies, both of whom stand to pay out substantial sums, and the charges are withdrawn even though the police know they are guilty. However, in the course of the trial, the lovers have turned on each other, Frank having been persuaded to swear out a complaint against Cora and Cora reacting by making a statement of confession to Katz and his assistant that implicates Frank. When they are set free, they are confronted with their mutual betrayals and life between them is difficult and bitter. When Cora goes away for a week to see her dying mother, Frank hitches to San Diego where he has a brief love affair with a circus performer, which Cora later finds out about. The lawyer's assistant attempts to blackmail them over the confession Cora has made, but Frank deals with him violently and effectively. This seems to bring them together again and their love is cemented when Cora announces she is pregnant and Frank appears happy about that. They are driving back to the diner in this happy frame of mind when they start kissing and Frank has to swerve to avoid a lorry; Cora is thrown out of the car and is killed. The last shots of the film have Frank sobbing uncontrollably beside Cora's dead body and the sound of a police car siren is heard in the distance. Fate has finally dealt with the couple and they are never to find the happiness they were striving for together. In the 1947 version, the film ends with Frank in prison charged with the murder of Cora and laughing sardonically about the fact that he got away with killing Nick and now he is going to be executed for a murder he did not commit. Rafelson and Mamet's version only hints at this and concentrates on the loss Frank is feeling, which reinforces a view of the characters as born losers in a system that is unfeeling and totally corrupt itself.

The Postman Always Rings Twice. Cora (Jessica Lange) and Frank (Nicholson) indulge in some steamy sex on the kitchen table.

Sven Nykvist's sombre photography elicits the seediness of the roadside diner and petrol station milieu in Depression America. It is a darkly pessimistic movie and this is reflected in the dark muted colours and interiors favoured by Rafelson and his cinematographer. *Postman* qualifies as an example of late film noir, as *Chinatown* did, and although it does not achieve that movie's quality, it is a memorable movie in its own right and one of the most unjustifiably neglected films of the eighties. When Nykvist's track record with Ingmar Bergman is considered, his contribution to the overall visual style of *Postman* cannot be overestimated. But for a lighting cameraman such as Nykvist to operate artistically and successfully, he has to be working with a sympathetic and skilled director, and that is what he had in Rafelson, who, again, has been one of the most underrated directors working in

the Hollywood film industry. When much lesser directors such as Ridley Scott or Mike Nichols are given serious critical attention and someone like Rafelson has to struggle to get his films made, then there is something truly wrong in the Hollywood film industry and among the critics who are apologists for the industry. *Postman* has been criticized by some critics for being too self-consciously arty, but would they have had the same reaction if the movie had been European? When a Hollywood director tries to make an arthouse film within the Hollywood mainstream, then he or she is very likely to encounter that kind of half-baked criticism.

Nicholson gives one of his convincing understated performances in this movie. He can never quite disguise his intelligence, however, and the only question mark over his playing of

The Postman Always Rings Twice. Frank Chambers thinks about his next move outside the diner.

the itinerant bum is whether someone as smart as Nicholson appears to be could so consistently foul up. I guess the answer to that has to be yes, if you see the characters of both Frank and Cora as inherently self-destructive and caught up in a train of circumstances where they feel trapped. They feel they have to take extreme measures to grab at one of the few chances of happiness that has ever come their way. As in Hitchcock's movies, we are drawn into a position where we want the murderers to get away with it, not that Nick, the husband, is portrayed as a bad man; that would be too easy and Mamet and Rafelson avoid that. Indeed, Nick, in his yearning to get on in this land of opportunity, and his awareness that he will always be treated as a foreigner, elicits the audience's sympathy, so that our willing Frank and Cora to escape from the trap is that more unsettling. Nick is played by Canadian actor John Colicos, who is of Greek extraction, and this care in casting avoids the usual crass representation of ethnic minorities in Hollywood movies.

The film, too, has an understated political subtext. It is set in the Depression and Frank's situation at the start of the movie exemplifies what happened to millions of Americans during the 1930s. The authorities, the cops, the legal system, the agents of big business, are all portrayed as hard, conniving or corrupt. Frank and Cora are not represented as being as they are because of their innate badness, but because they are products of this unjust and unequal system. During their trial, they have no control over events; their release is the result of a stitch-up between lawyers, the court and large financial interests. Cora has said she's tired of what's right and wrong, but it is the society that has no interest in rights and wrongs, only power, influence and money. Perhaps it was this subtly implied political content that alienated some American critics; certainly, it was an element completely absent from the 1947 glossy version, which many of them preferred.
I would rate Nicholson's performance in *Postman* as one of his best and the movie among the most successful, in an artistic sense, that he has made. I hope that in time the critical consensus will change and the movie will be given full credit for being one of the best that mainstream Hollywood produced in the eighties.

Reds (1981)

Director, Warren Beatty; Producer, Warren Beatty; Screenplay, Warren Beatty and Trevor Griffiths; Cinematography, Vittorio Storaro; Editors, Dede Allen and Craig Mckay; Music, Stephen Sondheim

Cast: Warren Beatty (John Reed); Diane Keaton (Louise Bryant); Jack Nicholson (Max Eastman); Jack Nicholson (Eugene O'Neill); Edward Herrmann (Max Eastman); Jerzy Kosinski (Grigory Zinoviev); Oaul Sorvino (Louis Fraina); Maureen Stapleton (Emma Goldman); Nicolas Coster (Paul Trullinger); Ian Wolfe (Mr Partlow); Gene Hackman (Pete Van Wherry)

Running time 200 minutes

America had just elected the extreme conservative Ronald Reagan President when *Reds* was released to general critical acclaim in 1981. Reagan, an ex-President of the Screen Actors Guild, had always been a red-baiter, a fellow-traveller with the notorious witchhunters of the forties and fifties when many of his actor colleagues were blacklisted by the studios for supposed Communist sympathies. Thirty or so years after those disgraceful events, times had changed and it was acceptable for a superstar like Warren Beatty to produce, direct and star in a movie about a left-wing journalist who had made his name by being in Russia at the right time and producing his story of the Russian Revolution, *Ten Days That Shook the World*. But then, that is a familiar pattern in the entertainment industry: rebels and agitators from the distant past are often sanctified when they are no longer any danger to the established order. Still, it has to be granted that Beatty was taking a chance by devoting so much of his time and energies to documenting John Reed's life and dealing sympathetically with the revolution that had produced the Communist regime which most of America, along with its President, thought of as the 'evil Empire'.

Beatty, still a pal of Nicholson's, persuaded him to accept the role of Eugene O'Neill, America's leading dramatist of the first half of the century. O'Neill had sympathized with

John Reed's political ideals, but had not been a joiner, being too much of a cynic about movements and human motivation. Along with Reed, he had been the lover of Louise Bryant, an early feminist and radical. The movie uses this love triangle to explore the themes of idealism in politics and the strains that political commitment puts on relationships. Being a Hollywood movie and having to appeal to a mass audience, it does stress the personal too much at the expense of the wider political canvas, and it is in danger of tipping over into being yet another romantic tearjerker about a doomed romance. However, there is enough politics in it (just!) to rescue it from this fate and it ends up as one of the most interesting, albeit deeply flawed, films of the eighties.

Trevor Griffiths, the radical British playwright, wrote the first draft of the screenplay, then Beatty worked with him over a protracted period to knock out a less 'political' draft. Griffiths then left the project and Elaine May and Robert Towne did some uncredited work tinkering with the structure. One of the interesting features of *Reds*, a feature that helps rescue the movie from just being a love story that happens to be set against the background of radical politics in America and the Russian Revolution, is the use of real-life 'witnesses' whose personal accounts of the events and the main protagonists are interspersed in the narrative. These witnesses include Henry Miller, Adela Rogers St John, Dora Russell and Rebecca West, and they help to give up a welcome distancing effect from the story of Reed and Bryant and to remind us of the really important aspects of this tale. Reed was interesting because he was an early American radical who fell for the Russian Revolution and was on hand to report it for the American public, and not because he had a lasting affair with Louise Bryant. Unfortunately, the film never really acknowledges that, because the commercial pressures were pulling in the opposite direction.

Reds. Nicholson as Eugene O'Neil.

It is irrelevant to speculate whether Nicholson's portrayal of Eugene O'Neill is anything like the reality of the man himself. In the first place, we have no definitive view of O'Neill, only different versions of him as ladled out through his plays, biographies and other testimonies. This is always the difficulty when a real life character is portrayed in any drama, especially a figure as prominent as O'Neill. The question is whether Nicholson as O'Neill works as a narrative figure within the movie, and the answer is a qualified yes. O'Neill is meant to counter Reed's naive enthusiasm with a world-weary cynicism about causes and political ideals. Reed is a joiner, or he wants to be, although his difficulty in trying to 'join' the comrades in the Russian Revolution is that he is an American and will always be seen as an outsider by the very people he wants to help. Lenin called these foreigner sympathizers 'useful idiots'. O'Neill is represented as a non-joiner, who nonetheless shares some of the ideals of Reed. Bryant is caught between the two men: on the one hand she is attracted by Reed's boyish enthusiasm and get-up-and-go, whilst on the other she finds O'Neill's brooding disenchantment and overt sexuality (as portrayed by Nicholson) seductive. Thus, it can be argued that the love triangle operates as a kind of metaphor for the opposing attitudes of the American Left to what was happening in Russia. Reed fervently wants the revolution to change the world for ever, and Bryant shares that wish, while to O'Neill that's just a pipe dream, and Bryant knows in her soul he is right. However, there is far too much stress on the romance rather than on the issues dividing the characters, and so this metaphor is somewhat submerged.

Nevertheless, within the parameters set by the romanticized script, Nicholson scores as O'Neill. This is one of his restrained performances where what he does not do or say is just as effective as his dialogue and actions. He is a contrast to the All-American, college boy gush of Reed/Beatty, and in his underplaying, he reinforces how naive Reed's hopes for the Revolution were, given the type of men who were in charge and the historical circumstances they found themselves in. Reed dies of typhus at the end of the movie, which may be seen as a metaphor for the death of his hopes for the Revolution. Nicholson portrays O'Neill as a realist and a survivor, who has seen too much and knows too much of human nature

to invest that much credence in political events that will inevitably end in tears. It is an effective performance in a movie that deserves some respect.

The Border (1981)

Universal: Director, Tony Richardson; Producer, Edgar Bronfman; Screenplay, Deric Washburn, Walon Green and David Freeman from a story by Deric Washburn; Cinematography: Ric Waite; Editor, Robert K. Lambert; Music, Ry Cooder

Cast: Jack Nicholson (Charlie Smith); Valerie Perrine (Marcy); Harvey Keitel (Cat); Warren Oates (Big Red); Elpidia Carrillo (Maria); Shannon Wilcox (Savannah)

Running time 107 minutes

Tony Richardson, the British film director, had made his reputation by directing British 'New Wave' films in the sixties such as *The Loneliness of the Long-Distance Runner*, *A Taste of Honey*, *Look Back in Anger* and *Tom Jones*. However, Richardson's real métier was the theatre and I think this shows in his films. Successful stage directors do not necessarily become creative film directors. The sixties British films Richardson directed have not worn particularly well and his American films even less well (*The Loved One*, *Sanctuary*, *Hotel New Hampshire*). Yet one of the reasons Jack Nicholson chose to participate in *The Border* was because Richardson was directing. Some American actors have what I can only describe as an over-reverential regard for the British stage and its leading lights, and Nicholson's misplaced faith in Richardson may have had its root cause in just such an attitude.

The Border isn't a total turkey, but it comes close. Like many upper-middle-class, ex-public schoolboy British lefties, Richardson basically saw the working-class and underclasses through sentimental and rose-coloured spectacles. This sentimentality pervades movies like *A Taste of Honey*, leading to a simplistic and one-dimensional representation of social divisions within British society. This kind of simplification finds its way into *The Border*, although clearly some effort has been made to avoid this. In this case, the 'wetback' Mexicans seeking illegal

The Border. In a border raid, Charlie (Nicholson) arrests a drug dealer who had tried to escape.

entry into Texas are the equivalent of the British working-class and the American Immigration Services are the agents of an oppressive ruling class. The mediating figure between the oppressed would-be immigrants and the powers-that-be is Charlie Smith (Nicholson), who, after succumbing to the corruption endemic among his fellow border guards, is transformed by the desire to save a Madonna-like Mexican young woman and her baby.

Apart from the opportunity to be directed by Richardson, Nicholson was obviously attracted to the project by the role of Charlie, which would provide him with the chance to play an 'ordinary Joe' ennobled by the dramatic circumstances in which he finds himself. Nicholson does a fine job: gone are the sometimes embarrassing over-the-top flamboyance and sheer ham of his performances in *The Shining* and *Goin' South* and instead, he gives one of his intuitive, restrained and sensitive portrayals where he often suggests more than the script offers. He is excellent at acting the

part of a fairly average guy, who is almost drowning in the surrounding corruption and bullshit, but manages somehow to find some kind of moral bearings again and to act on his higher instincts. He almost makes the drama believable, but his character is hemmed in by the cardboard cut-out villains (Harvey Keitel and Warren Oates) who are into brutalizing, and profiting from, the illegal immigrants whom they are charged to prevent from entering the States. There is a predictable ending involving a shoot-out between Charlie and his boss, Big Red (Oates) and Cat (Keitel), which is not only unbelievable, but far too reminiscent of the facile resolutions much favoured by cheap western oaters. Victorious in the shoot-out, Charlie crosses the Rio Grande, like a slighter and less macho John Wayne, to return her baby to the saint-like Maria. Hollywood has found itself one more happy ending.

It is a familiar strategy in Hollywood movies when representing some 'social problem' (in this case, illegal immigration and the corrupt practices surrounding it) to have one central figure (inevitably played by a star who can stand for integrity) who intervenes and puts things to rights. That way the system can be seen to be correctable, if only right-thinking individuals go against the trend and stand up for what's right. It is a reassuring message, but one that conveniently skirts hard realities. Deric Washburn's original script had originally portrayed Charlie as much more macho than he is in the final film, and it is clear that attempts have been made to give depth to the character. One of the reasons he is 'attracted' to the Madonna-like Maria is that his wife, Marcy, as portrayed, is such a materialistic bitch. The representation of the two main women characters of the movie reflects the film's deficiencies: on the one hand there is the victimized saint, complete with baby, and on the other, the grasping, vulgar harridan who stands for Middle American womanhood. The opposing poles are just too extreme: these are not characters but ciphers.

The Border only found studio financing when Jack Nicholson was brought on board. The script had been knocking about for some years and the intention had been that Robert Blake would star, but his name on the marquee would not, it was thought, generate enough audience interest. When Blake dropped out of the project and Nicholson agreed to play Charlie Smith, the money ($14 million) suddenly and miraculously appeared. With a substantial budget like that, it is unlikely that Universal did not influence the final shape and ending of the movie, but how much the studio can carry the responsibility for the facile manipulations of the script and how much that was down to Richardson and his scriptwriters is impossible to gauge.

However, not many Hollywood superstars, if any, would have chosen to play such a downbeat role as Charlie Smith. Here is Nicholson demonstrating once more his courage in accepting unglamorous parts where he plays morally ambiguous men operating in the grubbier corners of American society. It is not Nicholson's fault that *The Border* is not better than it is. Indeed, he is one of the main reasons for taking the time to see the movie. It does not date well and its moral simplicities seem even more unconvincing at the end of the nineties than

they did the early eighties. *The Border* is one of those Nicholson films where he is by far the best thing about it.

Terms of Endearment (1983)

Paramount: Director, James L. Brooks; Producer, James L. Brooks; Screenwriter, James L. Brooks, adapted from the novel by Larry McMurtry; Cinematography, Andrzej Bartkowiak; Editor, Richard Marks; Music, Michael Gore

Cast: Shirley MacLaine (Aurora Greenway); Debra Winger (Emma Greenway Horton); Jack Nicholson (Garrett Breedlove); Jeff Daniels (Flap Horton); Danny DeVito (Vernon Dahlart); John Lithgow (Sam Evans); Betty R. King (Rosie Dunlop); Kate Charleson (Janice); Troy Bishop (Tommy Horton); Huckleberry Fox (Teddy Horton)

Running time 132 minutes

Jack Nicholson, in terms of his Hollywood superstar status, now needed a monster hit, if that pre-eminent position he had carved out for himself was to be maintained. Hollywood can forgive almost anything except successive box-office failures and no picture starring Nicholson had really made any money since *One Flew Over The Cuckoo's Nest*. However, the picture that would restore his box-office credibility would not offer him the chance of playing a leading role, nor even top or second billing. The part of ex-astronaut Garret Breedlove in *Terms of Endearment* would be more substantial than a cameo role, but it was still a small part, and he only received third billing under Shirley MacLaine and Debra Winger. Yet Nicholson's instinct for juicy roles, and working with the right director, proved once again invaluable and the role would win him an Oscar for Best Supporting Actor.

James L. Brooks's experience at the time of his taking on *Terms of Endearment* was restricted to television, but he clearly had a knack for making bland, superficially smart, middlebrow entertainment, as the hugely popular and long-running *Mary Tyler Show* and *Taxi* had indicated. Later he would be responsible for the 'thirty-something' series on television, and he would direct Nicholson again a few years later

Terms of Endearment. Breedlove (Nicholson) chats up the reluctant widow Aurora (Shirley MacLaine) across the garden fence.

in another middlebrow movie, *Broadcast News*. As the director, producer and screenwriter of *Terms of Endearment*, Brooks was getting as close to complete control over a project as it is possible for any filmmaker to do within the Hollywood system. Of course, the movie was adapted from Larry McMurtry's novel (author of other novels that had already been screened such as *Hud* and *The Last Picture Show*) and the film was also working within the tradition of two Hollywood genres: the romantic comedy and the tear-jerker or 'woman's picture'. Although many critics praised Brooks for managing to successfully dovetail the two genres, the fact is that *Terms of Endearment* plays it fairly safe all the way down the line, never really challenging the expectations of audiences in any profound way, although it could be said that the script is somewhat more perceptive and adult than many other examples of the genres.

The character of Garrett Breedlove does not appear in the original novel. Brooks wrote the character into the screenplay as a kind of amalgam of several of Aurora's suitors. Certainly, the two remaining suitors that are left in the screenplay are no match for Breedlove, and Danny DeVito in particular is totally wasted as a lapdog admirer of the Texas widow. In fact, all the male characters in *Terms of Endearment* are rather flabby and wimpish, except, of course, for Breedlove, who is portrayed as the eternal hedonist and chauvinist, scared of emotional commitments and with a libido that seems all-consuming. As the picture was aimed predominantly at a female audience, this pandered to female prejudices along the lines of 'Men are just big kids at heart,' or 'Men are only after one thing.' The women in the movie are constantly looking for something that their men folk cannot give them and their most important relationships are shown to be with other women and/or their children. Essentially, *Terms of Endearment* is a film about the mother-daughter relationship or female buddyship, as seen through the eyes of two male artists, McMurtry and Brooks.

The setting is a suburb of Houston, Texas. The film opens with Aurora Greenway (MacLaine) newly widowed and the stern, ambivalent relationship she has with her young daughter, Emma (Winger), is immediately established. The action spans the next thirty years and explores the ebbs and flows of their sometimes stormy, sometimes loving interaction and interdependence. Aurora is a rather puritanical, forbidding matron who somehow gathers round her willing male slaves, whom she treats at best with patronizing superiority, at worst with contempt. Emma manages to grow up differently from her mother; she is warm, sexy and giving. She resents deeply her mother's interference in her life and her constant advice about how she should behave, especially in relation to men and sex. Her mother's opposition has something to do with Emma's decision to marry the feckless and unambitious Flap Horton (Jeff Daniels), a minor-league university teacher of literature. Aurora makes no secret of her basic contempt for her son-in-law; indeed, she behaves like the original mother-in-law from hell. When the son-in-law is offered a teaching job in Desmoines, the daughter, now a full-time mother of three children, reluctantly agrees to move because he may win tenure in his new post. The mother and daughter say a fond farewell, although Aurora is as usual undemonstrative in her behaviour. One of her grandsons refers to her as Mrs Greenway during the leave-taking.

In between times, Aurora has made the acquaintance of Garrett Breedlove (Nicholson), the ex-astronaut who lives noisily and publicly next door. She is appalled, but fascinated, by his constant flow of lovers and his general lifestyle. When she shouts a complaint over the garden fence about the noise he is making, Breedlove engages in conversation with her, more or less propositioning her immediately: 'Why not lie back and enjoy the ride?' Aurora caustically puts him down when he asks for a date by saying, 'Imagine you having a date with someone which wasn't necessarily a felony', in reference to the young age of some of his amours. Indeed, the

first scene Nicholson appears in has him falling out of a car drunk, bloodying his head, asking two teenage girls into his house and their replying that they had expected 'a hero' when they had offered to drive the astronaut home. Meanwhile, back in Desmoines, Emma and Flap are undergoing financial difficulties. She meets Sam Evans (John Lithgow), another wimpish male, and, partly because she suspects her husband of having serial affairs with his students, she starts an affair with him. When her suspicions about her husband are confirmed, she takes herself and her children back to Mama, who, by this time several years later, has succumbed to Breedlove's seductive ways and become his lover. The mother and daughter joyfully share this event together and the mother seems far less uptight and much more happy with herself. However, Breedlove, having been introduced to her daughter and family, feels encroached upon and he tells her he wants to back away from the relationship: 'I'm starting to feel an obligation here and that makes it rough.'

Flap gives Emma an ultimatum: he has been offered a head of department job in Nebraska and he's going to move there within a week. She rejoins him, but his pattern of affairs continues. The hand of fate, as in all standard melodramas, intervenes and Emma is diagnosed as having inoperable cancer. The rest of the movie is devoted to her getting her affairs in order, settling her relationships with her nearest and dearest, especially with her mother, and facing up to the grim reaper with chirpy courage. She dies and the last scene takes place after the funeral in Houston. Breedlove, who has surprisingly turned up in Nebraska to support Aurora in her time of need, befriends the forlorn eldest son of Emma and Flap, who has conceded to the dying Emma that Aurora should bring up his kids. The movie ends on this gentle, elegiac note.

Terms of Endearment, then, is a movie that intends to have its cake and eat it. It goes for its laughs and then suddenly it pushes the audience through the emotional wringer, or should it be Winger? For me, it is too blatantly manipulative, and the death of Emma through a sudden onset of cancer seems quite arbitrary. It is one way of resolving, or not resolving, the narrative, without resorting to having the daughter leave her husband finally and returning to the rather-less-stony bosom of the matron. In essence, it gives the movie an opportunity to squeeze the last drop of emotion from the final parting of mother and daughter, even though the mother figure is restrained in her display of grief. The husband is neither shown to be overwhelmed with sadness, nor even at the centre of the drama. The most affecting scene may be where the mother says farewell to her sons, the elder of whom emanates anger at his mother for dying and resentment that he loves her so much, a love he is unable to express.

The Nicholson character is allowed to be a bit of a softy too; when he turns up to console the mother, she says, 'Who would have expected you to be a nice guy?' Well, in terms of the movie's intentions, everybody could more or less expect it, because under the guise of being a smart, rather acerbic comedy mixed with adult tragedy, *Terms of Endearment* is fundamentally a fusion of old-fashioned romantic comedy and updated woman's weepie. The social values it embodies, however, are basically conservative. Although Emma and Flap are strapped for money, there is no question of the wife taking a job to help sustain the household; indeed, one of the ways in which the husband is shown to be a hopeless case is that he fails to provide adequately for his family. In a scene near the end of the picture, Emma is put out by some smart New York women who react with surprise that she is content with being a full-time mother and the movie's sympathies are clearly with the Emma character. A similar view of family politics was represented in the series, 'thirty-something', which Brooks later produced. The movie is blatantly geared to 'a woman's point of view' in which family life, setting up a permanent home and a stable marriage are the ideal, an ideal which is seldom achieved because of the childishness and general inadequacies of the male of the species.

Garrett Breedlove is not one of Nicholson's most challenging parts. It is a kind of training ground for his roles in *The Witches of Eastwick* and *Heartburn* and, to a certain extent, *Batman*. Once again, he shows he is a star who doesn't care too much about projecting a glamorous image. In his first appearance on screen, he is drunk and bloodied. The next time we see him he is exposing his naked paunch and his hair is mussed. He is represented as behaving crudely. When Aurora says she is not going to become

just one of his string of lovers, he replies, 'Not much chance of that unless you curtsy on my face real soon.' There is a certain sense of disbelief that a man like Breedlove would bother with a puritanical Texan widow, who dresses for a lunch date with him in a grotesque, girlish frock and with hair attachments. But he tells her, 'You do bring out the devil in me,' and the audience has to suspend disbelief, if the picture is going to work for them at all. On their first date, there is the now-famous scene where Breedlove/Nicholson drives along the shoreline precariously balancing on top of the driver's seat while steering the car with his foot. Aurora suddenly brakes and he tumbles into the ocean. They kiss and he immediately puts his hand in her bra; she recoils and his hand gets stuck in her bosom. At moments like these, the movie aims for farcical effect, the comedy depending on the contrast between the opposing moral views that the two characters represent. But Nicholson is also allowed to be more restrained in the representation of the character, especially when he tells Aurora that he feels the relationship is getting too heavy, and at the end of the movie when he consoles her and befriends the son as a substitute father for the distant Flap. So there is some variety to the role, otherwise the character, and Nicholson, would just become a one-joke bore for the duration of the movie. Nicholson has been quoted as saying that he wanted to represent a middle-aged man who was not going through a mid-life crisis and someone who was not an object of scorn and pity.

Terms of Endearment more or less swept the Oscars when they were presented in March 1984 at the Dorothy Chandler Pavilion in Los Angeles. The movie won Best Picture Oscar, Brooks won the Best Director and Best Screenplay awards, and these tell us more about the conservative tastes of Academy members rather than anything about the quality of the movie. Viewed fifteen years later, the film seems rather obvious and dated, although it has a certain wit and intelligence working for it. It is the kind of movie you can watch on a wet afternoon and think you haven't completely wasted your time. Nicholson once again emerges with credit from his participation in a movie, and the film's success, both at the box office and critically, as well as at the Oscars, certainly revived his career, if reviving it needed.

Prizzi's Honour. John Huston advises Nicholson and crew about what he wants from the next set-up.

Prizzi's Honour (1985)

20th Century Fox: Director, John Huston; Producer, John Foreman; Screenplay, Richard Condon and Janet Roach from the novel by Richard Condon; Cinematography, Andrezej Bartkowiak; Editors, Rudi Fehr and Kaja Fehr

Cast: Jack Nicholson (Charley Partanna); Kathleen Turner (Irene Walker); Anjelica Huston (Maerose Prizzi); William Hickey (Don Corrado); John Randolph (Angelo Partanna); Lee Richardson (Dominic Partanna); Robert Loggia (Eduardo Partanna)

Running time 129 minutes

Jack Nicholson had had a long-lasting relationship (by Hollywood standards) with Anjelica Huston, the daughter of 'old Hollywood' director, John Huston, by the time he came to make *Prizzi's Honour* with his quasi-father-in-law directing and his partner as one of his co-stars. Anjelica had been trying to establish a career as a movie actress and no

doubt that was a factor in Nicholson deciding to take the part, as well as the movie presenting an opportunity to work with the seventy-nine-year-old Huston, with whom he had a close relationship as well. Seemingly, he was reluctant at first to play the Brooklyn hit-man, Charley Partanna, because he did not understand the script, the role and whether it was meant to be a black comedy or a Mafia gangster genre movie. Huston assured him that it was a comedy, a satire on family values and honour, which was also meant to make a comment on eighties, Reaganite greed and corporate business ethics. The famous credo 'What's good for General Motors is good for America' was to be transposed as 'What's good for the Prizzi mafioso family is honourable and for the maintenance of family and the American way of life.' The family honour of the film's title was to be exposed as vicious and amoral.

The film starts with the birth of Charley Partanna, whose father (John Randolph) is an integral part of the Brooklyn-based Mafia family led by Don Corrado, who acts as the literal godfather to Charley. Years pass and the young Charley is initiated into the crime organization by a mingling of blood with the Don who enunciates the law: 'We are as one until death.' The actual narrative opens at a Mafia wedding of the granddaughter of Corrado. Charley spots a beautiful, blonde stranger (Kathleen Turner) and is immediately smitten with her. He spurns the approaches of Maerose Prizzi, another granddaughter of Corrado's, advising her to 'cook her meatballs'. Maerose is a 'family scandal' and ignored by her father, the son of the Don. Charley pursues Irene Walker (Turner) to LA. After he becomes her besotted lover, he discovers that she is a specialist 'hitman', in fact she had worked as such for the Prizzi family. However, he also discovers that she has been part of a scam that she and her husband had worked at a casino owned by the Prizzis. He seeks advice from Maerose about what she should do: marry her or 'ice' her. Maerose recommends marriage for

her own reasons, because she is determined not only to be accepted back into the family but to win back Charley.

The family asks Charley to carry out a kidnapping of a banker who has been cheating them and Irene volunteers to be part of the job. During the kidnapping, she shoots dead the wife of a New York cop, which upsets the local force, who withdraw their 'co-operation' with the family and put pressure on them to deliver up the murderer. Meanwhile, Maerose has told her father, who has had a long-standing hatred for Charley, that he has raped her, which means the father is honour-bound to avenge his daughter's honour. The father, not knowing that Irene is Charley's wife, contracts her to bump off her husband. The Don, however, pressured by rival mafioso, who are losing out because of the killing of the cop's wife, and

Prizzi's Honour. An off-the-set pose for Nicholson, co-star Kathleen Turner, director John Huston and Anjelica Huston.

also by the corrupt Brooklyn police, has to offer up a hostage to the cops and Irene is slated for the role, as it was her error in the first place that has caused all their problems. Charley is told that he must kill her and although he protests at first, the Don reminds him of his 'family' responsibilities and that the honour of the Prizzi family is at stake. Charley, who has already eliminated Maerose's father because Irene has told him that he has contracted her to ice him, assures Irene that all is forgiven and her demand that money she thinks the family owes her will be paid. She knows immediately that all is not well and flees to LA, pursued by Charley. They pretend rapture at meeting up again, but both know the other's purpose. As Charley waits for her in bed, she enters the bedroom and shoots at him, but he throws a knife which impales her through the throat. The last scene has Charley back in Brooklyn phoning up Maerose and asking her out for a dinner date. Maerose has won: she is back in the family and she is going to get Charley.

If the plot sounds complicated in summary, it is because it is so convoluted in the film. Underlying the failure of the movie, however, is the sheer improbability of the characters and the action. First of all, you have to accept the stylish and warm Kathleen Turner as a paid killer. This is impossible even within the satirical agenda of the movie. Then you have to accept the intensity of feeling between the two characters, which only the even more intense loyalty to the concept of the family can supersede. And then you have to accept that Charley and Irene could cold-bloodedly plan one another's murder and that Charley would seemingly emerge unscathed from the experience and turn to Maerose for consolation. The entire screenplay is made up of a series of unlikely events and coincidences with characters behaving in incredible ways. The excuse for all of this is that is black comedy, a supposedly searing satire on family and business methods. 'It's only business,' the mafioso repeatedly say and that is the extent and depth of the satirical aspect of the movie. The dealings of the Brooklyn Mafia family is likened to corporate business ethics and the conduct of the members of the crime family towards one another is represented as being similar to the intrigues and betrayals that pass for 'ordinary family life'. It clearly was intended as a comic version of *The Godfather*, but it isn't funny

enough, and there is a point where cold-blooded killings and hitmen going about their business as though it were just a run-of-the-mill, everyday type of job cannot be seen as comical.

Charley Partanna is meant to be a dumb Mafia killer who is competent only in his profession. Nicholson, as he showed in *The Fortune*, is not at his best when he plays a dumb character. His initial reaction to playing the role was almost certainly the right one: he shouldn't have done it. The character is badly enough written, however, without the embellishments he gives him. He added some tissue to his upper lip, which gives his face an unnatural look, and he pretends a frozen lip, which comes over as phoney and embarrassing in a kind of parody of Brando's performance in *The Godfather*, which at times itself teeters on the edge of caricature. Nicholson also mugs, arches his eyebrows, pulls faces, does a stereotypical twitch with his neck and shoulders and generally does actorish things which betray his lack of ease with the role. Actors always resort to tricks like that when they can't get inside a part. This is one of Nicholson's worst performances and yet it found favour in some critical quarters as did the movie itself, although many people hated it. There is a heartless quality to it, as there is about a number of Huston-directed films, but the main charge against it is its plentiful lack of wit.

Anjelica Huston won the Best Supporting Actress Oscar for her role as Maerose and I wish I could say she deserved it. The range of acting skills the role demands is extremely limited and thousands of actors could have done as well, if not better. William Hickey as the ancient Don gives a hammy performance and John Randolph is unconvincing as Charley's dad. Judging by the performances of the cast, Huston's attention to the actors must have been minimal, and he certainly let Nicholson get away with a stereotypical and surprisingly amateurish performance. Nicholson is often an actor who is either very, very good or very, very bad. His performance in *Prizzi's Honour* belongs to the latter category. However, it would be wrong not to point out that the movie and Nicholson's performance has its fervent admirers, but, then, that may be because there are fans out there for whom John Huston and/or Jack Nicholson can do no wrong.

Heartburn (1986)

Paramount: Director, Mike Nichols; Producers, Mike Nichols and Robert Greenhut; Screenplay, Nora Ephron, based on her novel; Cinematography, Nestor Almendros; Editor, Sam O'Steen; Music, Carly Simon

Cast: Meryl Streep (Rachel); Jack Nicholson (Mark); Jeff Daniels (Richard); Maureen Stapleton (Vera); Stockard Channing (Julie); Richard Masur (Arthur); Catherine O'Hara (Betty); Milos Forman (Dmitri)

Running time 108 minutes

Heartburn. Rachel (Meryl Streep) and Mark (Nicholson) enjoy one of the happier moments in their troubled marriage.

Why movie stars of the magnitude of Jack Nicholson come to choose the parts they do, in this case, the husband in *Heartburn*, after the actor originally cast in the role, Mandy Pantinkin, walked off the picture, is always interesting to speculate about. When Nicholson was offered the part of Mark, he may have welcomed the chance to work with director Mike Nichols again (despite the total failure of *The Fortune*), and to co-star with the then leading female star in Hollywood, Meryl Streep. In addition, the film had going for it that it was an adaptation of a best-selling novel by Nora Ephron, which everyone knew was based on her real-life marriage and divorce to Carl Bernstein, the journalist of Woodward and Bernstein fame, the *Washington Post* duo who broke the Watergate story. Bernstein had already been portrayed on screen by Dustin Hoffman in *All the President's Men*, but this portrayal was intended to be very different. Ephron's revenge novel had acquired a degree of notoriety of the 'kiss-and-tell' variety and the filmmakers clearly expected to cash in on the prurient interest of a mass audience in this very public washing of the dirty linen of a Washington gilded couple. Their expectations were not to be met, however, as the public stayed away in their millions.

It seems that Carl Bernstein, having been put through the wringer in his ex-wife's novel, had had enough. It was clearly one thing to be portrayed, albeit in the guise of a fictional character, as a lecherous, chauvinist pig in the pages of a novel, it was quite another to be immortalized in a major Hollywood movie. Cheap novels such as Ephron's have a relatively short shelf life and are largely forgotten by the following year, but movies in this age of cable and video go on forever. Thus, it appears that Bernstein used his muscle to affect how 'he' was portrayed on screen and the filmmakers, including his friend, Mike Nichols, and his bitter ex-wife, Ephron, who also wrote the screenplay, toned down the crudeness of the caricature of the husband until audiences were bound to wonder what the film wife (Rachel/Streep) had to bleat about so volubly. There is a soppiness at the core of *Heartburn* that probably had nothing to do with Bernstein's influence, however. Nora Ephron went on to write the screenplays of *When Harry Met Sally* and *Sleepless in Seattle*, both of which were immensely successful, but which suffer from terminal cuteness, sentimentality and, yes, conservative social attitudes. These are movies for Middle America: romantic comedies with 'safe' stars like Meg Ryan, Tom Hanks and Billy Crystal.

The story of *Heartburn* is thin. Rachel and Mark meet at a mutual friend's wedding, go to bed and get married shortly afterwards. She works in publishing in New York, he is a successful Washington columnist, who is always using his friends and social life as material for

113

his column. All goes well initially with the marriage, despite the fact they endure months of renovation by incompetent builders on their Washington home. A child is born, Mark proves himself a fond father, and another baby is soon on the way. Then Rachel discovers that Mark has been having an affair with one of their circle. Heavily pregnant, she briefly returns to her father's home in New York. Mark comes after her; he says he loves her and asks her to return to him. She returns to their Washington home and Mark is there during the difficult birth of their second child. Despite this seeming closeness, she finds out he is having another affair. This time she does not confront him directly, but waits till a dinner party at a friend's house where she pushes a cream pie in her husband's face to humiliate him publicly in front of their friends. She leaves by air for New York. The last shots of the movie are of her on the plane singing with her daughter and cradling the baby in her arms.

As a movie, *Heartburn* never seems to go anywhere. It is aimless and pointless. If it pretends to be about something universal regarding marriage or the relationships between men and women, then it significantly fails. The 'long-suffering' wife is played irritatingly by Streep in her victim mode and you could well understand why her general whininess would drive any husband into the arms of another woman. At the hollow core of the movie is this question: so what? A husband has an affair with another woman. Wowee! What! Shoot the bastard, castrate him, well, at least, stick a pecan pie in his face. Other than the infidelities, the hubby, as portrayed by Nicholson, is generally shown to be caring, supportive and charming. He gets the few good lines that are going (and there are very few of those) and the wife comes across as a mess – powerless, vindictive (she spreads the rumour that the other woman has a terrible vaginal disease) and prone to just the kind of gossip that is the original source for the movie. Hubby does go on somewhat about missing socks, she seems to do all the cooking and it is his work that seems to matter. What the movie does not address at all is why a supposedly adult and aware woman such as Rachel could possibly find herself in the situation where she is so dependent. You are bound to ask what she was thinking about and what her own responsibility for this parlous state of affairs is.

But the movie only deals in shallowness so perhaps such questions are irrelevant. Perhaps Nichols, Ephron and the producers believed that this peep into the home life of this media couple would by itself be appealing enough to a mass audience brought up on tabloid and television gossip about the wealthy and famous. If so, their attitude is deeply patronizing and this thin brew is served up in a take-it-or-leave-it style. Did anyone involved really believe they had made an amusing, affecting or even significant movie? I can hardly believe it, but there is an unmistakable smugness about the whole project that is distinctly unattractive. Smug Mike Nichols, plus smug Nora Ephron, equals smugsabord.

Generally, Nicholson gives one of his more understated performances. He is allowed a few of his famous rages, gives an extended rendition of Rodgers and Hammerstein's 'My Boy Bill' and is allowed to be winningly charming, as well as mildly grouchy. But so much of the movie meanders and there are sequences that could only have been included because of the makers' belief that they were amusingly cute: the already mentioned singing of a show tune (which Nicholson and Streep start off by singing together but which ends up being an extended solo for Nicholson), the difficulties the couple have in getting their shell of a Washington house renovated (meant, no doubt, to strike a chord with aspiring middle-class homeowners who have similarly suffered at the hands of recalcitrant, lower-class builders), and a totally unfunny stickup of the wife's New York therapy group (the only interest this scene has is that the thief is played by a young Kevin Spacey, who must wince every time the movie plays on television). Additionally, supporting actors Stockard Channing, as a friend, and Maureen Stapleton, as the therapist, are underused and their talents as comedy actors wasted. The biggest puzzle is the Jeff Daniels character, Rachel's publishing firm boss. He is attentive, supportive and at times appears to be on the edge of moving in on her, but there is no clear role for him in the scenario: is he the next lover waiting in the wings, a predatory male sensing an 'easy kill' or a supportive male friend with no sexual axe to grind? Perhaps he is there to represent the acceptable 'new man' so that the movie cannot be accused of being a man-hating rant.

The Witches of Eastwick. Sukie (Michelle Pfeiffer), Jane (Susan Sarandon) and Alexandra (Cher) all with really big hair, discover their witch-like powers.

Finally, *Heartburn*, like *When Harry Meets Sally* and *Sleepless in Seattle*, presents a vision of happiness as being happily married with children, which the husband ruins. The husband stands for polygamy and faithlessness; the wife for monogamy and fidelity. However, these opposing values are never explored with any depth and the ending is pure treacle, like the Carly Simon song that plays on the soundtrack. The movie has not communicated real pain or anger, just spite and pique. The characters are ciphers. Lifelessness is the word that best encapsulates the essence of the film.

The only contributor that comes out of this mess with any credit is Nicholson himself. If he does not exactly steal the picture, at best a doubtful privilege, he at least gives it some solidity. Otherwise it could be forgotten for the piece of candyfloss it is.

The Witches of Eastwick (1987)

Warner Brothers: Director, George Miller; Producers, Neil Canton, Peter Guber and Jon Peters; Screenplay, Michael Cristofer from the novel by John Updike; Cinematography, Vilmos Zsigmond; Editors, Richard Francis-Bruce and Hubert C. De la Bouillerie; Music, John Williams

Cast: Jack Nicholson (Daryl Van Horne); Cher (Alexandra Medford); Susan Sarandon (Jane Spofford); Michelle Pfeiffer (Suki Ridgemont); Veronica Cartwright (Felicia Alden); Richard Jenkins (Clyde Alden); Keith Jochim (Walter Neff)

Running time 118 minutes

When a novel by one of America's leading novelists is adapted for the Hollywood screen, then, comparisons, odious or not, are bound to be made between the resulting film and its source material and in most such cases Hollywood is accused of trivializing or commercializing literature because of the crass demands of Tinseltown's need for mass audiences. *The Witches of Eastwick* was adapted from the novel by John Updike, most famous as the author of the *Rabbit* trilogy and *Couples*; Updike has been chronicling the social and sexual anxieties of the American suburban middle-class for many years and has acquired a respectable position in the pecking-order of contemporary American novelists, though he is not everyone's favourite writer, especially among more hard-line feminists. The inevitable comparisons were made between the original novel and the film when *Witches* was released and the jury, again almost inevitably, found for the novel. Yet such judgements are almost always totally irrelevant. Screen adaptations of any source material must be judged for their intrinsic artistic merit, as films, rather than as versions of novels, plays, short stories or whatever. Once a writer signs away his or her rights to a literary work, the filmmakers may do what they like with the material and need only be judged on the worth of their final product. A film is a film is a film is a film...

Although it is very different in tone and intention, *The Witches of Eastwick* (the movie) resembles in some ways Arthur Miller's play *The Crucible*: both are set in New England, both deal with witchcraft and the devil, both show small town prejudice and deal with the theme of American puritanism. However, whereas the witches of Salem in *The Crucible* are the product of paranoiac fantasies, repressed sexuality and political opportunism, resulting in the persecution and judicial murder of those the community seeks to destroy, the contemporary New England witches (played by Susan Sarandon, Michelle Pfeiffer and Cher) do have witch-like powers, do indeed fornicate with the devil, delight in the fact and survive with their female power renewed after having expelled the devil figure from their lives. At their unconscious behest, the devil in the shape of Daryl Van Horne (Nicholson) comes to their small New England town. The three women, a spinsterish schoolteacher (Sarandon), a local

newspaper reporter and an abandoned wife with numerous children (Pfeiffer), and a widowed sculptress (Cher) are bored and frustrated with their lives, suffocating in the pieties of the puritanical New England small town. Van Horne (pigtailed and horny) comes to live in Lennox Mansion, which has somehow been associated with witchcraft in the past. One by one, the witches fall under Van Horne's spell and go to bed with him. He opens sexual doors for all three and soon they live in the mansion as a loving quartet indulging in every kind of heterosexual delight. Van Horne's initial approaches to the women have been crassly direct ('Use me! Make it happen!') and once he has woven his sensual spell, he behaves like a chauvinistic and hedonistic prince expecting the women to serve him in every way.

These high jinks do not go unnoticed by the town's leading puritan, Felicia (Veronica Cartwright), who is fighting the urgings of her own libido, but she begins to suffer from disgusting physical symptoms such as spewing forth cherry pits (in a parody of *The Exorcist*) and finally her nice-guy husband, driven to distraction by her madness, hacks her to death. The three women's idyll with the 'average horny little devil' cannot last in harmony; they quarrel and they realize that Van Horne must be rejected. Each has become pregnant by him and this seems to be the point at which they decide to reclaim their independence. By using their witches' powers they bring down terrible torments on Van Horne ('Cheap tricks that I taught them.' he complains) and they banish him from their lives and the town. In a kind of epilogue to the movie, they are shown eighteen months later together with their new-born babies. They admit to missing Van Horne at times but when his image appears on a multitude of television screens and he makes his plea to be restored, with the babies watching from their cots, the women switch the images off and the devil disappears. Beguiling as it has been occasionally to the three women, unregenerate male chauvinism is finally and comprehensively banished by them.

The Witches of Eastwick is a romp of a film; its forte is not subtlety, although it has a certain alluring visual appeal and a sprightly score by John Williams that signals its light-hearted intentions. It offers discourses on

The Witches of Eastwick. Nicholson as Daryl Van Horn looking distinctly browned off.

gender and sex, and despite its attempts to appear shocking and subversive, it is really quite conservative and even reactionary in its conclusions. The first shots in the movie of the three women associate them with motherhood: the sculptress (Cher) in sculpting an earth mother figure, the reporter (Pfeiffer) is surrounded by her brood of kids (the reason her husband has abandoned her is because of her compulsion to breed) and the schoolteacher is rehearsing the kids of the school orchestra. At the end of the movie, the women are reunited in the club of new motherhood and although they cast a regretful glance back at their recent sexually free past, they seem content now in the sisterhood of their friendship and their role as mothers. The horny little devil has served his purpose and his services are no longer required. Their rebellion is seen as a brief interlude of hedonism and indulgence. Van Horne is the stereotypical male figure (lecherous, domineering and untrustworthy) and their defence is found in child-rearing and sisterhood.

It must have seemed obvious casting to give Nicholson the role of the devil. An essential part of the Nicholson image is the devilish aspect, the loveable rogue, the charming seducer, the impish lout, the chauvinist hedonist. His suitability for the role is enhanced by the fact that Nicholson is not a traditionally handsome Hollywood leading man: he is balding, overweight and has features that more than hint at an overindulgence in the good things of life. At one point in the movie, the Cher character attacks Van Horne/Nicholson for his lack of physical and other appeal, and yet a few minutes later she is in bed with him. Van Horne's appeal to women, and by implication Nicholson's, is seen to be above conventional considerations of handsomeness. Van Horne/Nicholson leapfrogs over such perceived physical deficiencies and emerges as a triumphantly attractive male, confident in his own sexuality and power. There is inevitably a straight identification between the actor and the role, because an essential aspect of the Nicholson screen persona is that he is not Robert Redford nor Richard Gere; he is a larger-than-life version of your average guy with all his physical, emotional and moral shortcomings.

But *The Witches of Eastwick* is a film of the eighties and a kind of political correctness, which is not unlike the brand of puritanism the old Hays Office used to exemplify and impose and which the movie initially appears to want to reject, enters into the resolution so the women have to be seen to be content in their lone parenthood and, by implication, in their celibacy, whilst being only vaguely regretful about the bad old days with bad old Jack. The ghost of the sixties has been exorcized; in the 1980s, with the fear of AIDS and in the era of post-feminism, more 'adult' attitudes prevail. The male principle in this movie represents promiscuity, freedom from responsibilities and marriage, a *Playboy* vision of eternal self-indulgence. The female principle represents stability, nurturing, bonding and security.

Nicholson's performance in the movie is decidedly self-indulgent. It is a variation on his other devilish roles (in *One Flew* and *The Shining*, for example). The overall style of the film, however, would appear to force the actor towards delivering an over-the-top performance and in this context, it works reasonably well. The movie allows the star to teeter on the edge of appearing ridiculous, especially in the bizarre outfits (his tennis shorts, his absurd hats) he is allowed to wear. Look, the movie seems to be saying, this guy is so confident in his own attractiveness that he can wear these silly clothes and get away with it. Nicholson glories in his role as the arch chauvinist, the Playboy Club devotee, the insensitive manipulator and exploiter. It is almost as though the actor is cocking a snook at those puritans who have tut-tutted about his own real life shenanigans. It has to be said that most of the film's energy resides in his performance and in the scenes that he dominates. Finally, the movie is given over to an orgy of special effects that seem rather tired and obvious.

Overall, *The Witches of Eastwick* is a shallow but mildly entertaining movie. In a Hollywood that had largely given itself over to mindless action flicks or cute, anodyne comedies, *Witches* at least plays with ideas, however conventionally or stereotypically they are handled. George Miller, director of *Mad Max* was perhaps not the best choice for this material, but according to Hollywood lore, there was a continual confusion about what kind of movie the producers wanted to make and this is reflected in the final product. Compromises were clearly arrived at and the result is a hotchpotch, but with its entertaining moments, many of them supplied by its leading male actor. There is also a convincing portrayal of outraged Puritanism from Veronica Cartwright, who steals the picture from under the noses of the female stars. And any verve the movie has owes a lot to that John Williams score and the glowing photography of Vilmos Zsigmond

Broadcast News (1987)

20th Century Fox: Director, James L. Brooks; Producers, James L. Brooks, Penney Finkelman Cox and Polly Platt; Screenplay, James L. Brooks; Cinematography Michael Balhaus; Production Design, Charles Rosen; Editor, Richard Marx; Music, Bill Conti;

Cast: William Hurt (Tom Grunick); Albert Brooks (Aaron Altamn); Holly Hunter (Jane Craig); Robert Prosky (Ernie Merriman); Lois Chiles (Jennifer Mack); Joan Cusack (Blair Litton); Jack Nicholson (The Anchorman)

Running time 131 minutes

Nicholson asked to receive no billing for his cameo role in *Broadcast News* and for his name not to be exploited in any of the advertising material that accompanied the release of the film. He clearly took the small part of the famous news anchorman as a favour to the writer-director, James L. Brooks, with whom he had had such a success in *Terms of Endearment*. Brooks delivers superior soap operas and sitcoms for cinema release. His work is rather bland, inoffensive and definitely orientated for the 'middlebrow' market. There is lots of smart dialogue and what passes for sophistication in the movies. Generally, his films are agreeable entertainments that do not tug on either the emotions or the intellect. *Broadcast News* is a prime example.

Nicholson may also have been attracted to the opportunity of playing an overweening, smug

newscaster, who is treated as one of the nation's oracles, but who is simply the front man and mouthpiece for a television news industry more interested in ratings and advertising revenue than anything else. In Britain, thankfully, although we have well-known newscasters and they do become minor celebrities, these television journalists do not acquire the stature and trust they appear to do in America. There, newsreaders such as Walter Cronkite, Dan Rather, Barbara Walters and Chet Huntley are elevated almost to the level of seers, whereby whatever they say during a news broadcast, or in editorial comment, is seen to be the 'truth'. The portrait of the station's anchorman in *Broadcast News* is intended to puncture the solemnity and gravitas of television stars like these and show them up for being the self-important, inflated personalities they in reality are.

Nicholson appears in only a few brief scenes and has only about a dozen lines, but his appearances and the import he manages to invest in the small role says more about the television news world than all of the rest of the film. It is an underplayed performance and through the underplaying, much is said about the character's arrogance, ruthlessness and immense ego. It is too much to state that Nicholson steals the picture, but his brief participation has more resonance than the size of the part would appear to promise.

Otherwise, there are appealing performances from Holly Hunter, William Hurt and, especially, Albert Brooks. Hurt, too, is an actor who doesn't mind playing unsympathetic characters, although he is too intelligent an actor for him to be entirely convincing as the smooth but vacant Tom Grunick. *Broadcast News* is, then, a soft-centred look at the television industry that blends familiar sitcom elements with a smart wit. The result is a so-so movie which Jack Nicholson enlivens with his presence, albeit in his more restrained, and convincing, manner. The movie was a success both commercially and critically, with Nicholson garnering some favourable reviews. Once more he had shown that he was not scared of endangering his superstar status by accepting small parts in movie made by a buddy.

Ironweed (1988)

Tristar: Director, Hector Babenco; Producers, Keith
Barish and Marcia Nasatir; Screenplay, William
Kennedy from his own novel; Cinematography, Lauro
Escorel; Production Design Jeanine C. Opplewall; Art
Director, Robert Guerra; Editor, Anne Goursaud;
Music, John Morris

Cast: Francis Phelan; Meryl Streep (Helen Archer);
Carroll Baker (Annie Phelan); Michael O'Keefe (Billy);
Diane Verona (Peggy); Fred Gwynne (Oscar Reo);
Margaret Whitton (Katrina); Tom Waits (Rudy); Jake
Dengel (Pee Wee)

Running time 144 minutes

William Kennedy had written a series of novels
set in Albany in upstate New York, which had
recently been rediscovered by the literary
establishment in America. Kennedy had become
something of flavour-of-the-month not only in
literary circles, but also in Hollywood where he
had scripted *The Cotton Club*, which had been
directed without much success by Francis
Coppola. Despite that movie's lack of success,
however, when Hector Babenco, another flavour-
of-the-month at this time because of the Oscar
and commercial success of *Kiss of the Spider
Woman*, wanted to film one of Kennedy's
Albany novels, *Ironweed*, the financing was
found, especially when Nicholson and Meryl
Streep were brought on board to give the project
marquee credibility. The main characters were
down-and-outs in the thirties so the money men
must have been doubtful whether many of the
movie-going public would pay money to be
depressed by this story of derelicts without any
feel-good elements to alleviate the pain. This
was not going to be a *Miracle on 34th Street* or
It's A Wonderful Life.

There is something bizarre about super rich movie
stars like Streep and Nicholson being paid
millions of dollars to portray alcoholic bums and
homeless people. Is this the ultimate indulgence
for the Hollywood superstar: the chance to play
characters at the very opposite end of the social
spectrum to themselves? Do these characters in
some way represent their ultimate fears that all
their riches and fame will some day disappear and

they themselves might be swallowed up into the lower depths? Perhaps these questions have extra relevance in relation to this particular project in that the character Nicholson plays in the movie, Francis Phelan, had once been a successful baseball player with the Washington Senators, and Streep's role, that of Helen Archer, had once been a professional singer. Almost overnight the characters' success, their money, and their family life had disappeared and now they were the kind of people whom you try to avoid when you see them coming towards you in somewhere like Cardboard City in London's Waterloo.

Adapting literary novels to the screen always carries pitfalls, and Kennedy's novel was no exception. There is practically no action in the book. The drama is internalized inside the head of Phelan and there are many recollections of the past as the character tries to come to terms unsuccessfully with the weight of guilt he feels about past events in his life and his sins of omission. There is a strong Catholic dimension to all Kennedy's writing, which is not prominent in the movie version of *Ironweed*. The movie would have to find a way of externalizing the 'internalization'. However, it was to prove too much for the writers and the director, Nevertheless, *Ironweed* is not a negligible effort; it deserves respect and it contains one of Nicholson's better, restrained acting efforts.

Perhaps the restraint the role would need is one of the reasons Nicholson accepted the part after the bravura and exaggerated performance he had given in *The Witches of Eastwick*. Once more he was self-consciously bucking the conventional by choosing to play a derelict. In the old days of Hollywood, if a major star had played a bum, say Gary Cooper, William Powell or Bette Davis, then it was almost invariably in the context of comedy, and arising from the needs of a comic screenplay. Bogart had played a bum in *The Treasure of Sierra Madre*, but that had been in a western of sorts. *Ironweed* would be set in the not-too-distant past (1938) and this bum would not only be homeless but a drunk who had killed his 18-day-old son by dropping him when he had too much to drink. Thus, in terms of Hollywood superstardom, Nicholson was taking another risk in accepting the part of Francis Phelan, but then risk-taking had become of this actor's trademarks by now.

As for Meryl Streep, she had also acquired a reputation for taking on difficult parts, which included the Polish heroine of *Sophie's Choice*, the working-class rebel in *Silkwood* and the disgruntled Englishwoman in *Plenty*. Each of these roles required different accents, which Streep had worked at relentlessly but had somehow not integrated into her performances, so that you were forced to notice the technique rather than the characterizations. The same problem would arise with her performance in *Ironweed*: it is another one of her self-conscious roles, where the voice she uses and her general delivery somehow grate because she is parading them as technical skills she has honed to perfection. The trouble is she misses out on real life.

The action, then, such as it is, takes place in Albany in 1938, although flashbacks take us back to events thirty years before. We follow a day and night in the desperate lives of Phelan (Nicholson) and Helen Archer (Streep), who have been live-in lovers at one time. They care for one another, but Phelan in particular cannot tie himself down to one intimate relationship. We learn that Phelan is haunted by the death of his baby son and his accidental killing of a tram driver during a distant strike when he had been a union activist. We see their pitiful attempts to find shelter, food and alcohol. Francis returns to his family whom he abandoned twenty years previously. His wife (Carroll Baker) is forgiving and wants him to return; his daughter is bitter and accusatory, while his son is noncommittal. But the past is the past and Phelan cannot forgive himself for his sins and also knows that being tied down to a family life again would not work. He feels responsible for Rudi (Tom Waits), a friend and fellow bum, but Rudi is killed when a bunch of local 'raiders' attack the derelicts' temporary shelters in an attempt to clear them out of the area. Agony is piled on agony when Francis finds Helen dead in a rooming-house. The last sequence has Francis on a freight train heading out of town, trying through flight to escape the tortured memories that will never leave him.

A major error by the director is to attempt to visualize the ghosts that haunt Phelan. They are represented as brightly lit tableaux and these images belong to some other film, perhaps a version of *A Christmas Carol*, certainly not a Depression-era tale of down-and-outs.

Unfortunately, these sequences recur frequently during the movie and they interrupt what narrative there is and strike a very false note indeed. Better is the sequence where Helen/Streep is invited to sing to the audience in a local tavern. We see her sing with confidence as the perfect professional and the audience greeting her performance with rapt attention and applause. Then a cut shows us the reality: the last few bars sung by Helen in a tuneless parody of her voice and the spectators' embarrassed and indifferent reaction to the sad spectacle. This scene brings home the huge gap between the dreams these characters hold on to and the grim reality of their actual situation. By contrast, the tableaux that represent Phelan's guilty past have a carnival, sideshow effect, which jars.

Nicholson disguises himself in a broad-brimmed hat, baggy suit and three days' growth of beard. Indeed, at times, the hat hides his face and the lighting is so dark that there is danger of overkill. Nevertheless, no one could accuse the film of indulging in 'derelict chic', unless the whole project is seen in that light. Nicholson also does not overtly play for the audience's sympathy and, indeed, the movie is curiously uninvolving in that sense. Sad things happen, such as the deaths of Rudi and Helen, and the scenes when Francis returns to the family home, but not many tears are induced. This may be to the movie's credit in avoiding manipulating the audience to easy tears, or it may be seen as the film's failure to involve on any serious level. The 'family scenes' are the most affecting in the film, and apart from Nicholson himself, Carroll Baker (an underrated actress), and especially Diane Venora as the embittered daughter are highly effective. Tom Waits also gives a skilful performance as Rudi. In fact, the acting can scarcely be faulted, which makes it all the more curious that the film isn't better than it is. It may be that it is too unrelentingly grim, as though the makers had set their face against any suspicion of sentimentalizing or providing any uplifting resolution. Yet the two deaths at the end of the movie go for almost nothing, because they have been telegraphed to us from the start and the characters have not moved in any way so the loss seems negligible. I have never agreed with the thesis that tragedy should be uplifting and renewing for the spectator: there are grim realities in life that cannot be escaped and some situations that allow no chink of light, but *Ironweed* presents such a relentlessly bleak picture that it becomes a kind of indulgence on that very score.

Despite the lukewarm reception *Ironweed* received both at the hands of the critics and the public, Nicholson was given the Best Actor Award by the New York critics and was nominated for another Oscar, which he did not win. Streep was also nominated for an Oscar for her role. Playing mutes, handicapped people or derelicts obviously does you no harm as far as the Oscar stakes are concerned.

4

LATE FLOWERING

LATE
FLOWERING

Batman (1989)

Warner Brothers: Director, Tim Burton; Producers, Jon Peters and Peter Guber; Screenplay, Sam Hamm and Warren Skaaren; Cinematography, Roger Pratt; Editor, Ray Lovejoy; Music, Danny Ellman with additional songs by Prince

Cast: Jack Nicholson (Jack Napier/The Joker); Michael Keaton (Bruce Wayne/Batman); Kim Basinger (Vicki Vale); Robert Wuhl (Knox); Pat Hingle (Commissioner Gordon); Billy Dee Williams (Harvey Dent); Michael Gough (Alfred); Jack Palance (Grissom); Jerry Hall (Alicia); Lee Wallace (Mayor); Tracey Walker (Bob the Goon)

Running time 126 minutes

At a conservative estimate, Jack Nicholson has made at least $60 million from his role as The Joker in *Batman*, which is an obscene amount for any actor to earn for one movie. Granted the film grossed $425 million worldwide, and no doubt it is still coining it from shows on television and from video sales, but $60 million is an awful lot of loot for a few weeks' work. The word has it that Nicholson struck a very hard deal on *Batman*, as he still carried resentments that he had missed out on the merchandising end of the success that the Monkees enjoyed with *Head*. You can argue that the star of a movie who has the box-office clout has the right to a major share of the movie's take, more than perhaps the producers and the money men who finance the project, so in insisting on the contract he did, Nicholson was only holding out for his own justified interests

and the interests of other stars, but for a guy who has always stuck to his 'alternative' image, he certainly knows how to dip into the trough and to argue the toss with the representatives of corporate capitalism who ultimately back big-budget Hollywood movies. If *Batman* is about anything other than spectacle, it is about rampant Reaganite-era greed, where the power of capitalism is used to make richer people richer and where the ordinary citizens are bystanders in a world given over to corruption and chicanery of all sorts. The in-built contradiction is that the makers of the film sending out this message are themselves coining it in that world at the 'expense' of the gaping millions who make rich people richer by plonking down their money at the box office.

The four Superman movies had grossed big bucks and it was natural that Hollywood would turn in due time to his comic superhero stable-mate, Batman. Indeed, the movie had been on the cards for almost ten years and no one else but Nicholson had been seriously considered for the part of Jack Napier/The Joker. It seemed a natural for the actor, especially after his devilish parts in *The Shining* and *The Witches of Eastwick*. The casting of Michael Keaton as Batman, however, caused some controversy, especially among fundamentalist comic fans; no doubt they wanted someone considerably more macho in his style than Keaton, who had had a success in *Beetlejuice* directed by Tim Burton, the director slotted in for *Batman*. In the event, Keaton gave the role of Bruce Wayne/Batman some duality and depth, or as much depth as the part could carry. Because *Batman* is not about depth, it is about comic book grotesqueries and outsize effects, although, having said that, Tim

Batman. The Joker (Nicholson) raising money for good works.

Burton, backed by screenwriters Sam Hamm and Warren Skaaren, designer Anton Furst, cinematographer Roger Pratt and composer Danny Elfman, produced a movie that was not just all staggering special effects or mindless action. The sets of Gotham City are very impressive, part German expressionist, as in Fritz Lang's *Metropolis*, part Art Deco, part comic book fantasy. The film looks good, but, finally, the question has to be asked: is there anything here for the mind as well as for the eye, or is this just another example of the tyranny of pop culture whereby all is given over to spectacle, sensation and something labelled 'entertainment'?

Burton and the screenwriters could certainly have taken an easier route to riches. They could have excised any cerebral content completely and gone hell for leather for unending sensation. That they didn't is to their credit and this creative approach to the stuff of popular myths would serve Burton well in later movies such as *Edward Scissorhands* and *The Nightmare Before Christmas*. Indeed, in some ways, *Batman* is not

a kids' movie at all, and some of its violence could well frighten younger children, for example, the scene where The Joker shakes a gangster's hand and he is electrocuted to death, leaving a burnt-out corpse. The film also takes its intellectual pretensions rather too seriously, with quotes from Nietzsche, and its shock tactics of showing The Joker and his gang vandalizing some of the most revered paintings in the world in a Gotham City art gallery. It is this kind of scene that gives the movie a kind of ambivalence. After all, the Batman character is an apotheosis of comic book culture, the direct antimony of high culture as exemplified by 'great paintings' by Rembrandt and others. As The Joker goes about his joyful destruction of art treasures, what are the audience meant to think? Does the movie half-share The Joker's attitude and is it encouraging the audience, who have come to see a comic book hero in action on the giant screen, to empathize with what the 'villain' is doing? Could there be subtext of philistinism lurking beneath the glossy exterior of this romp?

Batman. The Joker is confronted by Batman (Michael Keaton).

It is worth noting that some critics saw the movie as generally right-wing in its attitudes: an article in the National Review credited the film as supporting many of the values that Reagan stood for, including a tough law-and-order stance. 'This Batman is a criminologist in the Pat Buchanan mode. He does not attempt to "understand" evildoers: he throws them off skyscraper roofs…Here is an reconstructed Reagan Republican if ever there was one.') But that seems a pretty obvious attempt to incorporate the movie into a particular political camp and it is generally not borne out by a close scrutiny of the film. Gotham City, standing in for New York, is shown to be a nightmare place, dominated by crime and corrupt and ineffectual officials, which is hardly a testimony to what Reagan had managed to do in his eight years of office. The driving motivations are power and greed, as typified by The Joker. Nevertheless, the movie has to subscribe to the myth of the lone crusader, the individual with superhuman powers, on whom the well-being and security of Gotham City will depend, a Nietzschean supermensch whom the Nazis might well have embraced as one of their own. The makers of the Superman series had been faced with similar problems and they had used gentle send-up and irony to defuse the inherent danger in such representations. Burton and his collaborators took a different route: they show Wayne/Batman as a tortured individual, almost unwilling to act out his destiny and unsure of his own self and identity. They suggest that The Joker and Batman are two sides of the same coin and that they are closer than they think. This is where the casting of Michael Keaton pays off, because his 'softness' belies the superhero image. This Bruce Wayne is the kind of Gotham City citizen who would attend men's groups and undergo therapy about what happened to him in his childhood. Indeed, we see the young Wayne witnessing the murder of his parents at the hands of the young Jack Napier, and we understand that this has been the formative influence of his life. So we have a psychological study of the superhero, an attempt to undercut the simplified comic book cipher and create a real human being under the Batman suit. No doubt this was all so much liberal bullshit to the Batman fundamentalists.

Nicholson has a field day as The Joker. It is not a subtle portrait, because subtlety is not on demand. He has been quoted as saying that he was not worried about going over the top in the role because as The Joker there was no top. Painted up for the most part in clown white, and wearing a outsize purple suit and sporting green hair, he comes over as a circus act, part-clown, part-freak, the geek of all geeks. He sings, he prances, he laughs a lot, he smiles villainously, he throws out his favourite line 'Ever dance with the devil in the pale moonlight?', and generally sinks his teeth into the role and never lets go. Is this great acting? Decidedly not. With that make-up and the licence to do it big, any number of actors could have performed similarly, but it is the Nicholson persona, the already-established image, that the star brings to the part. We are not just watching an actor embodying The Joker, we are watching Jack Nicholson doing his familiar act: he is a devil, a card, a seducer, a rat, a smartass, a cynic, a fiend, a practical joker, a sadist, a madman, an eternal child and an amusing rogue who encapsulates a lot about ourselves, or what we would like to be at times in our lives. Seemingly, he contributed his key line, 'Ever dance with the devil in the pale moonlight?' to the script, and that is pure Nicholson when he is intent of acting out the commonly held perception of himself as the devilish, dangerous, more than

slightly crazy, lock-up-your-daughters, bad old Jack. In *Batman* he is content to strut his stuff as bad old Jack and run all the way to the bank. It is not a role that stretched him, but it is a role that many people will always identify him by.

What did playing The Joker contribute to the Nicholson career? Well, it made him a very rich man indeed, ensuring once and for all that he need never take any part for hunger ever again. Secondly, it established his name and reputation with millions of younger filmgoers who might not have noticed him much hitherto, because they had not been seeing his films. Thirdly, it reaffirmed his superstar status. The Quillan list of top box office stars for 1989 had Jack as number one, relegating Tom Cruise to second place, Robin Williams to third and Michael Douglas to fourth. The top-placed female star was Kathleen Turner at ten. Michael Keaton, Nicholson's co-star in *Batman*, was listed at thirteen, so playing the superhero had not done any harm to his career. But there could be no doubt that the top drawing card for the movie, apart from the inbuilt box-office appeal of the subject, was the presence of Nicholson in the cast. Whatever the makers eventually had to pay him was paid back many times over in terms of the box-office takings. The danger would have been had Nicholson been tempted to be in Batman sequels (I know The Joker expires at the end of the movie but Hollywood has its ways), or to follow up with further showy but essentially unchallenging parts. However, his next film would a long-cherished project playing Jake Gittes again and directing himself in a movie with much less inbuilt commercial appeal and with financial rewards that were minuscule compared to what he made on *Batman*.

The Two Jakes (1990)

Paramount: Director, Jack Nicholson; Producers, Robert Evans and Harold Scheider; Screenplay, Robert Towne; Cinematography, Vilmos Zsigmond; Production Design, Jeremy Railton and Richard Sawyer; Editor, Anne Goursaud; Music, Van Dyke Parks

Cast: Jack Nicholson (Jake Gittes); Harvey Keitel (Jake Berman); Meg Tilly (Kitty Berman); Madeleine Stowe (Lillian Bodine); Eli Wallach (Cotton Weinberger); Ruben Blades (Mickey Nice); Frederic

The Two Jakes. Jack Nicholson as Jake Gittes discusses the situation with Harvey Keitel as the other Jake of the title.

Foreest (Newty); David Keith (Loach); Richard Farnsworth (Earl Rawley); Joe Mantell (Walsh); James Hong (Khan); Perry Lopez (Captain Escobar); Rebecca Broussard (Gladys)

Running time 137 minutes

Jack Nicholson, Robert Towne and Robert Evans had planned to film the sequel to *Chinatown* in 1985, with Towne directing his own script and Evans, who had played in a few Hollywood movies in the fifties (*The Sun Also Rises, Man of a Thousand Faces*), taking the role of the other Jake, Jake Berman. But Towne had become convinced that Evans would not be up to the part and this led to acrimony not only with Evans, who had been going through a very bad time in his producing career and personal life, but with Nicholson, who was fiercely loyal to Evans. Nicholson had not forgotten Evans's support when he was cast as

Gittes eleven years previously. The erstwhile pals could not agree and the project was cancelled, leaving debts of $3.5 million and lawsuits in its wake.

It is a testimony to the hold that *Chinatown* had on Nicholson and Towne that, even after this debacle, four years later they could get back together again and try to get the picture made. Probably both of them realized that neither of them had ever been involved in anything as artistically successful as *Chinatown* and they wanted to see if the chemistry could work its magic again. With the passing of time since *Chinatown*'s first release, the stature of the movie had increased, and Evans, in particular, after his failures in directing *Best Friends* and *Tequila Sunrise* needed a boost. *The Two Jakes*, however, would lead to further acrimony between Nicholson and Towne, with the screenwriter feeling aggrieved that the picture had not been done as he would have wished. But that's a familiar enough story in Hollywood, the centre of more inflated egos per square mile than any other place on the globe.

Towne had originally planned a trilogy of movies chronicling at eleven-year intervals (in narrative terms) the development and decline of southern California as the result of rapacious developers and tycoons. *Chinatown* had been about water rights, *The Two Jakes* was to deal with oil, and a third movie, set in the fifties, would deal with pollution caused by the building of the freeways. Whether the third movie of the intended trilogy will ever be made seems highly unlikely, given Towne's present relationship with Nicholson and the comparative failure of *The Two Jakes*. I stress 'comparative', because despite its commercial failure, the movie is no mean achievement, although it is no *Chinatown*.

One of the problems with *The Two Jakes* is that it too self-consciously carries the monkey of *Chinatown* on its back. Although the underlying theme of *Jakes* is that the past never goes away, perhaps it was a mistake to tie the plot of the movie so closely to *Chinatown*. Evelyn's daughter/sister reappears as Kitty Berman (Meg Tilly), the wife of Jake Berman (Harvey Keitel), and Jake Gittes is still haunted by his love for the woman he had tried to save, but had only succeeded in helping to destroy. Discovering that Kitty is in fact Katherine Mulwray draws Jake once more into a morass of intrigue and double-dealing involving real estate developments and oil drilling, earthquakes and organized crime, that is intended to paint a picture of Los Angeles in 1948 in its immediate post-war boom when the cry was to get America moving again and the flight to the suburbs had begun with the consequent need for miles and miles of soulless housing developments. The storyline becomes almost impenetrable, certainly at first viewing, and subsequent viewings only reinforce a reaction that the movie is weighed down by plot lines and characters that are not given time to develop. This is particularly true of the Noah Cross substitute of the story, Earl Rawley (Richard Farnsworth), the oil tycoon, who is drilling for oil under the housing development and causing gas explosions and earth trembles. He flits in and out of the movie, but has no real ominous presence comparable to the impact that Cross/Huston had in the first movie.

Other characters who reappear from *Chinatown* are Lieutenant Escobar, Khan the Chinese butler, now running a florist's business, and Walsh, Jake's assistant (Joe Mantell). Jake's private investigation business has flourished in the intervening years; he now has a really fancy office and owns the whole building where it operates. He even belongs to the golf club and has a fairly luxurious house. All these details add convincingly to the historical context of the movie: America by 1948 was well on its way to enjoying a post-war boom after the slight recession when the war had ended. Jake is still the sharply dressed private eye, not averse to cutting legal corners and full of smart aphorisms such as his comment to the other Jake: 'I never lost a husband yet'. The opening shots of the movie is an out-of-focus close-up of a camera, suggesting that Jake is still putting his misguided faith in trying to pin down reality through a camera lens. We hear Jake's voice in a voiceover telling us about the characters and about his feelings. Voiceover, of course, is an accepted convention of the movie detective genre and of film noir, so there is nothing unusual or artistically crass about using this cinematic technique. But somehow this voiceover does not gel with the rest of the movie, and it is no real surprise to learn that Towne did not write it and that it was added after the filming ended in an attempt to make the labyrinth plot lines more accessible to audiences.

There are too many self-conscious signals for the audience to follow, with 'philosophical' comments such as, 'Time changes things, but the footprints of the past are everywhere.' It would have been much better if the film had been allowed to make that point by implication through what was happening to the characters in the film, rather than by so explicitly spelling it out. Echoes from *Chinatown* like Jake Berman saying to Jake Gittes, 'You may think you know what's going on around here, but you don't' are also rather heavy-handed. The movie, indeed, does demand that the audience has a fairly intimate acquaintanceship with *Chinatown*, which is fine for us movie buffs, who can pick up on these nuances and reverberations, but for those members of a mass audience who may not even have seen the earlier movie, or who only have hazy recollections of it, it introduces elements that are bound to be

The Two Jakes. Jake Gittes is questioned by Loach (David Keith, right) and another detective (Tom Waits).

puzzling. For example, the scene where Gittes unearths the Evelyn Mulwray file and cries tears over the newspaper clippings that tell of her death in Los Angeles Chinatown eleven years previously can only make sense to an audience thoroughly acquainted with the 1974 classic.

Yet, despite these strictures, I find myself admiring the movie in many ways. There is a real sense of period and yes, there is an impression of a society and a town in a transitional phase with all the wrong decisions being made for purely commercial reasons. It does help if you can see the movie within its historical context. As *Chinatown* was a comment on the 1970s, although it was set in

the thirties, so *The Two Jakes*, set in the forties as it is, is making some kind of comment on Reaganite greed and the further despoliation of America. 'The name of the game is oil,' says one character, and what could be a more apposite comment on the eighties than that? The tone is wholly cynical. The LA basin on which the city is built is referred to as having been full of 'animals eating animals' and the voracious nature of the contemporary society is made clear throughout the movie. Everyone is compromised: when someone queries a lawyer's actions by asking 'Is that ethical?', Jake replies, 'Harry, he's a lawyer.' The corruption started by Noah Cross had come down a generation and Kitty

Berman, Noah's daughter by his own daughter, is a deeply compromised character, whom Jake Berman, dying of cancer, shoots himself for so that she will inherit his share of the real estate development, but she has been unfaithful with his partner and shows herself willing to become Gittes's lover at the end of the movie. It is a deeply racist society; the golf club doesn't want 'Mexicans or Jews around'. Jake Berman is Gittes's doppelganger, and like Gittes, he is a deeply flawed man, although not a bad one. He cares about his wife, but he is the partner of a vicious Mafia type, Mickey Nice. There is the required bad cop, Loach, a vicious, sadistic lout, who is the son of the cop who had shot Evelyn Mulwray. Bodine's widow (Bodine is the partner that Jake Berman has shot) seems to be motivated more by greed and revenge than by love for her dead husband, and Gittes has a mechanical sex bout with her. No one tells the truth, or the whole truth at least, as Jake Gittes admits about himself. In the end, Jake has to lie again so that 'Katherine can deal with her ghosts in private.' This way he has kept his promise to Evelyn to look after her daughter/sister.

Nicholson again inhabits the role of Gittes completely. Gittes hasn't learnt much in the intervening years. The Chinese butler tells him, 'Like her,' (meaning Katherine/Kitty), 'you are a person of the past.' Gittes says, 'I don't want to live in the past. I just don't want to lose it,' but Gittes's problem is he doesn't know how to live in the present. In fact, he doesn't know what he feels, and his continuing sentimentality over the death of Mrs Mulwray is a testimony to that. This kind of moral and emotional confusion, this eternal air of world-weariness, the defensiveness that is expressed in wisecracks, insults or outright violence, all are trademarks of this particular Nicholson screen persona and no one does it better.

The Two Jakes was not a success either critically or commercially, but it's a safe bet that it will outlast most movies of its time by a distance. Its status as a sequel to *Chinatown* works for and against it. By comparison, it is not nearly such a rich and multi-layered text, but, viewed on its own, if that is possible, it is a compelling and consistently interesting flick. It is a movie that is overdue for reassessment and my guess is that in years to come, it will slot into the category of minor Hollywood classics.

Man Trouble (1992)

Director, Bob Rafelson; Producers, Bruce Gilbert and Carole Eastman; Executive Producers, Vittorio Cecchi Gori and Gianni Nunnari; Screenplay: Carole Eastman; Cinematography, Stephen H. Burum; Production design, Mel Bourne; Editor, William Steinkamp; Music, Georges Delerue

Cast: Jack Nicholson (Harry Bliss); Ellen Barkin (Joan Spruance); Harry Dean Stanton (Redmond Laylis); Beverly D'Angelo (Andy Ellerman); Michael McKean (Eddy Revere); Saul Rubinek (Laurence Moncrief); Viveka Davis (June Huff); Veronica Cartwright (Helen Dextra); David Clennon (Lewis Duart)

Running time 100 minutes

Man Trouble raises one central question: how could Bob Rafelson, Carole Eastman and Jack Nicholson combine their talents in 1971 to make a movie like *Five Easy Pieces* and then get together in 1992 to produce something as dire as this turkey? If *Man Trouble* had been made by anybody else, it would have been simply dismissed as a crass, tasteless mess, which it is, but with the participation of this talented trio, it becomes something infinitely sadder: evidence of a total misjudgement on their collective part and it also raises a question mark about their previous collaboration. Was *Five Easy Pieces* just a happy accident? As with *Chinatown*, a movie can turn out infinitely better than the sum of the individual talents involved; it can almost take on a life of its own and end up being a collaborative triumph that goes well beyond what any of the individuals could reasonably be expected to have created. *Man Trouble* is the inversion of that: it ends up being infinitely worse, possibly because it brings out the worst in all of the major participants.

Buried deep in this sorry tale of Joan Spruance (Ellen Barkin) and Harry Bliss (Jack Nicholson) is a discourse about the dangers facing women in contemporary society, but the treatment of this submerged theme is so cack-handed and tasteless that it is truly wondrous that none of the three principals, never mind anybody else associated with the movie, could not see this during shooting and call for drastic changes.

Perhaps Rafelson did see it, because, by all accounts, there were great strains during the making of the film, but probably by that time it was far too late. Movie-making has an economic logic of its own and when you are in the middle of making a turkey like this, it must be well nigh impossible to call a halt and say let's start again or call the whole thing off.

Joan Spurance is a classical singer getting grief from her ex-lover who is also her conductor as she rehearses for a concert. Someone trashes her flat, she receives menacing telephone calls and she has unpleasant encounters with Neanderthal men. She hires Harry Bliss to advise her about security and guard dogs. Harry is a shady character, who has changed his name to evade his creditors. His marriage is in deep trouble, although unwillingly he is attending marriage guidance sessions with his bitter wife. In the wider context, there is a slasher loose in the city, who attacks women, and Joan sees recurring images of women-in-peril on her television. Gradually, Joan and Harry become involved; he pretends to love classical music and to have read Dente's *Divine Comedy*, although why Joan/Barkin could possibly believe either of those things defies credibility. There is a subplot of Joan's bimbo sister (Beverly D'Angelo) threatening to publish a scandal-mongering book about a millionaire, Redwood Laylis (Harry Dean Stanton). Bliss is drawn into this subplot and the whole narrative becomes more and more farcical until the slasher is revealed to be one of Joan's admirers, and the conflict with the millionaire is resolved. All ends up happily.

Watch the credits of *Man Trouble* and you know you're in for a dire time. Jokey credits are never a good sign, especially when accompanied with heavily jokey underscoring, and when a cartoon dog is involved in explaining what the plot is going to revolve around. These credits and the score tell you this is going to be real funny, but, unfortunately, they speak with a forked tongue. What ensues is as flat as the proverbial pancake, and Nicholson suffers as badly as everyone else. Once more we have the spectacle of Nicholson acting funny, instead of being funny within a comic situation. His desperation grows as the film progresses. He mugs, he musses his hair, he goes well over the top in his playing of scenes that need subtlety if they are to work, he tries to be shaggily cute and generally he delivers another parody of the archetypal Nicholson performance.

Ellen Barkin is all at sea in her role and by the end of the movie, you feel that if she flashes that crooked smile at you one more time, you'll start throwing things at the screen. Harry Dean Stanton is totally wasted, as are Veronica Cartwright and David Clennon. But the major tragedy of *Man Trouble* is that Bob Rafelson, nominally at least, directed this mess. He must have been tempted to take his name off the credits and seemingly he did minimal publicity for the movie. Why did he allow Nicholson to give such a bad performance? Did he just give up, or was his star out of control? Why, indeed, did Nicholson agree to make the movie in the first place? Was it a case of loyalty to old pals, Eastman and Rafelson? But Eastman had scripted that other tasteless flop *The Fortune* so it wasn't that he hadn't been warned. Sometimes you can carry loyalty too far and, anyway, one way of showing loyalty to a friend is to be able to say, hey, let's slow up here, this script is a no-no. The screenplay for *Man Trouble* had been on offer for most of the eighties and it wasn't until Nicholson lent his name to it that it was taken off the shelf. The budget ran to $30 million, but the movie disappeared quickly after short runs in major cities. Nicholson's name on the marquee no doubt drew in what few customers the movie attracted, but most Nicholson fans must have been disappointed with the film itself and their hero's role in it. This is definitely one of Nicholson's films that will not be due for reassessment in years to come. It is a blot on his career record, and a major disappointment from a director of Rafelson's talent and integrity.

A Few Good Men (1992)

Cattle Rock/Tristar: Director, Rob Reiner, Andrew Scheinman; Screenplay, Aaron Sorkin based on his own Broadway play; Cinematography, Robert Richardson; Production Design, J. Michael Riva; Editors, Robert Leighton, Steve Nevius; Music, Marc Shaiman

Cast: Tom Cruise (Lt. Daniel Kaffee); Jack Nicholson (Col. Nathan Jessup); Demi Moore (Lt. Cdr. JoAnne Galloway); Kevin Bacon (Capt. Jack Ross); Kiefer Sutherland (Lt. Jonathan Kendrick); Kevin Pollak (Lt.

A Few Good Men. The late J.T. Walsh as Lt. Colonel Matthew Markinson, Keifer Sutherland as Lt. Jonathan Kendrick and Jack Nicholson as Colonel Nathan R. Jessep.

Sam Weinberg); James Marshall (PFC Louden Downey); J. T. Walsh (Lt. Col. Matthew Markinson); J. A. Preston (Judge Randolph)

Running time 138 minutes

In making *A Few Good Men*, Castle Rock, a production arm of the Walt Disney Corporation, was playing it safe in several ways: the source material was a successful Broadway play and, therefore, the movie would have an in-built unique selling point, the subject matter was very contemporary and based on a notorious case of bullying that went too far in the American military, and the movie would fit comfortably into the genre of courtroom drama that Hollywood had mined for many years. Indeed, the plot and main character would certainly revive instant memories of *The Caine Mutiny*, which had been a successful novel, play

and, in particular, a 1954 movie starring Humphrey Bogart as the deranged navy Captain Queeg who played with his brass balls and was extremely nasty to everyone under his command. Into the 'Queeg' part, this time with the label Colonel Nathan Jessup, would step Jack Nicholson, not for the first time in his career taking on a role with strong Bogart associations.

As well as ensuring box-office success by hiring Nicholson in the lesser role of Jessup, the producers brought in two of the leading stars of the younger generation, Tom Cruise and Demi Moore. By doing so, they could not have made it easier for Nicholson to steal the picture. The drawing power that Tom Cruise undoubtedly has puzzles me. Of course, there have been huge stars in the past who could scarcely act, but the extent of Cruise's popularity (he has been number one box-office star, or thereabouts, ever since 1989) is staggering if, you believe, as I do, he lacks any depth, charisma or wit as an actor. Demi Moore, to put it mildly, is also a very limited actor. Whatever else they bring to their roles, the communication of intelligence is not one of the qualities these stars possess, and yet in *A Few Good Men* the audience are asked to believe in them as two razor-sharp, highly astute naval lawyers. An intelligent actor of the same generation as Cruise and Moore, Kevin Bacon, who plays the prosecuting attorney Ross in the movie, would have been far more interesting and convincing in the role of Kaffee and would have provided Nicholson with more competition on screen. As it is, although he is only in four scenes, the old devil Jack walks away with the movie.

The story concerns an incident at the US navy base of Guantánamo Bay in Cuba, where the marines are only a few yards away from potential enemies and where one false move by any of the parties could escalate into a conflagration. A marine, Santiago, dubbed a 'screwup' by his colleagues, has allegedly been murdered by PFC Downey and Corporal Dawson. The film opens with the scene of these two pushing a poisoned rag into Santiago's mouth, which, because he suffers from a weak heart, causes his death. We are also given the information that Santiago has written to his Senator begging for a transfer from his unit and Cuba because of the tropical climate, which he cannot endure because of his heart condition. In return for his transfer, Santiago offers the Senator evidence that there has been an illegal 'fence-shooting' incident whereby Corporal Dawson has fired at his Cuban counterpart a few hundred yards away. His commanding officer, Jessup, finds out about this 'snitching', and against the advice of his deputy Markinson, refuses Santiago's request for a transfer, and unofficially tells the automaton Lieutenant Kendrick (Kiefer Sutherland) to organize a 'Code Red' against Santiago. A 'Code Red' is the signal, sanctioned by superior officers, for the systematic bullying and physical torture of recalcitrants. It is a practice that has been explicitly forbidden by the higher military powers and commanding officers have been warned not to turn a blind eye to it. The bullying ends up with Santiago dying.

Lieutenant Kaffee (Cruise) is assigned to defend the two marines. He is the son of a famous navy lawyer and a subtext of the movie is the issue of whether Kaffee will live up to the old man's legacy of integrity and devotion to duty. Kaffee is known for his expert plea-bargaining, and for settling cases before they get into court. It turns out that this is why the authorities have handed him the case in the first place because they do not want the bad publicity attendant to such an incident. Initially, Kaffee takes his task light-heartedly, just stirring himself enough to ensure that his clients get a reduced sentence, but he is goaded to action by Lt. Commander Galloway (Moore), to whom he is attracted and irritated by. Galloway is convinced there is a cover-up going on linked to the practice of 'Code Red' that she thinks has been sanctioned against Santiago by Jessup. The two accused marines tell their lawyers that the Code Red was instructed by Kendrick acting on Jessup's orders, but they hold to their code of honour and believe that the practice is justifiable when someone like Santiago is screwing up or snitching on fellow marines. It emerges, too, that Kaffee could face a court martial if he accuses a commanding officer of a crime even under trial conditions, so it becomes a test of Kaffee's commitment to his profession and to the standards that had been laid down by his illustrious father whether or not he will put his career on the line by pursuing Jessup. He takes the decision to put the gung-ho colonel on the stand and then, in a grandstand finish, he provokes him into admitting that he had sanctioned the Code Red that had led to Santiago's death. The Colonel is arrested, the two marines are given two years and a dishonourable discharge and Kaffee emerges as the hero of the hour in the eyes of his colleagues, Galloway and, presumably, it is intended, the movie audience.

Undoubtedly, the movie has a certain power, especially when Nicholson is on the screen. This is another of his portraits of bad guys wielding power in an unacceptable way and justifying it in an orgy of self-righteousness and, with this character, by flag-waving and macho posturing. When Cruise first visits Jessup at the base in Cuba and gets up his nose, the Colonel refers to the 'faggoty whites' he is wearing and 'his Harvard mouth', which gives the confrontation a class motivation that is not explored further. In making Jessup the fall guy for the system, the

Hoffa. Jimmy Hoffa (Nicholson) explains himself to the assembled media while Bobby Ciaro (Danny De Vito) watches warily in case his boss mentions the Mafia.

movie takes the easy way out: he is shown to be a psychotic individual, an extreme oddball who is way out on his own. It is not implied that such outrageous bullying is endemic to the military, so the audience can be reassured, as they were in *The Caine Mutiny*, that such petty dictators will always be rooted out. Jessup's excuses for his actions are that the marines 'are in the business of saving lives', that 'we follow orders or people die' and that America has to be guarded against its enemies by trained professionals who obey a code of honour. Although Jessup's extreme point of view is attacked in the movie, Galloway explains why she is so keen to defend the two marines by saying, 'Because they stand on a wall and they say nothing's going to hurt you tonight, not on my watch.' So the movie, just as in *The Caine Mutiny*, has it both ways, offering a critique of an extreme militarism, and yet apologising for it in some ways at the same time. As the convicted Corporal Dawson says at the end, 'We were supposed to fight for people who couldn't fight for themselves instead of

victimizing one of them.' Thus, the threat from Cuba to America's existence is implicitly taken seriously and the military presence justified; all that is wrong is there needs to be a weeding out of bad apples like Jessup.

In the tradition of other Hollywood movies such as *Twelve Angry Men* and *To Kill A Mocking Bird*, it is a lawyer figure who stands alone against corruption and who rights wrongs on behalf of us all. Gregory Peck was a man in a white suit defending a wrongly accused black in *Mocking Bird*; Henry Fonda wore another white suit in *Twelve Angry Men* to persuade his fellow jurors that the Puerto Rican teenager had not knifed his father to death. Tom Cruise wears naval whites and blues to ensure that the system emerges whiter-than-white and restored to full health by making the buck stop where it ought to: at the door of members of the officer class who abuse their position. The final shot of the movie says it all: a close-up of the self-satisfied, nay smug, Kaffee/Cruise, almost wearing a halo, who has lived up to dear old dad's legacy at last and saved American democracy. The implicit message is that American justice and democratic ideals are just as safe in the hands of the contemporary younger generation as it was in the grasp of previous generations.

Nicholson does not have to use his full range of acting skills as Jessup, but those he does use are employed impressively. He is sardonic, megalomaniac, foul-mouthed, self-justifying and arrogant, and we know already that he can communicate all those characteristics on screen. But intelligence is one of the marks of a Nicholson performance and Jessup is clearly meant to be an intelligent man, which makes it all the more unconvincing that he would allow himself to be so provoked in the final courtroom scene by Kaffee's accusations that he would give himself away by blurting out the truth. This 'confession' is deeply unconvincing, but Nicholson carries it off with conviction because he is such a good actor in this type of role. 'You fucking people,' he screams at Kaffee after he has given the game away, 'you have no idea how to defend a nation. All you did was weaken a country today.' Because it is the bad guy saying this, we know by implication that the good guy (Kaffee) has strengthened the nation by exposing sadists like Jessup and restoring order to the ranks. Nicholson manages to keep his performance from going over the top and easily wins any acting honours that are going. Up against Nicholson, Cruise points a lot, jabbing his index fingers into the air for emphasis and otherwise using his hands in a style that is usually a mark of an actor who doesn't know what to do with them. Cruise is playing a flip character, but there is something basically cocky about this actor which is off-putting and smacks of college boy jock. Perhaps that is why he appeals to so many movie-goers of his generation.

A Few Good Men was a box-office smash and was a welcome restorative to Nicholson's market value after the failure of *Man Trouble*. He was nominated for the Best Supporting Actor Oscar but did not win, which may not have been too much of a disappointment, because he had the compensation of a $5 million fee for his four scenes in the movie, plus a percentage of the gross profits. Nice work if you can get it.

Hoffa (1992)

20th Century Fox: Director, Danny DeVito; Producers, Edward R. Pressman, Caldecot Chubb, Danny DeVito; Screenplay, David Mamet; Cinematography, Stephen H. Burum; Production Design, Ida Randon; Editors, Lynzee Klingman, Ronald Roose; Music, David Newman

Cast: Jack Nicholson (Jimmy Hoffa); Danny DeVito (Bobby Ciaro); Armand Assante (Carol D'Allesandro); J. T. Walsh (Fitzsimmons); John C. Reilly (Pete Connelly); Frank Whaley (Young Kid); Kevin Anderson (Robert Kennedy); John P. Ryan (Red Bennett); Robert Prosky (Billy Flynn); Natalija Nogulich (Jo Hoffa); Nicholas Pryor (Hoffa's Attorney); Cliff Gorman (Solly Stein)

Running time 140 minutes

In Britain, crooked union leaders with connections to organized crime are thin on the ground. That is not to say we haven't had our share of corrupt union officials, but the corruption has never reached the proportions of their American counterparts, where, for a long time now, the Mafia control of trade unions has been undisputed. In the States, Jimmy Hoffa has achieved almost iconic stature as an example of that kind of labour leader who, perhaps, sets out with the interests of his members at heart, but along the way picks up some very dubious pals indeed and lines his own pockets as well. In the American pantheon of bad guys, Hoffa ranks alongside Richard Nixon, who interestingly granted him a pardon and released him from prison. However, as Oliver Stone's *Nixon* showed, no one is all bad, and this was clearly the intent behind *Hoffa*: to present a more positive, or, at least, more complex portrait of the man than had hitherto been offered. David Mamet, the screenwriter, and Danny DeVito, combine, however, to deliver a picture of a flawed man who invites our sympathy, understanding and admiration. Both Mamet and DeVito are guilty of sentimentalizing sheer thuggery and idolizing the tough guy.

David Mamet is generally perceived as one of the leading playwrights of the contemporary theatre. He had already scripted *The Untouchables* which had purported to be about the life of Eliot Ness. There is in that movie the same ambivalent attitude to violence and the thug, for example, in the representation of the character played by Sean Connery playing Sean Connery. Mamet's world is an entirely male world, where women are either sidelined or suspect, and where male violence is the currency that buys power and influence. It could be argued that that is how it is, but what is missing in Mamet's work is any critique of that. He seems to endorse it and he is open to the charge of being one of those intellectuals who are more than a little in love with lowlifes and the tawdry bullying thuggery that inevitably attaches itself to them.

Just as the script for *The Untouchables* had been sprawling and unstructured, so Mamet's screenplay for *Hoffa* has the same faults. The framing device is a proposed meeting at a Mafia-connected roadhouse between Hoffa (Nicholson), accompanied by his henchman, Bobby Ciaro (DeVito), and a Mafia boss, D'Allesandro (Armand Assante). As Hoffa waits and waits, we are treated to flashbacks that are intended to elucidate how this disgraced union leader has reached this point in his life and career that he could be having a furtive meeting with a gangster shortly after having been released from prison. As we discover at the end of the movie, what awaits Hoffa is death, because the assignation has been set up for a young hit man (Frank Whaley), who has been planted at the roadhouse, to eliminate him. Hoffa has become too much a liability to his Mafia controllers.

Hoffa's story spans over thirty years: we see him in his early years recruiting members for the teamsters by fair means or foul and becoming immensely popular with the membership, who love him because he is 'a working man' like them, and because he has balls. He uses his fists, clubs his opponents viciously, is a party to sabotage and generally behaves like a fascist, except that is not how the film sees it. He is just doing what a man has to do when his enemies are out to get him. It is more difficult for the movie to gloss over the cosy arrangement Hoffa makes with the Mafia, whereby half the lorries driven by Teamster members will be driven to warehouses where the contents will be removed,

or complicated transactions where Teamster pension funds will be involved in 'loans' to the Mafia and vice versa. There is even the ludicrous implication that Jimmy here is only looking out for the interests of his members, and that the union as a whole benefited from these deals with organized crime.

The movie also portrays Hoffa's enemies as vindictive or craven. Bobby Kennedy is represented as an arrogant wimp, whose main objective was to destroy a working-class hero. Well, maybe, because the Kennedys were certainly no friends of organized labour, but the representation in *Hoffa* is so slanted in Jimmy's favour that it manages to evoke some sympathy for Bobby in this viewer, at least. Then there is the Detroit reporter who threatens to use some incriminating evidence against Hoffa, but drops the article when Hoffa, or his minion Ciaro, sends him a detached penis and testicles as a present and as a graphic warning to lay off. The casting of the actors playing these enemies, and the way they are represented, tells us all about the movie's intentions. What seems to be admired above all is cojones, an extreme model of brutish masculinity, and Hoffa is shown to have a excess of testosterone-driven power.

Whereas Oliver Stone's *Nixon* (a much better film than *Hoffa*) showed how the President's early family experiences and his emotional isolation made him the leader he turned out to be, *Hoffa* eschews all that internalized stuff. Suddenly, in the movie we find that Jimmy is married and we see him with his spouse, but that is as far as it goes. Perhaps Mamet and DeVito thought it would be 'sissy' to reveal anything about Hoffa's personal life, but the lack of it seriously diminishes the picture of the man. A startling omission too is not to give a clue as to his real motives. He talks a lot about the working man and his rights, but are we meant to think this is genuine or merely the rhetoric of an ambitious man who was willing to exploit the justified grievances of workers to feather his own nest and create a power base for himself where he is mixing with important politicians, business tycoons, show business celebrities and Mafia dons? If the movie left you to make up your own mind about that, then that would be acceptable, but it doesn't, because, with Nicholson giving one of his 'star' performances, and given the generally sympathetic and partial representation of the hero, the dice are loaded.

Nicholson's performance as Hoffa was generally admired by critics, whereas the movie itself received very mixed reviews. However, for me, Nicholson's acting never gets beyond the merely technical. His much-praised make-up (the wig, the jowls, the nose) remains make-up, external signs of the character he is playing, a character he never truly inhabits. Indeed, his performance is all externalized with tics, shrugs, vocal inflections, accent, walk and the use of the eyes all contributing to a portrait that resolutely stays outside the character but never gets inside. This is partly due to the script and the opportunities it grants Nicholson, but it is also to do with the actor's status as a star turn whereby he has to give a showy performance in

the one role in the movie that has any real substance. There is very little variety in the acting because the portrait is so one-dimensional. At times, too, Nicholson does overdo, as is his wont, the tics and the mannerisms, until we're bound to think, 'Ah, we're being acted to here.' That's fatal. However, Nicholson does bring power and presence to the part, but it is a pity that the material he is given to work on is so limited, and that DeVito's direction heads straight for the sensational and superficial rather than for balance and restraint. Anthony Hopkins was excellent as Nixon in Stone's film, but if he had not played the part, then Nicholson would have been the natural next choice.

Wolf (1994)

Columbia: Director, Mike Nichols; Producer, Douglas Wick; Screenplay, Jim Harrison and Wesley Strick; Cinematography, Giuseppe Rotunno; Editor, Sam O'Steen; Music, Ennio Morricone; Production Design, Bob Welch

Cast: Jack Nicholson (Will Randall); Michelle Pfeiffer (Laura Alden); James Spader (Stewart Swinton); Kate Nelligan (Charlotte Randall); Richard Jenkins (Detective Bridger); Christopher Plummer (Raymond Alden); Eileen Atkins (Mary); David Hyde Pierce (Roy); Om Puri (Dr Vijay Alezias)

Running time 121 minutes

In a shortlist of established Hollywood directors who might be able to handle successfully a werewolf horror movie, Mike Nichols' name might well not feature in may people's lists, but, nevertheless, Nichols was handed the *Wolf* project by producer Douglas Wick who had produced the Nichols-directed corporate business comedy starring Harrison Ford and Melanie Griffiths, *Working Girl*. The reasoning may have been that, as *Wolf* was to have the setting of a New York publishing firm, it would appear fertile territory for a director with Nichols' track record. The trouble is that whereas *Working Girl* had been a traditional Hollywood romantic comedy set in the milieu of a business corporation and given a post-feminist twist Hollywood-style, *Wolf* was initially a genre film straight out of the classic Hollywood genre stable. There was nothing intrinsically wrong-

Wolf. Will Randall (Nicholson) on his way to becoming a wolf.

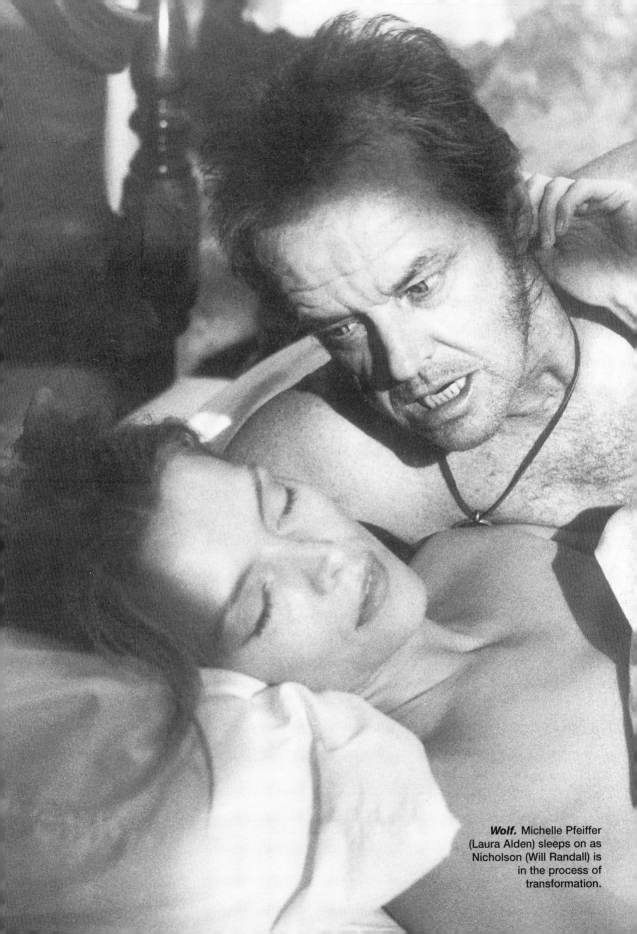

Wolf. Michelle Pfeiffer (Laura Alden) sleeps on as Nicholson (Will Randall) is in the process of transformation.

headed about setting a werewolf genre flick in a New York publishing setting, but it would certainly have been wise to have commissioned a director who had some feel for the horror genre, perhaps someone like Stanley Kubrick or the Coen brothers.

The script was an original screenplay by Jim Harrison, the novelist, whose writing content usually dealt in extremes of violence and other kinds of mayhem, and certainly not the stuff of middle-class angst that characterized the subject-matter of most of the movies Nichols had directed. Eventually, Harrison departed from the movie, though he shares the screenplay credit with Wesley Strick, writer of the remake of *Cape Fear*, who was brought in to redraft Harrison's script. It was apparently Nichols' decision to make the setting a New York publishing house and his decision also to add Elaine May, his one-time comedy partner, to the roster of writers. May produced a final draft of the script, but she declined a screen credit. Doubtless, too, Nichols and Nicholson had their own script input and the final screenplay has all the landmarks of a script produced, if not by a committee, certainly by too many hands. Harrison's fingerprints can be detected in the generic aspects, possibly Strick's in the thriller elements and definitely May's and Nichols' in the representation of the New York publishing world. But with so many hands on the tiller, it is hardly surprising that the disparate elements do not gel and that the movie, although it has its moments, never really lives up to its potential.

The movie opens with Will Randall (Nicholson), a New York executive in a high-powered and prestigious publishing firm, driving along a snowbound Vermont road at night. His car hits a wolf (yes, in Vermont!) and when he approaches with extreme trepidation what he thinks is the dead animal, he is bitten. Back at the publishing house, smooth but ruthless tycoon Raymond Alden (Christopher Plummer), whose multinational corporation has just acquired the firm, is intent on shunting Randall aside, because the latter's cultured tastes, integrity and loyalty to his authors is out of tune with contemporary corporate business practices. Randall is liked by his authors (Prunella Scales plays an Edna O'Brien-type novelist who dotes on Randall), but is of the old school in publishing terms. He is courteous, a bit hangdog and unlikely to put up much of a fight for his job. By contrast, Stewart Swinton (James Spader) is younger, ambitious, fawning, scheming and disloyal, all characteristics valued by the publishing house's new owner. Although Swinton pretends friendship towards Randall, he has in fact been plotting to take over Randall's job as senior editor and has also been sleeping with Randall's wife (Kate Nelligan). However, Randall suddenly develops a ruthless streak, which he gradually realizes is connected with the wolf bite. He refuses the worthless sop of being in charge of 'Eastern Europe' and threatens to leave the firm, taking his authors with him. The magnate concedes, Randall is reinstated and he pees over Swinton as a sign of his contempt for his hypocrisy and disloyalty. He also moves out of his family home when he discovers his wife's affair. Meanwhile, he is becoming involved with the tycoon's aimless daughter, Laura (Michelle Pfeiffer) and he finds his sexual and sensual urges are much enhanced since the encounter with the wolf. The only drawbacks seem to be an excess of facial and bodily hair, plus a desire to devour defenceless animals. He consults an expert on lycanthropy, the condition by which a human being takes on the characteristics of the animal that has bitten him. The wise old doctor tells Randall there must be 'something wild within' for this to happen. Randall then performs *Death Wish* type heroics on a Central park mugger and gradually he descends into pure wolfdom, as does Swinton. There is a climactic tussle between the two and Randall, the victor, now completes the transformation from human to wolf and is last seen hanging out in the Vermont woods near to where it all began for him. Laura/Pfeiffer, too, develops glowing eyes, a sign that the sheep she appears to be to the world is developing wolf characteristics.

Wolf seems to imply that there is a wolf in all of us, even in the mildest and most sophisticated, and further, that in the American business world, you have to act like a wolf to survive: predatory, unfeeling, ruthless and solitary. However, as the Randall character is meant to be likeable and he is played by the star of the movie, the movie also seems to encourage the idea that, when under ruthless attack, it is acceptable to use the same weapons as your attackers to defend yourself. There are 'good wolves' (Randall and Laura) and there are 'bad wolves' (Swinton and Alden). It is a variation on the good guy–bad guy opposition, except that, as in contemporary Hollywood westerns as typified by Clint Eastwood movies, the good guys have to employ ruthless murderous methods to restore balance and justice. The movie's superficial cynicism, indeed, as represented in the publishing-firm scenes, presents the audience with its best sequences and it is a pity that it has to revert to its generic roots. It could have been a smart comedy about modern business ethics, a less soft-centred *Working Girl* with better lines and more interesting actors than Ford or Griffiths, but the makers had to deliver a werewolf movie and it is in these sequences that it is at its most unconvincing. The physical transformation of Nicholson from man to wolfman is fine on a technical level, but these generic conventions seem to have strayed in from some other movie entirely and the climax to the film, like the ending of *The Witches of Eastwick* is given over to an orgy of shock special effects, as though no American movie of this era can afford not to produce computer-driven visual wonders for our uncritical eyes. These special effects, however, seem merely routine and the movie comes close in its latter stages to descending into mindless fodder, which is a pity.

However, Nicholson emerges with credit, especially in his portrayal of the victimized Randall and when he turns nasty in the human sense of the word, but he can do nothing much in the sequences when he is covered with hair and his teeth become badly in need of urgent dental work. Nicholson is an actor eminently suited to play a wolfman; he emanates danger and repressed anger and, given the limitations of the movie, he does a very creditable job of lending credence to the concept of the character. James Spader is also excellent as the creepy, two-faced young pretender to Randall's throne, whilst Christopher Plummer does his smooth villain act to the letter. Michelle Pfeiffer does not have much to do, although her role was reputedly strengthened by Elaine May's participation in the screenwriting, and the admirable Kate Nelligan as the straying wife is on the screen far too briefly.

Thus, *Wolf* is at best only a partially successful movie because of the confusion inherent in its final concept and direction. Nevertheless, Nicholson's track record as an actor is certainly not damaged by his part in it; indeed, his presence gives yet another film some weight which it might not have had if another actor had played Will Randall.

The Crossing Guard (1995)

Mirimax: Director, Sean Penn; Producers, Sean Penn and David S. Hamburger; Executive Producers, Bob Weinstein, Harvey Weinstein and Ricard Gladstein; Screenplay, Sean Penn; Cinematography, Vilmos Zsigmond; Production Design, Michael Haller; Editor, Jay Cassidy; Music, Jack Nitzsche; Costume Design, Jill Ohanneson

Cast: Jack Nicholson (Freddy Gale); David Morse (John Booth); Anjelica Huston (Mary); Robin Wright (JoJo); Piper Laurie (Helen Booth); Richard Bradford (Stuart Booth); Robbie Robertson (Roger); John Savage (Bobby); Priscilla Barnes (Verna); Kari Wuhrer (Mia)

Running time 114 minutes

Sean Penn had already directed one movie *The Indian Runner* before he managed to get Mirimax backing for *The Crossing Guard*, for which he also wrote the screenplay. *The Indian Runner* had not been a commercial success and had attracted only subdued critical approval, but Nicholson knew Penn as a friend and there was clearly a mutual admiration society operating so Nicholson, coming off the back of *Wolf*, agreed to take the part of the self-loathing, self-destructive jeweller, Freddy Gale, a part that would require him to tone down the familiar Nicholson 'over-dramatics' and inject more restraint and realism into his performance. His choosing to make this particular movie is perhaps another instance of Nicholson loyalty to Hollywood pals, but this time the gesture paid off in terms of his own performance and the quality of the movie created by the collaboration.

The Crossing Guard is almost remorselessly bleak, perhaps too much so. Freddy Gale (Nicholson) is an LA jeweller whose little daughter has been killed in an traffic accident involving a drunken driver, John Booth (David Morse). Gale's life has been so upturned by this event that he has sunk into totally self-destructive patterns of living. His marriage to Mary (Anjelica Huston) has broken up and he is a stranger to his two remaining children who look upon Roger, Gale's successor, as their father. Freddy drinks too much, neglects his business and spends much of his time in a lowlife strip joint with equally lowlife companions. He is either always on the edge of violence or tipping over into it. In his state of bitter misery, he sets himself the task of shooting Booth when he is released from prison. He goes to Booth's parents' house one night and points the gun at the calmly resigned Booth, but the gun jams and he tells Booth he will return in three days. The movie records his joyless encounters with strippers, a bitter argument with his ex-wife, his alienation from his business (including a savage encounter with an irritating customer) and his fights in bars. Three days later, on his way to kill Booth, he is pulled over by the cops who arrest him for driving under the influence of alcohol, the very crime that Booth had been guilty of when he ran over his little girl. He runs from the cops, goes to Booth's parents' house again, but finds Booth, who has found a renewed interest in life, pointing a rifle at him. A chase through the city streets ensues and Booth leads him to his daughter's grave, a place Freddy, for all his outraged grief, has never visited. There the two men kneel and, holding hands, express their shared grief and remorse.

As the tone of what has gone before has been so pessimistic, this ending may seem overly optimistic, given the depths of hopelessness and hatred towards Booth that Gale has expressed. However, this resolution is just acceptable within the parameters of the film's agenda, part of which is to show that Freddy's hatred of Booth is more about his own self-hatred than motivated by revenge. As Mary/Huston says to him, 'It has nothing to do with our daughter.' This has wider social implications than just this narrative about a drunken driver and a revengeful father: it says something about how society projects its own self-loathing onto groups and individuals, thereby demonizing them and making them scapegoats for its own deep dissatisfactions and self-recrimination. Booth is represented as a deeply wounded individual; he has to come to terms with what he has done and want to live again. As the woman he has a passing affair with says, 'Your

guilt is a little too much competition for me. You must let me know when you want life.' Booth has made one great error in his life: he has got behind a wheel when he was drunk and a little girl has been killed. Because of his reckless action, lives have been destroyed, including his own. Everyone is a victim in these circumstances: the dead girl, the mother, the father, the perpetrator, even the supportive and loving parents of Booth who have to endure their son being in prison for six years and watch as he struggles to get his life back again.

The Crossing Guard is, at the very least, a refreshing change from standard Hollywood revenge movies where the good guy tracks down the bad guy who has done him or those close to him harm and eliminates him to the accompanying cheers of the movie audience. Those psychotic heroes played by Eastwood, Stallone or someone of their ilk are thrown into relief by the representation of Freddy Gale: his violent instincts come from an inner violence and a profound alienation from self and the society he operates in. The sleaziness of his lifestyle is convincingly portrayed and even when one of his casual lovers wants more than just money or sex from him, he is totally unable to meet her needs. He treats everyone with contempt because he is full of contempt for himself.

There are two scenes with Mary/Huston that are memorable: one near the beginning of the picture when he visits the house they used to share. Her bitterness at his lack of support at the time when she most needed it, and at his sinking into a state of bitterness where the only thing he has to offer her is the promise that he will kill their daughter's 'murderer' is strongly portrayed. Then there is a night-time meeting in a coffee shop that starts off with fond recollections of better times between them and ends with his hurling crazy accusations at her and her leaving him angry and hating. Naturally, it was commented on that, as the Nicholson/Huston relationship had broken up amidst mutual recriminations a few years previously, the two actors were working off that shared history. Well, whether or not they were, this scene and the previous one at the house have a convincing and chilling bitterness to them: 'I hope you fucking die,' he screams at her. We are reminded of how two people who have been very close can become so estranged that all they can do is behave as though they had always hated one another.

Nicholson is entirely convincing as Freddy Gale. When he does erupt in anger and violence, as in the scene in the house, or the sequence in the bar when some joker tries to muscle in on his women, it is justified by the dramatic situation. In one brief telling scene when he measures a troublesome customer's ring finger and then almost violently sticks the ring on her finger, everything he feels about the way he makes his living, about people and himself is expressed succinctly. Nicholson allows himself to show extremes of emotion that he has seldom shown on screen before, particularly when he is explaining to Mary/Huston on the phone a terrible dream he has had about the death of his daughter. He breaks down in real tears and Nicholson has never exposed himself emotionally in such a raw way before on screen. It is to Sean Penn's credit, and a testimony to how much Nicholson trusted his director, that he was willing to show that much feeling.

Anjelica Huston, too, gives one of her best performances as Gale's ex-wife. Since her early appearances in films, she has progressed considerably as an actress, and no doubt she has used her personal experience of the ups-and-downs in her own life as the springboard for her acting on screen. David Morse as Booth has a sensitivity and a quality of stillness that communicates the character's wounded nature perfectly. Other actors who score in the movie are Piper Laurie and Richard Bradford as Booth's parents, Robbie Robertson as Roger (Mary's new husband) and Priscilla Barnes as Verna, the stripper who wants something more from Gale than he can provide. Although, then, Nicholson's performance is of outstanding quality, it does not cause an imbalance in the picture, as he is surrounded by other actors who also know what they are doing. It could be claimed, indeed, that Sean Penn coaxed an ensemble performance out of a well-chosen and committed cast. *The Crossing Guard* is not a masterpiece of the cinema, but in the Hollywood of the mid-nineties, it was one movie that attempted to say something meaningful and that did not resort to stereotypical characterization, glib moralizing or sentimentalization.

The Evening Star (1996)

Paramount/Rysher Entertainment: Director, Robert Harling; Producers, David Kirkpatrick and Polly Platt; Screenplay, Robert Harling adapted from the novel by Larry McMurtry; Cinematography, Don Burgess; Editors, Priscilla Nedd-Friendly and David Moritz; Music, William Ross

Cast: Shirley MacLaine (Aurora Greenway); Bill Paxton (Jerry); Juliette Lewis (Melanie); Miranda Richardson (Patsy); Ben Johnson (Arthur); Scott Wolf (Bruce); George Newbern (Tommy); Marion Ross (Rosie); Mackenzie Astin (Teddy); Donald Moffat (Hector); Jack Nicholson (Garrett Breedlove)

Running time 105 minutes

Thirteen years after *Terms of Endearment*, the hankies were out in force again when the sequel *The Evening Star* was released, but this time the reception was muted and there were to be no Oscar awards and no great box-office bonanza. Larry McMurtry had written a second novel based on the same characters, minus the daughter, and Robert Harling did the adaptation for the screen and directed it himself. The movie has the same mixture of 'laughter and tears' as the original and with three of the main characters dying in the course of the narrative, it certainly could not be accused of not going for the emotional jugular.

The action has moved forward to 1988. Aurora (MacLaine) has brought up her daughter's four children with varying success: Tommy is in prison for a third drugs offence, Teddy is saddling himself with a partner and children without the benefit of marriage, and Melanie (Juliette Lewis) has an unfortunate taste in boy friends and doesn't listen to her grandmother enough. 'You're suffocating me!' she shrieks at her. Rosie, Aurora's housekeeper, arranges for her to meet a therapist, Jerry (Bill Paxton), who is much younger than her but with whom she has an affair. Jerry also sleeps with Aurora's best friend/enemy, Patsy (Miranda Richardson), whose own children have left home. The rivalry between the two women over their mutual lover and their parenting of Melanie leads to a farcical fight on a flight back from LA to Houston. Aurora also surrounds herself with several hapless elderly male admirers, but gradually her entourage thins out as the movie strains for emotional effect by killing off characters to show how time has passed and how bitter-sweet life is. The General (Donald Moffat) croaks first, then Rosie, the faithful and self-sacrificing housekeeper, dies, followed finally by the great matron herself. Just before the end of the movie Jack Nicholson pops in as Garrett Breedlove, the ex-astronaut, who now lives in Milwaukee, is married and proudly shows Aurora snapshots of his children. Garrett still has a twinkle in his eye, having chosen a woman much younger than himself for his wife. She's 'pretty swell', he tells Aurora, 'but you'd hate her guts.' He is in four brief scenes and it is the type of cameo Nicholson could do in his sleep. Clearly, it was important to the makers to have his presence in the movie so that they could milk the connection with the megahit that *Terms of Endearment* had been, but his entry that late in the movie seems contrived and extraneous, and although it is a pleasant enough 'turn' on Jack's part, it doesn't add up to very much.

Anyone who knows anything about Nicholson's private life could not but help be aware of the resemblance between what is supposed to have happened to the character's life in the intervening years and how Nicholson's own life had developed since *Endearment*. Nicholson had settled down with a woman much younger than himself and now was a proud dad himself, so the movie seems to be playing off that 'reality' in that shameless way that Hollywood has. The subtext seems to be that even bad old Jack Nicholson has settled down into a long relationship and become a respectable dad. Family life may be painted as claustrophobic in *The Evening Star*, but there is no doubt about the values the movie seeks to propagate: women like Aurora (and by implication the middle-aged women who will make up most of the movie's audience) are at the core of family life, handing out advice and practical aid, sometimes unwanted and frequently misunderstood, while the men are either feckless, promiscuous, almost always selfish or absent, unlike the matrons of this world who give themselves to those they love without seeking reward or thanks. The movie oozes sentimentality and

evasiveness, masks real pain and resentments with farcical confrontations, and sets out to flatter its target audience outrageously, particularly by serving up Aurora with a young lover and several slavish elderly admirers. Its emotional manipulations are far too obvious to wring tears other than from elderly ladies who have identified completely with the central character.

Blood and Wine (1997)

Fox/Searchlight: Director, Bob Rafelson; Producer, Jeremy Thomas; Executive Producers, Chris Auty and Bernie Williams; Story by Nick Villiers and Bob Rafelson; Screenplay, Nick Villiers and Alison Cross; Cinematography, Newton Thomas Sigal; Editor, Steven Cohen; Production Design, Richard Sylbert; Music, Michal Lorenc

Cast: Alex Gates (Jack Nicholson); Suzanne Gates (Judy Davis); Jason (Stephen Dorff); Victor (Michael Caine); Henry (Harold Perrineau Jnr.)

Running time 110 minutes

There were those who had predicted that Bob Rafelson's career would never recover after the disaster of *Man Trouble*, but a few years later here he was once more directing his pal and Hollywood superstar Jack Nicholson in a thriller adapted from a story created by Rafelson and Nick Villiers, who shared the screenwriting credit with Alison Cross. Nicholson has a reputation for being loyal to old Hollywood buddies and Rafelson's direction had undoubtedly helped him establish his reputation as an actor way back in the early seventies, so his participation in *Blood and Wine*, hardly a front-rank, big-budget Hollywood movie, may have had something to do with his innate loyalty and his wish to pay off old dues. If so, then it was not that much of a sacrifice because the movie provided him with an interesting role in a film that was a creditable effort to work within the thriller genre and create something entertaining and intelligent at the same time.

Nicholson plays Alex Gates, a Miami wine merchant, trapped in a loveless marriage with the alcoholic Suzanne (Judy Davis) who had married him eight years previously when her first husband had died. Suzanne had financed the Gates wine business which was not producing enough money for their needs. Suzanne's son from her first marriage, Jason (Stephen Dorff), is employed by Alex, but his real love is for the sea and fishing. Stepfather and stepson loathe each other, Gates bullying the young man into looking 'respectable' and attending to his duties at the store. Gates and Jason deliver an order of wine to the Reeces, a rich but vulgar couple who employ Gabriella, an illegal Cuban immigrant as their nanny. It turns out that Gates is having an affair with the beautiful Gaby to whom Jason is immediately attracted. Gates is planning to rob the Reeces (while they are away on their yacht) of a million-dollar necklace with the help of the seedy and tubercular Englishman, Victor, who is a burglar and an ex-con. Victor knows he is dying, but he wants one last big score to ensure he doesn't die in the public ward of a state hospital. Alex wants the money from selling the necklace to a fence so he can vanish with Gaby. Gabriella's motives is that she sees Alex as her best hope of bringing her family over from Cuba. Victor and Alex manage the robbery, but Victor wants Alex to go to New York to negotiate with the fence, because he no longer has the 'bottle' for it. He tells Gaby to come with him and books two first-class air tickets. When he is packing to go to New York, Suzanne discovers the air tickets and guesses he is going away with a woman. They have a terrible fight and she strikes him with a golf club, knocking him unconscious. She empties the suitcase hurriedly, not knowing that the necklace is in a compartment, and fills it with her clothes. She escapes with Jason to a boat of a friend in a nearby port. Alex and Victor join forces to track them down. Meanwhile, Jason has found the necklace and had its value confirmed. After a high-speed car-chase, Suzanne is killed and Jason ends up in hospital, but Alex still does not know where the necklace is. He asks Gabriella to use her charms to get to Jason. Jason lies to Victor that he has given the jewels to Alex, whereupon Victor attacks Alex viciously and Alex smothers him with a cushion. Things have got completely out of hand now and in the final confrontation between stepfather and stepson, Jason rams the boat into Alex's legs as he hangs from the jetty, crippling him. Jason escapes in the boat, having phoned for an ambulance. Alex, unable to move and knowing he cannot be found helpless with the jewels in his possession throws them into the sea. All his efforts to carve out a new life for

himself have to come to naught.

As in *The King of Marvin Gardens*, Rafelson, as writer and director, is once again dealing with people on the edge, driven to wild schemes so that they can find their way out of the trap they have created for themselves and so fulfil their dreams. Alex Gates is not a wholly bad man, but he is a deeply frustrated one who hates his marriage, his lack of money, his way of making a living and his whole lifestyle. Gabriella, the young and beautiful Cuban refugee, offers the promise of a new start in life which will be financed from the proceeds of the robbing of the unlovely couple to whom he delivers wine. When Suzanne crashes the car and his wife is lying there in a critical condition, he is torn between concern for her and the need to know where the necklace is. In his anguish, his greed wins out and her response to his desperate pleas is 'Fuck you!' Indeed, almost all the relationships portrayed in the movie are full of resentments, doubts, betrayals and accusations. Gates and his wife have reached that stage in a marriage when they can only hurl insults and accusations at each other. Jason loves his mother but hates Alex. Even his best friend, Henry, turns against Jason when Victor beats him up. Victor and Alex are only friends because they are planning the heist together, but no love is lost when Victor suspects Alex of double-crossing him. The frustration Gates feels with his life explodes in his violence towards his wife and his smothering of Victor. Gabriella is ambivalent in her attitude to Alex; at times she seems genuinely fond of him, at other times self-interest rules and she acts as though he is her meal-ticket and the means through which she is going to get her family out of Cuba. Even Jason, who has no real interest in the jewels and hands them to Gabriella during the final confrontation (initially she drives off with them but then returns to give them to the crippled Alex), is represented as a resentful character. Suzanne, the wife, has broken her ankle and walks with a stick, a symbol of her crippled emotional state. She has played her part in creating the hell of the marriage Alex and she are sharing. There are no reassuring, untarnished good guys in this movie. It adds up to a bleak picture of human nature and loyalties.

By no stretch of the imagination could *Blood and Wine* be described as a major Rafelson-directed movie, nor one that Jack Nicholson will long be remembered for. However, it is a well-above-average example of the thriller genre, although some of the set-piece elements (the robbery itself, the car chase, the fights) only get in the way of our interest in the representation of the seedy lifestyle and the analysis of the motivations of the main characters. Nicholson is perfect as the cynical Gates and communicates the man's desperation very convincingly. Judy Davis does one of her 'grungy' parts, avoiding playing for the audience's sympathies and managing it. Michael Caine is eminently seedy and ugly as Victor and Stephen Dorff is at least adequate as Jason. This is the downside of the American dream again, where wealth, happiness and love elude the characters. The setting of Miami is suitably soulless and anonymous, only the sea offering an escape to peace and solitude. This is where Jason ends up at the end of the movie contemplating the immediate past and his future and facing up to life without his mother and Gabriella. There is a hopeless quality to the movie and an inevitability that the pressures the characters feel will finally crush them. It is implied that one has to flee this society in order to survive it, but taking refuge in illusions of starting again with nubile young women and

stolen riches remain only that, the sad illusions of the deluded. *Blood and Wine* makes a welcome change from all the 'feel good' movies Hollywood churns out. It has some of the look and ambience of a film noir, mainly because of the pessimistic view of human nature it represents and the doom-laden nature of the narrative. The film attracted some favourable critical attention when it was released but it did not survive long on the circuits. It is the kind of American movie that will soon be dubbed a classic by the French and, in some ways, it will deserve that accolade.

Mars Attacks! (1997)

Warner Brothers: Director, Tim Burton; Producer, Tim Burton; Screenplay, Jonathan Gems; Director of Photography, Peter Suschitzky; Visual Effects, James Mitchell, Michael Fink, David Anrdreas; Martian Visual Effects/Animation, Industrial Light and Magic; Music, Danny Elfman; Editor, Chris Lebenzon

Cast: Jack Nicholson (President James Dale/Art Land); Glenn Close (Marsha Dale); Pierce Brosnan

Mars Attacks. President James Dale (Nicholson) finds himself under the gun after the Martian girl (Lisa Marie) reveals her true identity.

(Professor Kessler); Sarah Jessica Parker (Nathalie Lake); Annette Bening (Barbara Land); Danny DeVito (Rude Gambler); Martin Short (Jerry Ross); Martian Girl (Lise Marie); Tom Jones as himself; Michael J. Fox (Jason Stone); Rod Steiger (General Decker); Lukas Haas (Richie Norris); Natalie Portman (Taffy Dale); Jim Brown (Byron Williams); Sylvia Sidney (Grandma Norris); Joe Don Baker (Glenn Norris)

Running time 103 minutes

Tim Burton had served Nicholson well when he directed him as The Joker in *Batman*, so when he was offered a dual role in Burton's sci-fi spoof it must have seemed a safe bet to accept. However, although *Mars Attacks!* did reasonably well at the box office, it was generally received with disappointment among Tim Burton and Nicholson fans. *Mars Attacks!* has its fervent defenders, but on the whole it is a very flat affair with real laughs few and far between.

How can you parody a parody? That is the main problem facing the makers of this send-up. *Mars Attacks!* makes clear references to *Independence Day* and *Close Encounters* among recent space movies, but its chief point of reference is the fifties alien invasion genre, movies such as *The Day The Earth Stood Still*, *Invaders from Mars* and Ed Wood's *Plan 9 from Outer Space*. These movies contain more than their fair share of unintentional laughs so Burton's 'target' is too easy, and his and screenwriter Jonathan Gems's attempts to lampoon the already risible get progressively more desperate.

Nicholson plays a President who, advised by a professor of astronautics (Pierce Brosnan), welcomes the invading Martians with open arms, only to find that the bug-eyed monsters are full of destructive intent. Once open warfare starts, only Jim Brown, as an ex-heavyweight champion of the world working as a greeter in a Las Vegas casino, and Slim Whitman-like records stand in the Martians' way. It is the latter, the yodelling sounds of Slim Whitman music, that finally see off the invaders, their brains exploding with the sheer horror of having to listen to such cacophony.

Nicholson's other part is as a dude cowboy millionaire intent on building a luxury casino called the Galaxy. These Las Vegas sequences seem detached from the rest of the movie and Nicholson's character just an excuse for the star to do another rather unconvincing turn. Tom Jones, surely a serious rival to Roger Daltry in the non-acting stakes, is dragged in to sing 'It's Not Unusual' in a Las Vegas casino, I hope with satirical intent, but it is not clear. Annette Bening wanders through the film, her comic acting abilities stretched to their restricted limit by a script that does her no favours. Pierce Brosnan ends up as a disembodied head in love with a female character whose body is a hairless tiny mutt. Rod Steiger goes over the top (the only thing to do in the circumstances) as a nutcase General. Glenn Close has nothing to do as the First Lady intent on refurbishing the White House and removing Eleanor Roosevelt's chintz.

The Martians in all their computer-driven glory become very irritating after a while with their comic book grunts, and the action sequences seem surprisingly routine, although Burton clearly extracted some pleasure from destroying Congress and most of Las Vegas. An authentic Burton touch is for the world to be saved by the 'retard' son of a redneck, trailer family, whose father (Joe Don Baker) proudly sends his other thicko son off to fight the Martians. The John Wayne-like macho grunt dies crying 'You alien shitheads!', while the retard son realizes that his grandmother's favourite music, the ghastly, synthetic country and western yodelling, has lethal powers. This Burton outsider, played by Lukas Haas, teams up at the end with the President's daughter, an alienated, cynical youngster who finds her parents hard to bear and thinks of the White House as a prison. The ancient Sylvia Sidney, a star in the Hollywood of the thirties and forties, plays the granny.

And what of Nicholson's turn as the President? Is he playing a variation on Richard Nixon? It's really hard to tell what he is trying to do. He pulls faces, acts smooth, goes into rages, and reacts a lot, but his style of delivery is funereal and his mugging too obvious and familiar. It's one of those Nicholson comic turns that falls embarrassingly flat. The script shows a plentiful lack of wit, but Nicholson needed a director to tell him, come on, Jack, stop giving us that hand-me-down Nicholson turn, and put some pace into it. However, the pace is so slow throughout, the performances so generally misjudged and the gags, both verbal and visual, so laboured, that nothing could have changed this dud performance into a winner. *Mars Attacks!* certainly will not rank high in the CVs of either Tim Burton or Jack Nicholson.

As Good As It Gets (1998)

Tristar Pictures: Director, James L. Brooks; Producer, James L. Brooks; Screenplay, Mark Andrus and James L. Brooks, from a story by Mark Andrus; Director of Photography, John Bailey; Production designer, Bill Breszki; Editor, Richard Marks; Music, Hans Zimmer

Cast: Jack Nicholson (Melvin Udall); Helen Hunt (Carol Connelly); Greg Kinnear (Simon Bishop); Cuba Gooding Jnr. (Frank Sachs); Skeet Ulrich (Vincent); Shirley Knight (Beverly); Yeardley Smith (Jackie)

Running time 138 minutes

Reunited once more with writer-director-producer James L. Brooks, Nicholson obviously thought he was on to a good thing when he chose to play the misanthropic, compulsive and obsessive Melvin Udall in *As Good As It Gets* and so it proved, at least in terms of the success the film would enjoy and the Oscar for Best Actor he would receive. Brooks makes safe, sophisticated, relatively undemanding mainstream movies and perhaps after *Blood and Wine* and *The Crossing Guard*, neither of which had been conventional Hollywood movies, Nicholson felt he had to reach for the mainstream audience again to re-establish his box-office credibility.

Melvin Udall (Nicholson) is a writer of romantic fiction, which is in itself a joke, because he is a misogynist, a cynic, a racist and an anti-gay fanatic. His reactionary views and his compulsion to dominate everyone in his vicinity through put-downs and insults are established early on in the movie and Nicholson clearly relishes the chance to be witheringly sarcastic and politically incorrect. He is offensive to his gay neighbour Simon (Greg Kinnear) and puts his Brussels Griffon pooch down the garbage chute of the apartment block they both live in. Udall brings his own plastic cutlery to the diner where he has his breakfast every day because he is obsessed with other people's germs. Only Carol (Helen Hunt) is willing to serve him and put up with his barbs. She, a single mother struggling to bring up a severely asthmatic son, holds her own in the repartee stakes with Melvin, which clearly intrigues him, as most people simply give up or steer clear of him. Their lives become entangled through various plot devices to do with the dog and Simon's career as a fashionable New York artist, and gradually Melvin shows that under that extremely waspish and supposedly repellent exterior, he has a heart of gold. The movie ends with Udall caring for both Simon and Carol, with the promise of a permanent relationship between the writer and the waitress.

As Good As It Gets pretends to be more hard-bitten than it ultimately is. The opinions and prejudices that Udall expresses about women, gays and other issues are somehow softened because it is loveable old Jack Nicholson who is expressing them. We just know he's going to turn out ace in the end, because it's that kind of feel-good movie. However, a character this crazy (he walks along the street neurotically avoiding any contact with passers-by and not stepping on the pavement cracks) would in real life be diagnosed as severely maladjusted and in dire need of some medical treatment. In the movie, it takes a dog, a sympathetic gay and an attractive, warm waitress to turn him around and make him a human being you would want to be around. Only in Hollywood!

The movie, as with all Brooks's big screen efforts, is an example of superior sit com transferred to the big screen. It has the same built-in pleasing elements as long-running Brooks's television shows such as *Taxi*, *The Mary Tyler Show* and *The Simpsons*. Brooks's most recent film before *As Good As It Gets* was *Jerry Maguire* starring Tom Cruise as an agent for top sports stars. It too pretended to a hard edge that it did not possess and the same sentimentality and theme of saving a lost cause through the intervention of a good woman, a kid and sundry others (including a character played by Cuba Gooding Jnr., who plays Kinnear's agent in this one) lead to a feel-good movie that is slick and superficial. There are incidental

As Good As It Gets. Melvin (Jack Nicholson) and Simon (Greg Kinnear) realise they have more in common than they once thought.

pleasures along the way in both films (witty one-liners, interesting comic situations), but there is an impression of formulaic entertainment and of the narrative being channelled in a certain direction to reassure audiences that finally scuppers any 'serious' intent.

Nicholson growls, leers, insults and generally delivers his crafted one-liners with aplomb and relish. When a fan asks him how he manages to create convincing female characters in his fiction, he says, 'I think of a man, I take away reason and accountability', and it is clear that Jack is enjoying himself. It is one more role that will probably offend hard-line feminists and that is what he has been doing for most of his screen career. The trouble is he is too likeable in the part and that is where the film cheats. The publicity tag-line for *As Good As It Gets* was 'Brace yourself for Melvin', promising a character who is 'to be avoided at all costs, but

some victims cannot escape'. But the movie never delivers on that promise. Nor does it fulfil its other boast, 'A comedy from the heart that goes for the throat'. More a comedy from sit com that goes for the comforting.

Nevertheless, *As Good As It Gets* is reasonable entertainment and Nicholson had one more mainstream success under his belt. His Hollywood peers acknowledged his skill in performing this kind of material and his status as a top box-office star was reinforced at the ripe old age of 61. Can't be bad! When it was announced at the Oscars that he had won, old show-off Jack did a Melvin Udall glide onto the stage, and in his acceptance speech he dedicated his award to the recently deceased Miles Davis, Robert Mitchum and Luana Anders among others. Then he left the stage on the arms of two attractive women. Jack was back on top and still playing Jack in front of the gaze of the world.

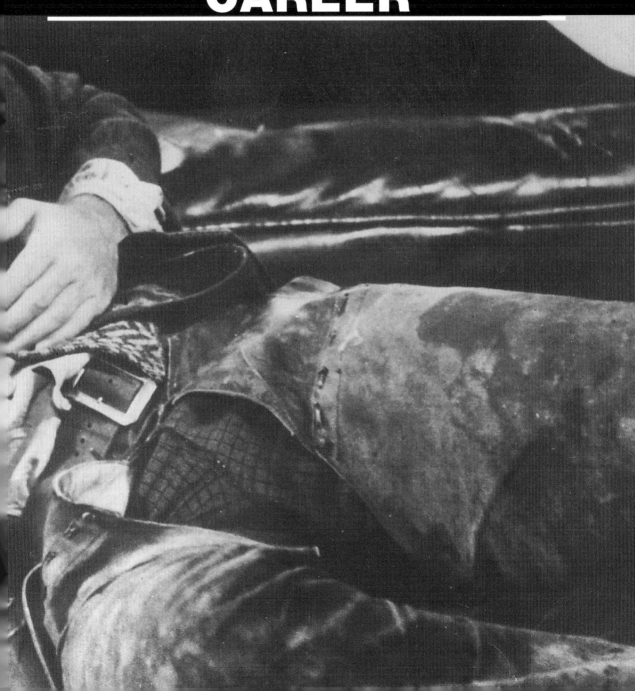

5
AN OVERVIEW OF JACK NICHOLSON'S CAREER

AN OVERVIEW OF JACK NICHOLSON'S CAREER

Jack Nicholson's career as a superstar shows no signs of fizzling out despite the fact he is now well into his sixties and that he will soon be entering his fifth decade at the top of the Hollywood pile. By any standards, Jack Nicholson, the movie star, that is, is a phenomenon, and his continuing success is almost unparalleled in its longevity. No doubt he will continue to reinvent himself over the next ten to twenty years, but it is likely that he will cling on to his reputation as Hollywood's resident rebel for as long as he can, even though Tinseltown took him to its flinty mercenary bosom and completely incorporated him in the American film industry a long time ago.

What, then, does an overview of the Nicholson career show us? Judgements about his performances and the movies he has appeared in are clearly a matter of personal preference, so in this summation I am sure to offend some readers by omission, exaggerated praise or criticism. Nevertheless, the task is worthwhile as a means of putting his achievements in some kind of perspective.

In the very first rank of these achievements is his part in *Chinatown*, one of the best movies Hollywood has ever made. Add his roles in *Five Easy Pieces*, *The King of Marvin Gardens* and *The Passenger* and he has already chalked up more major acting landmarks than the vast majority of movie stars. Just behind these come *The Shooting* (not so much for his performance, but as a movie), *The Last Detail*, *The Postman Always Rings Twice* and arguably *The Two Jakes* (both as actor and director).

Then there are *Ride in the Whirlwind*, *Ironweed*, *The Crossing Guard* and *Blood and Wine*, which are certainly all flawed films but boast strong performances by Nicholson. In this category must also come *One Flew Over the Cuckoo's Nest*, for which Nicholson won an Oscar and in which he gives one of his 'personality' performances. In *Easy Rider* he was far and away the best thing in the movie (apart from Laszlo Kovacs's photography), while in *Carnal Knowledge* he was convincing in a dislikeable picture. He performed cameo roles in *Reds*, *The Last Tycoon* and *Broadcast News* with aplomb. He was competent in difficult circumstances in *Missouri Breaks*, *The Border*, *Heartburn* and *Wolf*. He had fun as The Joker in *Batman*, and as that bad old devil Jack in *The Witches of Eastwick*. He also gave crowd-pleasing performances in *Terms of Endearment*, *A Few Good Men* and *As Good As It Gets*.

Now we must make a tally of his mistakes or when, in my opinion, he was just not very good or downright hammy. Outstanding in this list is his performance in *The Shining*, which I like as a film despite his outrageous mugging. Mugging also makes his part in *Goin' South* one of the minuses in his career, whilst he was totally miscast in *The Fortune* and *Prizzi's Honour*. He

showed desperation in *Man Trouble* (and no wonder), whilst *Mars Attacks!* had him taking on two parts and doing both of them badly. We can draw a veil over his participation in *On A Clear Day You Can See Forever*, *A Safe Place*, *Tommy* and most of the low-budget movies he made before *Easy Rider*, when he was learning his craft and also appearing in dross, as he himself has admitted many times.

Thus, the pluses far outnumber the minuses in Nicholson's long career. He has made his mark in Hollywood primarily as an actor, but he has two directing credits he can be proud of (*Drive, He Said* and *The Two Jakes*), and as a writer he scripted one of the most interesting westerns of the sixties, *The Shooting*). It is some record and in the process of forging a hugely successful career, Nicholson has become almost certainly one of the richest actors who ever strutted their stuff on the silver screen. He has retained his integrity by choosing difficult roles in movies that were clearly not meant to be popular

successes and although he continually plays the ass for the benefit of the media and acts up to his image of bad old Jack, he remains his own man, although he may have a problem, like many actors, of knowing of who exactly that man is. He is an actor who seems to appeal to all age ranges, to both men and women, to liberals and conservatives alike, to the rebel and the insider. That is why mainstream Hollywood has honoured him so many times. He provides Tinseltown with evidence that it is a broad church, that it can embrace wildly different personalities, attitudes and lifestyles, and that its heart is indeed bigger than its wallet. Jack is good old, bad old Jack for almost everyone. But the bottom line, of course, for the film industry is that Nicholson draws the customers in, and for that Hollywood will honour him till Death sends his calling card. Be careful, Jack, of that invitation to accept that inevitable Lifetime Achievement Award. It means they know something you don't.

6 WHAT JACK SAID

ON CHOOSING HIS ROLES

"I like making beautiful things. Maybe that sounds ridiculous, but when I choose a film to do, it's because it interests me in that way rather than in any other."

ON *TOMMY*

"Let me say at least I sang better than Oliver Reed. I'm available for touring. All the American record companies are in the hands of friends of mine, but not one of them has signed me up yet. I guess that's self-critical enough."

ABOUT *THE LAST DETAIL*

"I want to please the peer group. I'm a Navy man in *The Last Detail* and I want Navy men to say that's the way it is."

ABOUT POT, COCAINE AND ORGIES

"Hell, I wouldn't want you to think I'm an authority. I still smoke pot, but I don't dig cocaine. It is weird and dangerous. I haven't come across a sex orgy in years. Anyway, I think it is overrated."

ABOUT MAKING *HEAD* WITH THE MONKEES

"All my friends said, what are you doing working with The Monkees, are you crazy? But I like Curly [Rafelson]. Thought the guy was very honest, very open. I said, let's write a fair movie and do the best job we can. We made exactly the film we wanted to, an honest expression about a particular phenomenon, the suicide of The Monkees."

ABOUT HONESTY IN EMOTIONS

"Certain situations arise and for some reason or another, even at an early level, I can't keep it honest. Ten seconds later, I'll realize that whatever I said or did wasn't really the truth. Too late to correct it, though. And I never get it back."

ON HIS MOODS

"Sure I can be moody and appear vulnerable. So what's new in life? You stick around in this business for more than five minutes and it's easy to get like that."

ON BEING PHOTOGRAPHED

"For years it was my teeth. That's all photographers ever wanted to see. Now it's my eyebrows. It's an example of Reichian particularism. People are dismembered in order to negate them."

ON A BAD TRIP

"I gave up drugs when Dennis Hopper and I found ourselves up a tree after spending the night before on top of D. H. Lawrence's tomb."

ON THE FAMILY

"I have a lot of anti-family feelings. I think a lot of the things that people get fucked up about can be traced back to family structures."

ON BECOMING A STAR

"What got me is the change that happens when they suddenly notice you, like you haven't been around at all till those notices came in. I was shocked at the change it made for me. Your name becomes a brand image like a product."

ON STARDOM

"I don't minimize stardom, though if I had my choice I'd rather be thought of as nothing than as a mere showman."

"The system is geared toward overworking the stars. There aren't that many stars around to haul the freight."

"I aimed for stardom when I went into films. I figured if you were going to act on screen, there was nothing much else to be except a star."

ON MONEY

"The minute someone signs a deal with me, they've made money so what does it matter? The most expensive item in a film's costs that people complain about – the star's salary – is merely a guarantee against financial failure. I've made forty or fifty movies – only three haven't gotten more than they guaranteed me. In other words, I'm not out there destroying the movie business – I am making the movie business."

ABOUT COMMERCIALISM

"It's what I call the post-literate generation that is most disturbing to movie-makers: the explosions and the knifings. I worked as a producer very early on and I talked to the philistines. 'We like the movie, Jack, it's not that we don't like it, but it doesn't pay for us to distribute it."

ON HIS NEED TO BE FREE

"I don't like to be told what to do. It's central to my nature, period. It's a problem as an actor and it's a problem at home at night, I'm sure."

ABOUT INFLUENCING PRESIDENT CLINTON

"I'd like to have a positive influence on the President – a close and humanizing friend. I see myself as a kind of Sir Jack Falstaff to Clinton."

ON PSYCHOLOGY

"My psychological theory is Reichian. Liberty. I don't falsify sensuality. But I don't like the way society is at present. People having medical examinations so they might be allowed to have sex. It's all symbolic of pleasure denial and fear of freedom."

ABOUT SETTLING DOWN

"The other day in Paris I was with Warren Beatty and three other guys, all Playboys of the Western World and guess what we talked about? Babies."

ABOUT DIRECTING

"I have that director's arrogance. I've made three films where you could say 'What went wrong?' And I think they're all just dandy."

ON *BLOOD AND WINE*

"Here's a film without that saccharine, sentimental character development, begging the audience to admire you. There's no one in the film who asks to be liked."

ON THE GENDER WAR

"So, yes, I understand the resentment or rage of women, but nature's a balancing element. Women still control men. Not necessarily in the sense of gross national product or income, but if you look at relationships, the everyday walking-around nature of life, I think you'd see that the female controls the home. And in a relationship the woman has the power that comes from man's inability to think about anything but women."

"You have to understand that women are stronger, smarter and most important, they don't play fair. A female's initial impulse is not to tell you the truth, to make something up. There's nothing moral or relative about it, it's just gender difference."

"Women are always trying to reinvent you. That's happened a couple of times in my life, seriously that is."

ABOUT *THE POSTMAN ALWAYS RINGS TWICE*

"There was a shot I wanted to do when he first makes love to her, when he backs her off the chopping block I wanted to have a full stinger because they'd never seen that in the movies. Well, I went upstairs and worked on it for forty-five minutes, but I couldn't get anything going because I knew everyone was waiting down there to see this thing."

ABOUT *THE TWO JAKES*

"I wanted people to have to work harder to have to solve this film. There aren't a lot of popcorn stops in it. This is a real movie."

ON ANJELICA HUSTON

"I've learned as much from her as anyone. She's got a mind and a literary sense of style and imaginative energies. She's absolutely unpredictable and very beautiful."

ON CATHOLICISM

"Catholicism was the only official dogma training I've had. I liked it. It's a smart religion."

ON ACTING

"Acting is life study and Jeff Corey's classes got me into looking at life as – I'm still hesitant to say – an artist."

"Actors do play their own lives. What else do they have? It's not more painful – in some ways, it makes it easier."

ON HIS RELATIONSHIP WITH JUNE, HIS SISTER/MOTHER

"Once, I didn't speak to June for a year or so. She thought I was wasting my time on the theatrical profession, that I was lazy, a bum, wasn't trying, and that I should take my very fine mind and put it in a profession. She thought I'd had enough time to experiment, that all I was interested in was running around, getting high, and pussy."

ABOUT REDS

"I hadn't done any biographical acting, and I really felt I got brain contact there with Eugene O'Neill."

ON WORKING WITH DIANE KEATON

"I took great relish in doing Reds. I was meant to be in love with Miss Keaton, which isn't hard. I had the Pro (Warren Beatty) there as my boss and I was playing a fascinating character. So I had a real nice time."

ABOUT CRYING IN A SCENE FROM *FIVE EASY PIECES*

"Rafelson was now nakedly saying to me, 'Hey, I want you to cry in this movie.' Now that's one thing, as an actor, you never say. You don't go for emotion – or one doesn't if they work the way I do. And this is the last kind of direction you want to hear. But everything is not acting class. This is the professional game."

ON THE NICHOLSON GRIN

"People get hung up on the smile. It's so signatory."

ON MISSING OUT ON PLAYING GATSBY IN *THE GREAT GATSBY*

"I think I was righter than Bob Redford. He looks like a privileged person. He would not worry about chopping his way up. He would not worry about being well-groomed."

ON RANDALL MCMURPHY IN *ONE FLEW OVER THE CUCKOO'S NEST*

"This guy's a scamp who knows he's irresistible to women and in reality he expects Nurse Ratched to be seduced by him. This is his tragic flaw. This is why he ultimately fails."

ON HIS ACTING IN *THE SHINING*

"When the material is as unusual as The Shining, dealing with ghosts and spirits, the acting has to be larger than life. I play the character as a guy who's deeply pathological in the area of his marital relationships. The book had that intimation to begin with, and then I just blew it up."

ON POLITICS

"Is labor God? Is a job God? People vote like it is. Ronald Reagan is a vote to return to the company store. Let's go back in there and let's buy shoes down at the conglomerate. Let's get our movies down at the conglomerate. Let's let the big guy – the pin-stripe suit run things – 'cause it'll be quiet then."

ON FAME

"I was lying on the beach with Danny DeVito the other day and a guy comes staggering up and walks directly up to Danny and – I'm lying right next to the man – and says 'Are you Jack Nicholson?' To Danny. Danny gives me a look and says 'Yeah!'. And people ask me if it's a problem being recognized."

ON HIS WORK

"If there's a constant in my work, it is the principle of affirmation. It's the little guy and sometimes he may be moved back, squeezed down by the system, but he tries to creep back up, move forward, affirm his life. That's where the vitality and sense of adventure has to come from, that affirmation of basic human values. It's not anti-anything; it's pro, it's positive."

ABOUT CARNAL KNOWLEDGE

"I was just doing my job and anyway, it was a legitimate representation of male attitudes at the time. I myself try to duck conversations about feminism. It is all so dehumanizing."

ON ANTONIONI, WHO DIRECTED HIM IN *THE PASSENGER*

"He drives you crazy when you're working for him, but he's one of the greatest influences on film-making in the past three decades. They told me I was the first actor who got along with him in twenty-five years, probably because I gave him the performance he wanted. The one you see is exactly what he wanted."

ON ROMAN POLANSKI

"His situation is a very interesting case of what notoriety can do to you. I always felt that Roman was exiled because his wife had the bad taste to be murdered in the newspapers."

7 WHAT THEY SAID ABOUT JACK

Nicholson is a past master at the Hollywood psych, a vocational tool for professional survival he employs with a streetfighter's energy and a gunman's cunning.

Time

Jack Nicholson may be a superstar but until he unhoods his twinkling eyes and opens up his big ring of confidence grin you'd never know it. He wouldn't stand out in a crowd at your local.

Sue Pollard, journalist

There is a darker side to Nicholson. He is a loner terrified of being attacked by a crazed fan. He is an aggressive, moody table thumper. He is a reclusive multi-millionaire who dreams of even more millions.

Ivan Waterman

You had to stand well back when his temper went. He could be foul and rant and rave. It was frightening. Then seconds later he would smile and be all charm.

Karen Mayo-Chandler, ex-friend.

He is more hip than any man I know. I've never known anyone who enjoyed being himself more than Jack. He brings out the child in himself and everyone else.

Mark Canton, film executive

He's the most highly sexed individual I've ever met. He's just the devil.

Kim Basinger

It gave him a real deep hurt inside. There's no way of resolving it, ever.

Peter Fonda on the effect of the revelation that Nicholson's 'sister' was his mother

It was as if he was afraid he would wake up the following day and find everything back just the way it was in 1967.

One of Nicholson's friends

When I first met Jack, I decided I did not want to work for a year and then it became two. Before I knew it, I hadn't worked for five years and when I was living with him, it was to all intents and purposes as a housewife without my own centre.

Anjelica Huston

We both attended the west coast branch of the Actors Studio when we were starting out, but I hadn't seen much of him since. If the audience felt chemistry between Jack and me, it's because it genuinely exists. Jack is a prince, but to me he was and is just as great as when I first knew him.

Carrol Baker co-star in Ironweed

You know, Jack, what the public likes about your characters is that you're always playing the guy who has this tremendous ability at any given moment to say, 'Why don't you go fuck yourself?'

Billy Wilder

Jack was serious about acting in a way that somebody coming from New York such as myself would expect from a stage actor, but not from a movie actor.

Jules Feiffer

What women see in Jack Nicholson, I don't know. But what men like about him is precisely that mystery: he's fat, old, slovenly, selfish, he's losing his hair and he still pulls the chicks. He's a hero for an ageing population that badly wants to feel sexy. Somehow, despite the Picassos and Matisses and the reputed $60 million paycheck for Batman, Jack remains a man of the people, a prole demi-god.

Robert Leedham

I once got into a physical fight. I was in a small town where I'd spent a number of years and I went into the bar where I knew the bartender. He said, 'Set up a drink at the bar for the guy who discovered Jack Nicholson.' I leapt over the bar and knocked him flat out. I was insulted. I didn't want to be identified in that way.

Bob Rafelson

Earlier this year Nicholson leapt from his car and started hammering the windscreen of the Mercedes alongside him with a golf club, while the driver, Robert Scott Blank, cowered inside. The actor explained that Blank had carried out a 'crazy piece of driving that almost ran me off the road.' Blank filed for vandalism and assault. Nicholson settled out of court. 'Why, I was never going to kill the guy, I was just angry,' Nicholson explained.

Newspaper report

If Jack isn't in bed by 3am, he goes back to his hotel to sleep.

A friend

Jack's on the wild side. He loves going out nights, never gets to bed before the small hours, listens to music and smokes grass. Early morning calls are even more agonizing for him than they are for me; but he comes on the set knowing his lines and everybody else's, and he's such an exceptionally fine actor that the worst piece of Hollywood dialogue sounds crisp when he delivers it.

Roman Polanski

Jack carried himself like he was a movie star, and should be a movie star, almost from the get-go. He was deadly serious about his acting, although he didn't wear it on his sleeve. There was a little bit of the old athlete's attitude that acting is not something to talk about or carry on about.

Fred Roos, producer

You think you know your old friends. You read about them everywhere, they're public figures. But perhaps you have a feeling of false intimacy, as a fact that we're exposed indirectly to our friends in the same way the public is.

Robert Towne, reflecting on his soured relationship with Nicholson

He is a very great actor. The bravest, I would say. He has gone from being admired to liked, to appreciated and celebrated, to beloved. He is now beloved.

Milos Forman, director

AN A-Z OF NICHOLSON

A

American International

Roger Corman's production company that gave Nicholson his first screen acting roles in low-budget, quickie genre flicks aimed at the youth market and initially the drive-in circuit. Corman gave other Hollywood luminaries such as Coppola, Bogdanovich and Scorsese their first opportunity to direct. Corman has become a cult figure in his own right and some early Corman movies are even taken seriously in French critical circles. Penned a highly coloured account of American International's growth in book called *How I Made a Hundred Movies in Hollywood and Never Lost a Dime*.

Anspach, Susan

Nicholson's co-star in *Five Easy Pieces*, playing the woman Bobby Dupea has an affair with when he returns to the island. Reputedly had a torrid affair with Nicholson during the shoot and later claimed that a child born in 1970 was Nicholson's. Nicholson has never publicly accepted paternity.

Antonioni, Michelangelo

Italian film director with whom Nicholson made *The Passenger*, one of the films the star is most proud of. Antonioni's style is based on visual meaning, 'signs', sparse dialogue and narrative, and a deeply pessimistic view of contemporary life. His best known film is *L'Aventurra*, which is the movie that will probably earn him posterity's approval.

Ashby, Hal

Nicholson's director on *The Last Detail*. Made *Harold and Maude*, *Shampoo*, *Coming Home* and *Being There* before his career slumped.

B

Beatty, Warren

Nicholson's buddy, rival and occasional co-star. Acted in the disastrous *The Fortune* with Nicholson, but offered his friend the part of Eugene O'Neill in the much more successful *Reds*. Born in the same year as Nicholson, Beatty has acquired a Hollywood lothario reputation that even outdoes Nicholson's. Unlike Nicholson's career, however, Beatty's shows signs of slump.

Belmondo, Jean-Paul

French movie actor who made his name in Godard's *Breathless*. Nicholson greatly admired Belmondo and has been likened to the Bogart-like star, or is it the other way round?

Bernstein, Carl

The Bernstein of Woodward and Bernstein fame, the journos who 'broke' the Watergate story in the *Washington Post*. Nicholson played the role of the erring husband in movie based on ex-wife Nora Ephron's novel, *Heartburn*, despite Bernstein's demands for changes to the script.

Black, Karen

Black had been one of the gang that Nicholson associated with before she was cast as Rayette in *Five Easy Pieces*. After being totally miscast in *Day of the Locust*, a movie version of Nathaniel West's novel directed by John Schlesinger, her career stalled and she has never achieved stardom despite her excellence in *Easy Pieces*.

Brando, Marlon

Nicholson shared a driveway with Brando as their homes were adjacent to one another. Nicholson is often cited as Brando's natural successor in Hollywood. Acted with his hero in *Missouri Breaks*, but was less than enamoured with Brando's casual approach. Was around to help with the aftermath of the shooting of Brando's daughter's boy friend by Brando's son, Christian.

Broussard, Rebecca

Nicholson's current partner, with whom he has had two children. Declares himself very happy with Broussard's company, partly because she agrees with him more than anyone else. Nicholson's fathering of Broussard's first child helped to bring about break-up of his relationship with Anjelica Huston. Broussard was at that time the best friend of Nicholson's daughter, Jennifer.

Camus Albert

French existentialist philosopher and writer. Contemporary rival of Sartre and Beauvoir. Camus' *Myth of Sisyphus* said to be big influence on Nicholson. Symbol of individual rolling huge rock to top of mountain, then it rolling down again for the process to start all over again.

Catholicism

Nicholson comes from part-Irish stock and was influenced by Catholicism when growing up. He still has soft words to say about the religion, but his general 'outrageousness' could be seen as his attempt to break free from Catholic strictures.

Corey, Jeff

The Hollywood supporting player who was blacklisted for a time during the fifties for his leftist sympathies. To make a living, Corey started an acting class, which Nicholson attended and met people such as Robert Towne, Robert Evans and Corman there.

Corman, Roger

See above under American International.

Dern, Bruce

'Dernsie' to Nicholson, this talented actor has never quite made it in Hollywood, despite being favoured over Nicholson by Roger Corman in casting decisions early in both their careers. Said to have a highly volatile and competitive relationship with Nicholson, Dern is reputed to be Republican in his political sympathies and generally rather conservative, which makes it odd that he played all those counterculture people for Corman. A very gifted actor who should have made it as a star if there were any Hollywood justice.

DeVito, Danny

Long-time Nicholson buddy who appeared in minor roles in numerous Nicholson films until he shot to fame himself and could play star parts. Co-starred with, and directed Nicholson in *Hoffa*.

Drive, He Said

The 1972 movie Nicholson directed that was unfavourably received and bombed at the box office, but which claims a place high in Nicholson's affections and which you criticize at your peril in his presence.

Dupea, Bobby

The character Nicholson played in *Five Easy Pieces*. Dupea's run-in with reluctant waitress and his subsequent unorthodox clearing of the diner table has become a quintessential Nicholson scene.

E

Eastman, Carol

Sometimes writing as Adrien Joyce, Eastman scripted *The Shooting* and *Five Easy Pieces*, but has never fitted into Hollywood mainstream and her career has not developed as it should have. Also wrote *The Fortune* and *Man Trouble*, both rather tasteless and unfunny scripts, which may reflect something about her generally jaundiced view of life and Hollywood.

Easy Rider

The seminal movie in Nicholson's early years and the film that launched him to superstardom. Now can be viewed as a rather embarrassing and glossy portrait of sixties counterculture (it was embarrassing then, too!), but has a certain historical importance. In the movie Nicholson acts Dennis Hopper and Peter Fonda off the screen, but he has faced more difficult challenges.

Epitaph

The unfilmed script that Nicholson wrote with Monte Hellman. Reputedly based partly on Nicholson's relationship with his wife Sandra Knight, the script dealt with the theme of abortion, which Roger Corman felt was a no-no at that time. When Corman turned down *Epitaph*, he financed two cheapie westerns as a kind of consolation prize: *The Shooting* and *Ride in the Whirlwind*.

Evans, Robert

Sometime indifferent actor, Evans made it big time in Hollywood executive producer at Paramount, backing *Chinatown*, *The Great Gatsby*, *The Cotton Club*. A one-time close associate of Nicholson, Evans fell from grace after being linked to the murder investigation of producer Roy Radin, but Nicholson stayed fiercely loyal.

F

Fonda, Peter

Son of Henry, brother of Jane, Peter has seemed to suffer from a severe lack of talent by comparison. That deficiency, however, he has never allowed to stand in his way. Becoming seriously rich after the huge success of *Easy Rider*, which he helped to write and produce, Fonda's Hollywood career largely stalled as he became identified as a time warp sixties icon, now irredeemably tarnished. Nominated for an Oscar as Best Actor in 1998. Wow!

Forman, Milos

Czech director who remained an exile after the Soviets invaded his country in 1968. Directed Nicholson in his major hit *One Flew Over The Cuckoo's Nest*, but his best work remains the Czech comedies *A Blonde in Love* and *The Fireman's Ball*. Also directed *Taking Off* and *Amadeus* in Hollywood.

Furcillo-Rose, Don

One of the two strong candidates as the father of Jack Nicholson. Song-and-dance man Furcillo-Rose claimed he had fathered Jack during an affair he had with June, Nicholson's sister/mother. Later in life, after he had learned that June was his mother, Nicholson contacted Furcillo-Rose by phone, but the two never met.

G

Gittes, Harry

The character Nicholson played in *Chinatown* and *The Two Jakes*. Bogart would have played this role in the forties, as the cynicism, intelligence and world-weariness would have suited his style. Nicholson added an extra layer of vulnerability and superficial cockiness, and one of the definitive Nicholson roles was born.

Godard, Jean-Luc

Godard is a director that Nicholson much admired and whom he got to know when Nicholson and Hellman went to France to find a distributor for *The Shooting* and *Ride in the Whirlwind*. At that time, anyway, a idolater of B-movies and so-called Hollywood auteurs, Godard gave the two films his enthusiastic support.

H

Hansen, George

The character Nicholson played in *Easy Rider*. The famous Nicholson drawl came into full operation with this character, perhaps because he was reputedly stoned during the filming of some of the sequences, notably the famous camp fire scene when Hansen talks about America as having been a 'helluva country' at one time.

Hawley, June

The married name of June Nicholson, Jack's 'sister' who turned out to be his mother. She died without telling him the truth about his birth, which says a lot about the stigma attached to Catholic young women in the fifties who became pregnant in an unmarried state. June was a talented and beautiful singer-dancer and Nicholson clearly inherited his mother's penchant for show business. When June divorced Murray Hawley, she moved to LA and invited her son to stay with her. This 'visit' to LA extended itself and that is where Nicholson lives to this day.

Hellman, Monte

Nicholson's friend and associate in his early days in Hollywood, Hellman directed Nicholson on *The Shooting* and *Ride in the Whirlwind*, as well as in *Flight To Fury* and *Back Door to Hell*. Hellman's Hollywood career never took off perhaps because of his uncompromising artistic

stance. Only *Two-Lane Blacktop* of his later films made any splash.

Hopper, Dennis

Long-time associate of Nicholson, Hopper, along with Peter Fonda, became a counterculture icon in films such as *Easy Rider* and *The Trip*. Directed *Rider* as well as *The Last Movie*, *Kid Blue* and *Out of the Blue*. Appeared as the stoned, gibbering photographer (acting?) in Coppola's *Apocalypse Now* and in recent years has played heavies in mainstream Hollywood movies such as *Blue Velvet* and *Red Rock*. A man whose pretensions outdistance his talents by some mileage.

Huston, Anjelica

The daughter of John Huston's fourth marriage to a ballet dancer, Anjelica was Nicholson's long-time partner until they famously broke up when Rebecca Broussard came on the scene. After misfiring in her first acting role in *A Walk with Love and Death*, directed by her father, she retreated from a career in movies until the mid-seventies, when she gathered confidence again and later won an Oscar for *Prizzi's Honour*. Since then she has been effective in *The Grifters* and *The Crossing Guard*. Very much her own lady in later life, it could not have been easy to come out from under the shadow of her famous father and later her equally famous lover, Nicholson.

Huston, John

The father of Anjelica and director of *Treasure of Sierra Madre*, *The Asphalt Jungle*, *The African Queen*, *The Misfits* and *Prizzi's Honour*. A verbose bully, emanating loads of suspect machismo, Huston survived and prospered in Hollywood by playing the Hollywood game while pretending to be one of its rebels. Sounds familiar!

J

Jaglom, Henry

Writer-director, longtime buddy of Nicholson since his acting-class days. Wrote and directed *A*

Safe Place in which Nicholson appeared. Went on to make rather eccentric, rambling movies such as *Tracks*, *Sitting Ducks* and *Can She Bake A Cherry Pie?*

K

King, Eddie

The other main contender for the paternity of Nicholson, King was mother June's partner in a song-and-dance act. Some people claim there was a striking resemblance between King and Nicholson. The case rests.

Knight, Sandra

Nicholson's ex-wife whom he married in 1962 in a Unitarian Universalist ceremony. Harry Dean Stanton was Nicholson's best man, Millie Perkins was bridesmaid. Knight appeared with Nicholson in *The Terror*, but the marriage ended in divorce in 1968 with Knight citing extreme cruelty against her husband and being awarded sole custody of their four-year-old daughter Jennifer. Knight. who never resumed her film career, moved to Hawaii and married again.

Kovacs, Laszlo

Cinematographer on *Easy Rider*, *Five Easy Pieces* and a few of the Corman cheapies. Usually brought a distinction to schlock the material scarcely deserved. Has worked with top directors Peter Bogdanovich (*Paper Moon*), Martin Scorsese (*New York, New York*), *The Last Waltz* and Spielberg (*Close Encounters of the Third Kind*).

Kubrick, Stanley

Nicholson's demanding director on *The Shining*, demanding in terms of time spent on the shoot, but perhaps not demanding enough in terms of Nicholson's performance. Not an actors' director, Kubrick has made some of the most significant movies of the last five decades: *Paths of Glory*, *Dr Strangelove*, *2001*, *A Clockwork Orange* and *Full Metal Jacket*. Either a very talented oddity or a pretentious bore, depending on point of view.

L

Landau, Martin

Nicholson joined Landau's Method-influenced classes in LA, based on 'sense memory', where he worked with Bruce Dern, Dean Stanton and Sandra Knight among others.

Lippert, Robert

A producer in charge of B-movie unit at 20th Century Fox, Lippert reputedly supervised the making of hundreds of low-budget schlock from sci-fi to horror flicks and westerns. Lippert produced three of the cheapies that Nicholson appeared in, *The Broken Land*, *Flight to Fury* and *Back Door To Hell*. Lippert was a more downmarket Roger Corman, if that can be imagined.

Los Angeles Lakers

The LA Basketball team that Nicholson enthusiastically supports from the courtside.

M

Manasquan High School

The high school in Spring Lake, New Jersey, where Ethel May moved her home and business from nearby Ashbury Park. Nicholson graduated from high school having a reputation for not having put everything into his education that he should have. He was mischievous rather than 'bad', acted in school plays without special distinction, tried hard at sport and wasn't especially successful with girls. How things have changed!

MGM

Nicholson's first employer in Hollywood, not as an actor, but as mail clerk in the Hanna-Barbera cartoon division.

Money

A very important commodity for our hero, who has been known to drive a very sharp bargain with the suits in Hollywood. Nicholson has always admitted freely that money was important to him, because it brought him freedom, the right to choose what he wanted to do. One of the richest actors who ever drew a pay cheque or cornered his share of the grosses, Nicholson's personal wealth has an estimate of between $300 and $400 million.

Nichols, Mike

One of Nicholson's favoured directors who directed him in *Carnal Knowledge*, *The Fortune*, *Heartburn* and *Wolf*.

Nicholson, Ethel May

Nicholson's grandmother, whom he thought was his mother when he was growing up. She built up a successful hairdressing business, which elevated the family's standard of living beyond its humble beginnings.

Nicholson, Jennifer

The daughter of the marriage between Sandra Knight and Jack. Though Knight got full custodial rights over their daughter, later Jennifer got to know her father well in Hollywood and it was through her friendship with Rebecca Broussard that her father met the woman who has shared his life for the last decade or so.

Nicholson, John Joseph

Nicholson's grandfather, whom he thought of as his father as he was growing up. An alcoholic, Nicholson was frequently absent from the New Jersey family home during Jack's formative years.

O'Neill, Eugene

America's first important playwright, a disenchanted radical and friend of John Reed, the subject of *Reds* and the lover of Louise Bryant. Nicholson played the role in the movie directed by Warren Beatty. One of only two 'real-life' characters Nicholson has played on screen, the other being Jimmy Hoffa.

Oscars

Nicholson has won the Best Actor Oscar for his roles in *One Flew Over The Cuckoo's Nest* and *As Good As It Gets*, plus Best Supporting Actor for *Terms of Endearment*. He was nominated for his roles in *Easy Rider* (Best Supporting Actor), *Five Easy Pieces*, *The Last Detail*, *Chinatown*, *Reds* (Best Supporting Actor), *Prizzi's Honour*, *Ironweed*, *A Few Good Men* (Best Supporting Actor).

Perkins, Millie

The actress who shot to fame when she played Anne Frank in George Stevens's 1959 movie *The Diary of Anne Frank*. She was Sandra Knight's 'maid of honour' when Knight and Nicholson married in 1962, and she also starred in the back-to-back westerns *The Shooting* and *Ride in the Whirlwind*. But somehow her career disappeared.

Polanski, Roman

The Polish-American director who directed Nicholson in *Chinatown* and later had to flee America after statutory rape charges had been laid against him. Nicholson and Polanski have a tempestuous professional relationship, but Jack has remained loyal to his friend and colleague.

Rafelson, Bob

After his success in the Rafelson-directed *Five Easy Pieces*, Nicholson reputedly agreed to appear in any movie Rafelson wanted him for. Unfortunately, this led him to starring in *Man Trouble*, but the account is well into the black when *Five Easy Pieces*, *The King of Marvin Gardens*, *The Postman Always Rings Twice* and *Blood and Wine* are credited. Rafelson's career, however, has stumbled, not through lack of talent, but because Hollywood is largely into feel-good movies and spectacular special effects.

Rush, Richard

The director of three early Nicholson films: *Too Soon To Love*, *Psych-Out* and *Hell's Angels on Wheels*. Of his later films, *The Stunt Man*, starring Peter O'Toole is probably the best known and liked.

S

Screenwriting

Nicholson's early ambition was to be a writer, specifically for the screen, but his success as an actor has completely overshadowed his achievements in this sphere.

Smith, George 'Shorty'

Married to Nicholson's sister/aunt, Lorraine, Smith became something of a surrogate father to Jack when he was growing up in New Jersey.

Smith, Lorraine

Nicholson's sister-aunt, who was very close to Jack and after whom he named the daughter he had with Rebecca Broussard.

Stanton, Harry Dean

Long-time buddy of Nicholson's who has appeared in numerous of his films and has carved out for himself a reputation as a quirky character actor. Probably best known for *Paris, Texas*.

T

Television

Like most struggling Hollywood actors in the fifties and sixties, Nicholson looked to television roles to earn bread. He appeared in *Matinee Theatre*, and series such as *Sea Hunt*, *The Barbara Stanwyck Theater*, *Mr Lucky*, *Tales of Wells Fargo*, *Bronco*, *Hawaiian Eye*, *Dr Kildare* and *The Andy Griffith Show*. Since becoming a major star, he has not appeared in a dramatic role in a television play or TV movie.

Theatre

While working as a mail clerk at MGM, Nicholson joined the Players Ring Theatre in LA, where he generally 'mucked in' and played small parts. Nicholson also founded with some friends the Store Theatre which lasted for one production. He has never returned to the stage since becoming a name.

Towne, Robert

The screenwriter of *Chinatown* and *The Two Jakes*, and also the director of movies such as *Personal Best*, *Tequila Sunrise* and *The Still of the Night*. Had a bad falling-out with Nicholson over *The Two Jakes*.

W

Welles, Orson

Legendary director of *Citizen Kane* and *The Magnificent Ambersons*, Welles wanted Nicholson to star in *The Big Brass Ring*, a screenplay for which Welles had written himself. However, although Welles and Nicholson admired one another, Nicholson reputedly would not lower his asking price as an actor and Welles, impecunious as usual, could not afford the star's services. The film was never made.

T